Getting Lost On My Way

Getting Lost On My Way

SELF-DISCOVERY ON IRELAND'S BACKROADS

Diane Hartman

SWP

SHE WRITES PRESS

Published in 2025 by
She Writes Press, an imprint of The Stable Book Group

SWP

32 Court Street, Suite 2109
Brooklyn, NY 11201
https://shewritespress.com
Library of Congress Control Number: 2025908962
ISBN: 978-1-64742-976-8
eISBN: 978-1-64742-977-5

Interior Design by Andrea Reider
Photos in book courtesy of the author

Printed in the United States

Names and identifying characteristics have been changed to protect the privacy of certain individuals.

For my daughters

Prologue

BLACK DOG was at my heels again, and I was running as fast as I could across an open field in the dark hoping I wouldn't trip. I could hear his terrifying growl getting closer. I pictured his sharp teeth and the slobbering white foam dripping from his panting mouth. Petrified, I ran faster, but my legs gave out, and I tumbled to the ground. I woke up screaming as Black Dog pounced.

I inherited the Black Dog of depression from my father and from ancestors from both sides of my family tree. But it was my father's depression that impacted my life the most. My father's depression was the severe, disabling kind. The family story is that his downward spiral began when, at the age of eighteen, he lost his mother to breast cancer, but I suspect that Black Dog arrived in his life long before then.

The Black Dog has made frequent, unwanted appearances in my dreams for many years. I pictured myself turning to face him, telling him to stay out of my dreams and to quit invading my waking life too. But the dream was the same. I always ran away from him in fear.

Black Dog made his appearance in my life during my early adolescence, but unlike my father's depression, mine was mild. I could hide it, but Black Dog was always there in the guise of the inner critic, the voice whispering in my head that I wasn't good enough, that no one loved me. I discovered years later that my type of depression has a name—dysthymia—a persistent mild depression that can be controlled with the new miraculous antidepressants and cognitive therapy.

My father wasn't as fortunate. Those miracle pharmaceuticals, not to mention therapy, weren't available to him. The few photos I have of him tell the story. There is a photo of a tall, thin handsome man smiling for the camera on his honeymoon in Colorado, and there is a photo of him twenty-five years later sitting on the front porch swing looking extremely overweight and sad, a shell of the man he used to be. By then, he was spending most of his time shuttered in his bedroom. My three brothers and I instinctively knew not to disturb him.

I have very few memories of him actively engaged with us, but I vividly recall the last time I spoke to him on April 17, 1964, when I was ten years old. In those days, we walked home for lunch from our nearby elementary school. He was ascending the stairs to his bedroom when I entered the house on that unseasonably warm, sunny day.

"Look what I did, Daddy," I said. He turned and smiled at me as I handed him two pieces of paper, one a crayon drawing and the other a story. He gently took the papers from my outreached hand and gazed at them for what seemed like an eternity to a little girl. Slowly, he handed the papers back to me and with a look that was both affectionate and sad, a look that to this day still pierces my soul, he said, "I like it when you draw pictures and write stories, Sissy. Keep doing it. Promise?"

"I promise, Daddy," I said. He continued up the stairs, and I joined my eight- and twelve-year-old brothers in the kitchen for lunch before we headed back to school. We were jealous of our sixteen-year-old brother, who ate his lunch in the high school cafeteria.

Not long after we returned to school, my mother left to visit a neighbor down the street, and my father went to the basement and shot himself with a 12-gauge shotgun he had borrowed from a neighbor.

But this story isn't about my father's suicide. It's about the hole that his suicide left in my heart, indeed in the hearts of everyone in my family. It's about how I carried the weight of losing him and feeling abandoned deep within me into my adulthood. It's about how, despite the miracle drugs and therapy, I continue to wrestle with the Black Dog. It's about how my father's abandonment led me to think less of myself, consequently making relationship decisions that didn't serve me, including marrying the wrong man at nineteen and committing myself to a twenty-two-year-long marriage that gave me two beautiful daughters, but left me hurt, angry, and distrustful.

Most importantly, it's about my conscious decision in middle age to keep my promise to my father, to make pictures with my camera and to weave words into stories. This is the story of a middle-aged woman who set out on four solo journeys to Ireland, a country I had yearned to visit for several years, to conquer fears, take risks, and tame the Black Dog of depression that thwarted my ability to feel happy.

It's about how a moment of synchronicity with the Irish writer John O'Donohue convinced me to stop waiting for a fellowship that would pay my way and to take a risk and travel to Ireland anyway.

I could have taken any road toward self-discovery, but I chose Ireland because my study of Celtic spirituality and music convinced me that Ireland was my spiritual home. I had an intuition that traveling to Ireland would lead to some much-needed emotional healing from my painful childhood and my unhappy marriage, which had ended in divorce six years earlier.

This is the story of my twisting, turning journey toward self-discovery on the back roads of Ireland.

PART ONE

The Journey Begins

Get up off your arse and drive!

CHAPTER ONE

Encounters with John O'Donohue

I HAD BEEN sitting in a hard folding chair for more than an hour and my butt hurt, but I didn't care. It seemed a small price to pay to hear a lecture by the renowned Irish writer, John O'Donohue, author of *Anam Cara: A Book of Celtic Wisdom*. Anam cara is Gaelic for "soul friend." Far more encompassing than the cliched "soulmate," it refers to a teacher, companion, or spiritual guide with whom you share your innermost self and by whom you are understood and loved in a way that transcends time and space. I loved the premise of the book, the beauty of O'Donohue's writing, and I felt lucky at being able to see him in person. His book had given me hope during the dismal time following my divorce. I didn't want to be cynical about love, and his words convinced me that having an anam cara, whether it be a romantic relationship or a close friendship, was possible. I jumped at this rare opportunity to see him in person. I wanted to hear those soothing words straight from his mouth. I was so unsure of myself and of what was in store for me post-divorce. I wanted some of his Celtic awareness, the flow of life and love, to rub off on me.

O'Donohue was speaking in the beautiful Alison Mansion, with its gorgeous mahogany paneled walls, at Marian University in Indianapolis. As he ended his fascinating lecture with an Irish blessing, he announced that there would be a book signing in the adjoining conservatory. With my well-worn copy of *Anam Cara* in hand, I stood up, simultaneously trying to massage my aching butt with the required amount of discreetness while making my way to the ever-growing line forming in the conservatory. I watched the windows being illuminated by a harvest moon as I waited my turn. I was alone and struggled with what I was going to say. Not the platitudinal "I love your work." Something more significant and personal that would reflect my love of Ireland and my unrequited desire to travel there.

Suddenly there he was, taking my book and asking my name without glancing up. When I told him, he quickly looked up and stared into my eyes. Startled by the intensity of his stare I mumbled, "I love your work, and I really want to travel to Ireland."

"Diane," he said earnestly in his beautiful western Irish lilt, "ye *must* travel to Ireland and then ye *must* write about it. It's important, ye understand?"

His gaze seemed to hold me for an eternity as he handed the book back to me. Before I could manage to respond I heard the woman behind me gush "I absolutely love your work" as she handed him her book.

Wow! How does he know I'm a writer! Weird! This totally freaks me out! Does he possess a sixth sense? Does he know that the emotional turmoil that's assaulted my spirit has caused me to lose my muse? That I'm struggling to write? How does he know about my unrequited desire to travel to Ireland? I felt like my soul had been pierced by a kindred spirit who understood. An anam cara. I stood there, frozen, for a few more seconds, long enough for him to look at me and smile and for me to smile back. *This is crazy. Why would someone like John O'Donohue single me out?*

"Right," said my inner critic in the voice of my ex-husband. "You're nothing special."

Several years later, after I had taken his advice and made four solo trips to Ireland, experienced a lifetime of adventures, made friends (some of whom knew John O'Donohue personally and shared their grief at his early passing), and come to feel that County Clare and the Beara Peninsula were my second homes, his ghost came to visit in a dream.

I was walking the path along the Cliffs of Moher in western County Clare, something I had done many times and never lost the wonder of. I glanced up the path and saw a middle-aged man with dark curly hair and a beard approaching me, his black coat blowing in the ever-present wind, and I knew that it was him. I stopped as he approached and he said, "Diane, ye have traveled here, ye know that it's affected yer heart and mind, but ye don't understand it. Now ye must write about it."

"But I have written about it," I said. "You know that!" I didn't know how he knew, but I knew that he did.

"Ah, ye mean those essays about climbing Croagh Patrick, meeting the fake nun, sitting at Yeats's grave? Good initial efforts, but they're not complete. Not enough heart."

"What do you mean not enough heart?" I shouted. "I've sweated over those essays for years, pouring my heart and soul into them."

"So ye say, but are they finished? Have ye submitted them for publication?"

"No," I mumbled.

"Right so, and why not? I'll tell ye why."

Oh great, I thought. *Just what I need. Another man with all the answers.* I didn't hate men, but the emotional abuse by my ex-husband had devastated my trust in them.

"By all means, illuminate me," I said.

He ignored my sarcasm and went on.

"It's the black dog," he said. "You know, depression. The old melancholy that runs in your family's veins. The hungry ghost that gnaws at your soul and leaves ye feeling empty and useless. Yer ability to hide it is admirable, but ye must wrestle that black dog out of the shadows, stare it in the face and wrestle it to the ground. Let it know who's really in charge. Let it know that yer using its secrets to stoke yer inner fire and illuminate yer life."

"But how?"

"Ah, 'tis the secret is it not? But ye already know it, and ye know that it's about more than Ireland. Ye will figure it out," he answered with that damn Irish glint in his eyes.

"Write, Diane," he said. "Write."

With that he turned and walked back toward O'Brien's Tower.

"But wait," I cried.

He turned around and looked at me with amused, but affectionate, impatience.

"You mean I can fix the melancholy that holds me back through my writing?"

"Indeed, that's what I did."

"I know, but you died so young, so unexpectedly. You had just found your true love, your anam cara."

He smiled sadly and said as he walked away, "Ye'd best get started."

In the years following that profound, unforgettable dream, I wrote about my experiences in Ireland. I took writing classes and went on writing retreats. I developed close friendships with like-minded writers. Finally, my muse returned. I welcomed her back, and every day I say thank you to John O'Donohue's spirit.

CHAPTER TWO

Driving Green

I WAS TRYING my best to stay on the left side of the road, my knuckles white, my left foot riding the clutch, and my left hand on the stick shift, ready to throw it into the wrong gear at a moment's notice. Suddenly, there it was. The dreaded roundabout to Limerick. I knew what roundabouts were, but I had never driven on one. I held my breath and, as I entered into its maze, I spotted a stocky middle-aged man swinging his arm in a circular motion and yelling something I couldn't understand. He was looking at me.

"What?" I mouthed as I approached. I was too afraid to take my hand off the wheel to roll down the window.

"Yer goin' the wrong way, woman!"

"Oh, crap!" I yelled out loud as I veered around him. I didn't realize that in Ireland I should navigate roundabouts in a clockwise direction. Fortunately for me, the other drivers recognized another first-time tourist just in from Shannon Airport suffering from jet lag. They stopped as I weaved among them taking the exit onto N21 south toward my ultimate destination, the Dingle Peninsula, ninety-five miles away.

I steered the car over to the side of the road after reaching the other side of Limerick, put the gear in park, and tried to relax a little. At least the weather was cooperating. It wasn't raining, and, for now, the sun was shining on this warm June day.

Deep breaths. Deep breaths. Recite your mantra you learned from the writings of the 12th-century saint Julian of Norwich: "And all shall be well, and all shall be well, and all manner of thing shall be well."

It wasn't working, and I felt my crazy-maker inner voice taking over.

What the hell were you thinking coming over here by yourself? What have you gotten yourself into? You can't even drive on the main highways! How are you going to handle the narrow, curvy back roads?

It was true. Maybe I had overestimated my ability to travel in a foreign country by myself. Here I was: a middle-aged divorced woman from Indiana with two teenage daughters and the rest of my family and friends worried sick about me. I had never been overseas before, and I didn't know anyone.

So, how had I gotten myself into this situation? It had been years in the making, complicated by many layers and even more curves, detours, and sharp turns. Beginning with the childhood encouragement from my father to foster my creativity, fermenting through my child-bearing years, and finally blossoming in middle age.

I became obsessed with all things Irish when I was in my forties after discovering traditional Celtic music (or "trad" as it is known in Irish lingo) and reading every book about Ireland

I could get my hands on—everything from Celtic spirituality, William Butler Yeats's poetry, Irish folklore and history to the memoirs of Pete McCarthy and Niall Williams. Ireland had become my passion, and I felt driven to travel there. I sensed that it was my spiritual home, though I didn't understand why, and I had an intuition that going there would lead to some much-needed emotional healing from a painful childhood, an unhappy marriage, and an even more painful divorce six years earlier. I wanted to get away from my life as a school librarian and a single mother of two often rebellious teenage daughters and all of the responsibility that came with it. So I did the responsible things before I left. I arranged for my daughters to stay with their best friends under the watchful eyes of those friends' parents, took my two greyhounds to the Greyhound Resort, their favorite home-away-from-home, paid the bills, and mowed the grass.

The thrill of sitting at the computer in my pj's while planning my trip was over. I was really here. I was on a journey of self-discovery and independence. This was an opportunity to become acquainted with my true self and to liberate myself from the demons in my past that were holding me back. I wasn't interested in taking the tourist route, riding on a bus and stopping just long enough to kiss the Blarney Stone or drink a few pints of Guinness. I wanted to see the real Ireland, get to know its people and immerse myself in its rich culture of music, pub life, and natural beauty. I was tired of being turned down year after year for a teacher creativity fellowship that would have covered the cost of my trip, and I was tired of waiting for the right person to travel with or the right moment to do it. This was the moment. I threw caution and my finances to the wind and decided to go for it. I had rented a car with the intention of exploring the back roads of western Ireland—alone.

Now the dream was quickly turning into a nightmare. I stared at the emerald countryside with its rolling hills in shades of green I'd never seen before. What was I supposed to do? How was I going to handle these roads, these fears? What if I was in an accident? What if I ended up in the hospital? What if I ended up dead? What if I caused an accident and ended up in jail? Maybe I'd be better off just driving to one place and staying there.

Fortunately, the "what-ifs" quieted down as my rational inner voice took over.

Now, here's the deal, Diane. You have the right to fulfill your dream. You've been through hell with your divorce and with being a single mom. You deserve to live your own life. You can either sit here in the car feeling terrified and sorry for yourself or you can get your arse in gear and get on with it, fear and all.

Fighting the fear. The fear that I would botch the journey. The fear that I would be discovered as an impostor. Not as the strong, confident woman I wanted to be, but as the insecure little girl I perceived myself to be. The fear that I would never find love again.

Fighting the pain. The pain from my depressed childhood. The pain from marrying the wrong man when I was far too young. The pain from not giving up on that marriage that I should have given up on long ago. The pain from being the only "present" parent to my two daughters.

"Guardian angels, please stay with me and guide me safely," I muttered as I put the car in gear, let up on the clutch, and continued to drive.

CHAPTER THREE

Ding-Dong in Dingle

SO MANY shades of green were blasting through my eyes that my brain could hardly absorb them. I was, as the Irish say, gobsmacked. I wanted to really look at those colors, but that would require pulling off to the side of the road again, and since there was no side to pull off to, I kept the car in gear and continued to drive southwest in total awe toward the Dingle Peninsula. I did park awkwardly in a few of the small towns along the way to find a toilet. Due to my nervous state, my gut was working overtime despite the deep breathing and mantra.

One of my favorite little towns was Adare, with its thatched cottage–style shops and, most importantly, a tea-room with a toilet. After checking out the toilet, I made my way to a table and ordered tea with milk and a small scone.

"Nothing else for you then?" said a young smiling waitress with a moon-shaped face, saucer-shaped brown eyes, and her long hazel hair clipped back.

"No thank you. But can you tell me how long it will take me to drive to Dingle town?"

"Ah, it shouldn't take longer than a few hours, ma'am. What? Are ye driving by yerself?"

"Um, yes I am," I admitted.

"So this is yer first trip is it?"

"Yes."

"My, yer a brave one. I mean, it's safe and all, but a woman traveling alone is considered a bit odd."

"Brave or stupid," I said.

"So, yer headed to Dingle town, eh?"

"Actually, Ventry, just south of Dingle town."

"No worries. When you enter Dingle town just take the roundabout onto Slea Head Road. It will send ye into Ventry. Now, to get yer tea and scone . . ."

She made it sound so easy and, like everyone else I had met so far, she was so friendly.

The scone stuck in my throat, so I washed it down with the tea.

Dang. I've really got to get a handle on this. I can't believe how stressed I am about the driving. It's taking everything out of me. I just want to curl up in a ball and be able to transport myself to where I need to go. Oh well, stay on the left side of the road, don't scrape your side-view mirror on the stone walls, and remember to enter the roundabout clockwise before exiting onto Slea Head Road. Easy peasy.

I hemmed and hawed my way out of my parallel parking spot and hit the road, figuratively speaking.

What the helpful waitress forgot to mention was that first I would have to maneuver the narrow streets through the town of Tralee, and second, that all of the road signs would be in Gaelic!

Panic time again. To help me navigate pre-GPS without taking my eyes off the road, I had taped a note on my dashboard with the names of all the roads in the order I would take them:

N21 to Tralee

N86 to Dingle

Slea Head Rd to Ventry

Holy crap! Why didn't any of those Irish travel guides mention this? Rick Steves recommended a special sign I could place in my car's back window announcing that I was a "student driver." I might as well put a "baby on board" sticker on the car for all the good it would do. "Illiterate driver" would have been more appropriate, but I doubted that they sold those. Thanks for nothing, Rick Steves!

Finally, I came to the infamous roundabout in Dingle, entered it clockwise and proceeded to drive around and around and around because I couldn't figure out which exit was Slea Head Road. I was getting curious stares from the other drivers, especially from those waiting to enter. After about twenty times around (I'm not exaggerating) I took the exit for Slea Head Road. *This has to be it.* I remembered the waitress saying something about it being beside a gas station and there was one. Or did she say just past the gas station?

I drove and drove into a more and more isolated mountainous area. Since no other cars were around, I pulled over to look at my map. Nothing I was looking at, beautiful though it was, matched what was on my map.

Double panic time. I was lost and the road ahead revealed higher and higher terrain. I was too far away from the roundabout to turn back. *There's got to be somebody out here who can help me!* I didn't even think about whether or not I should trust strangers. *Just get me out of the middle of nowhere!*

In tears, I pulled back onto the road and drove on. A few miles later, I spotted a building up ahead. I pulled into the drive next to a nondescript small white building and read the sign in the window: Michael's Pub. Kegs lined the side of the building, indicating that it must be a popular watering hole for whomever lived around here, but, unfortunately, the parking lot was empty and the pub was closed.

I took out my map and looked again. Hadn't I seen a sign back aways for Murreagh? *Why don't I see it on my map?* By now I was in full panic mode, briefly considering the folly of breaking into the pub and getting hammered on Guinness. I could see it now in the village paper: "An American woman has been arrested for breaking into Michael's Pub. She was found passed out under the bar having consumed mass quantities of Guinness. She said she was lost and panicked when she couldn't find anyone to help her. Her court date is set for next week."

Just then a white delivery truck pulled into the drive. Amazed, I jumped out of my car, map in hand, and ran toward the truck. Out jumped a young man in a navy-blue fleece jacket, carrying a set of milk bottles. He dropped the bottles off quickly at the front doorstep and headed back toward his truck.

"Sir!" I yelled. "I'm trying to get to Ventry, and I think I'm lost."

"Ventry is it?" he asked. "Well, yes luv, you are a bit out of yer way, like."

I stepped back a little as he approached. He was the most gorgeous man I had ever seen. Dark hair, blue eyes, easy smile. He looked so out of place and yet, at the same time, like he belonged here. What the hell was he doing out here? A milkman out here?

I tried to compose myself.

"Here," I said, pushing my map at him. "Can you show me where I am?"

He took the map, headed over to my car and flattened the map on the hood.

"Look here, luv. Yer here, way north of Dingle town at the foothills of Brendan Mountain."

"Oh no!" I yelled. "How did I end up here and how do I get down there?" I pointed to Ventry on the map.

"Not to worry, luv," he reassured me. "It will take a bit of time but ye can take this road here and then turn here . . ."

While he was talking, I opened my car door and rummaged for my notebook and pen.

"Here, will you write down the route for me? And write it big please, so I can read it as I'm driving."

He slowly shook his head and smiled slightly, then wrote the directions in big letters. I was relieved that he wrote in English instead of Gaelic.

"This should get ye there. The first turn is just up the rood aways. On yer way now. You'll be fine."

With that, he dashed back into his truck, anxious to keep his deliveries on time to God knows where.

"Thank you!" I yelled as he pulled out of the drive, heading in the opposite direction. I watched his truck as it headed around the curve and disappeared into the foothills, wondering if he was an angel sent to rescue me. It seemed obvious to me that he was.

The directions he gave were heaven-sent. I had no trouble following them back to the roundabout in Dingle and then taking the correct exit to Ventry. The drive was so beautiful. Row upon row of stone walls and green hills with sheep grazing along the sides. It was misting now and the scenery looked ethereal.

So, this is what the Irish mean by a soft day.

When I reached the Gregorys' Farmhouse Bed and Breakfast, I greeted Mrs. Gregory with such enthusiasm that she seemed a little taken aback.

"I'm sorry," I said. "I'm just so happy to be here because I've been driving all day, I got lost, and a handsome milkman rescued me up by Mt. Brendan."

"My, my then," she laughed. "Yer indeed ready for a bite to eat and some rest. Let me show you to your room."

Mrs. Gregory's face was worn, but she had a big smile and well-coifed beautiful white hair that curled around her face. The home was a white two-story farmhouse with green shutters. As we made our way up the narrow stairs to my room with slanted eaves and pink flowered wallpaper, she mentioned a couple of places I might want to visit toward Slea Head.

"It's rained heavily over the past few days and there's water on parts of the road, but ye should be all right getting through."

"That's good," I said, though I wasn't keen on fording any flooded roads.

"I mainly want to see the beehive huts and Blasket Island Heritage Centre. Are those very far from here?"

"Oh no, luv. Just up the rood aways."

I was exhausted, probably a combination of jet lag and the stress from driving, but I had a lovely stay there, and I wished I had planned to stay longer than one night. Naive on my part. I took photographs of the Gregorys' backyard, especially along the stone wall lined with pink flowers. Mr. Gregory, short, thin, sporting a tweed cap and carrying a walking stick, greeted me at the dairy barn, but I wasn't allowed past the gate due to the hoof-and-mouth epidemic plaguing Ireland at the time. Instead, he came around the gate and talked to me about his dairy cows and his loyal border collie, Fred.

"So how long is yer holiday, deah?"

"Only a week this first trip," I answered.

"Ah, das too short, too short," he said.

I agreed, loving his accent and friendliness.

Early that evening I headed south on Slea Head Road to visit the beehive huts at Fahan. It was drizzling as I sloshed around the steep hillsides lined with grazing sheep and perfectly formed stone huts in the shape of beehives. These huts were built and occupied during the 12th century when the Normans forced the Irish off the good land, forcing them to flee to the periphery of the Dingle Peninsula. Their occupants were thought to be monks and followers of St. Patrick.

Putting my exhaustion and wayward stomach aside, I became intrigued with these structures and the people who had created them. What had motivated them to come to this farthermost part of Ireland to live in a stone hut with no amenities whatsoever? The huts weren't even tall enough for a short adult to stand upright. The mist, dampness, and dreariness, punctuated by the steep hills, gave little hope to this desolate landscape in June. What about the torrents of rain in the winter months? How did they survive? What kind of protective clothing, if any, did they wear? What did they eat? How did they spend their time? Little is known about the people who lived here or even exactly when they lived here. No doubt they were aesthetic to the extreme, but what mysterious, timeless structures they left behind! So much so that they were used in two Star Wars movies. I admired the people's discipline and dedication. They must have felt that they were called to live this way, and they embraced that calling. Had I truly been called to come here? Would I embrace it?

I sat next to one of the huts. There were lessons here for me, I was sure. This was holy ground. I could feel it in the atmosphere and on the ground I sat upon. I was being called to do something, but what? Travel outside my comfort zone for sure. Feel the fear and do it anyway? I was trying. In fact, I was already finding reserves of strength and resolve that surprised me. What would be on the other side of the fear? Freedom to be who I am without having to apologize to anyone for taking up space on the planet? I hoped so and, truthfully, I was already on that road. I was feeling the Black Dog, the depression, retreating. I felt lighter, freer. I thought again of my mantra from the 12th-century anchoress, Julian of Norwich, and repeated it several times as the grazing sheep huddled close by: "And all shall be well, and all shall be well, and all manner of thing shall be well."

I felt a sense of peace and comfort as I made my way back to the car. I drove a short distance to a roadside café, where I ordered broiled salmon and French wine. It was the first real meal I'd had since I began my journey. A woman's beautiful, ethereal voice flowed from the café's speaker singing the classic Sandy Denny folksong, "Who Knows Where the Time Goes?" I was here at last, a lot of time had passed, but it was not too late. I felt hopeful that all would be well.

CHAPTER FOUR

Driving to Doolin

AT TEN THIRTY in the evening it was still light outside, and I was sitting by the window in my room at the Doolin Farmhouse B&B in Doolin, County Clare, watching a full moon emerge from behind the hills across the road. In a few more hours the moon would travel across the sky, hover over the Cliffs of Moher just three miles up the road, and sink into the horizon of the Atlantic Ocean. I wouldn't witness its descent. I'd be sound asleep after experiencing one of the most exhilarating days of my life.

I had risen that morning at the Gregorys' to the sun streaming through the lace curtains and the sound of cows mooing. Mr. Gregory was busy moving the cows to pasture while Mrs. Gregory prepared a delicious breakfast for me and my fellow guests, a young couple from Amsterdam and an older couple from Virginia. The Amsterdam couple and I talked about our shared interest in Celtic music, and both couples teased me about my inability to back my car out of my parking spot without killing the engine.

"We stood at the window watching you leave last evening," said the Dutch man.

"Yes," said the man from Virginia. "It was very entertaining."

"Oh, don't give her such a hard time," said his wife. "Remember, we made the mistake of renting a manual our first trip over, and we wouldn't be caught driving anything but an automatic now."

"I'll never rent a manual again either," I smiled. "But in the meantime, I'm glad I could provide some comic entertainment for you."

Reluctantly, I said goodbye to the Gregorys and my fellow guests and headed north toward County Clare, where I expected to spend most of my time exploring the uniquely beautiful limestone landscape of the Burren and the majestic Cliffs of Moher. It was these landscapes that had drawn me to Ireland in the first place. Traditional Celtic musicians had been writing and playing songs about them for centuries, and I was enamored with the new Irish musicians, such as Luka Bloom and Maura O'Connell, who were continuing the tradition. Luka Bloom's "Fertile Rock" and Maura O'Connell's "West Coast of Clare" were among my favorite songs. I would be staying at the Farmhouse Bed and Breakfast in Doolin, a village considered by many to be the home of traditional Irish music, and I was immeasurably excited about the prospect of listening to traditional Irish music in the local pubs at night and exploring the Cliffs of Moher and the Burren during the day. It sounded like pure paradise to me.

I was nervous about more long-distance driving, of course, but it proved to be less frightening than I had imagined. Still,

I found myself calling on Julian of Norwich's words again and reciting in my head over and over, *And all shall be well . . .*

I was the last one to pull my car up the ramp and onto the Talbert Ferry to cross the Shannon River into Clare. It was my first time on a ferry, and I was thankful that I was able to follow the hand gestures of the ferryman directing me up the ramp and not drive off the ramp into the river. As it happened, the Dutch couple were on the ferry too. We stood along the railing, gazing at the sun-dappled water while the wind blew our hair to smithereens, and they continued to rib me about my driving.

I said goodbye to the Dutch couple and exited the ferry without incident. I had been driving for a few hours, and as the road became more isolated, I was beginning to wonder if I was on the correct road. I wasn't taking any chances this time. There were houses dotting the landscape, so I stopped at one to ask directions. A middle-aged man in a County Clare football jersey answered the door and was happy to help. It turned out that I was on the correct road and that Doolin was "just up the rood aways."

There was quite a ruckus coming from the house. A large group of adults and kids were gathered around the TV watching a football match between County Clare and Mayo.

"Would ye like to come in for a cup of tea?" the man asked. "The game is on and Clare is up by seven points!"

"Oh, that's very kind of you, but I don't want to interrupt you during the game, and I really need to get to Doolin. Thanks again!"

"Yer most welcome, luv. Have a wonderful holiday. Bye now."

"Bye. Slainte," I answered, using the Gaelic word for "Cheers" and hoping I had pronounced it correctly.

The sunny day transformed into another soft day as I maneuvered the narrow, curvy road toward the Cliffs of Moher. Windy too, I noticed as I made the turn into the lot and found a place to park. *So this is really it. I'm really here.* The place I had wanted to travel to for so many years. The massive cliffs rose more than 700 feet, constantly battling with the Atlantic Ocean below. I couldn't believe I was finally here. Would it live up to my expectations? Would it hold for me the spiritual energy that these ancient places of pilgrimage held for others? I pulled on my royal-blue raincoat and walked to the visitor center. There was the ever-needed toilet and a small café inside. I ordered some tea and sat on a high stool at a table overlooking the cliff path. I watched the other visitors, people of all ages and nationalities, walking toward the cliffs. I wasn't ready to go there yet. I wanted to take my time and center myself before making the short trek. I just sat there sipping my tea, smiling to myself and thinking that I'd really done it. I'd made it here on my own terms. Mine alone.

The sidewalk path to the cliffs was filled with musicians and artists. I walked past a young man playing a fiddle, his green parka bellowing out behind him, and a woman with long salt-and-pepper hair playing the Celtic harp, its magical tones wafting into the mist.

Turning left and down a few steps, I found the railing for the side view of the cliffs. My breath stopped. Then I inhaled deeply and let out a huge sigh. What a sight! I soaked in the panoramic view of each cliff followed by another, as if nature had arranged them in perfect symmetrical precision. My gaze then followed the cliffs down, down 700 feet to the roiling sea below. I stood there mesmerized, losing all track of time, my eyes welling up with tears.

Dear God, thank you for bringing me here.

I was standing next to a small group of French tourists. One of them, a man with graying hair and beard and wearing a bright-red jacket glanced at me.

"Look," he said, handing me his binoculars and pointing toward the narrow cliffs, "there are puffins in the holes in the cliffs. They burrow in them and lay their eggs."

"Wow!" I said, focusing the binoculars on the cliff face as numerous puffins flew in and out of the holes, then cascaded into the sea. "I've studied Atlantic puffins at an Audubon camp in Maine. Aren't they amazing? And when they fly, they make a sound like a chainsaw," I said, laughing.

"Yes, they are funny seabirds."

"Look," I said, bringing the binoculars to my eyes again, "there are guillemots too!"

I handed the binoculars back to him. He pulled them to his eyes and laughed. "You're right. Lovely birds, all of them, and so busy, busy, busy."

The others in his group were moving away toward the steps. Reluctantly he said, "I must go now. Enjoy your visit."

"Merci," I answered in what was probably my worst attempt at French. "And merci for sharing your binoculars with me. Au revoir."

"Au revoir."

The wind was picking up and so was the mist. I focused the long lens on my camera and took some shots, but I knew they wouldn't do the cliffs justice. They were too majestic and mysterious, something that I knew would be difficult to capture with my camera. I took more shots anyway, hoping for that one lucky, perfect photo. Then I packed my camera into my camera bag and leaned against the rail overlooking the cliffs. I don't know how long I stood there. Time seemed to stand still as I watched the sun peek in and out of the clouds, changing the light on the cliffs from dark brown to indigo blue and back to dark brown. Even with the angry sea below and the wind screeching through my hair, I felt a sense of peace and calm overtaking me like a long-lost friend from far away. I reveled in it. The Black Dog was at bay for the moment, and the feelings of joy, love, and gratitude gelled into a feeling of oneness with the majestic landscape that surrounded me. Everything felt so familiar, like I had been here before. And once again the comforting words came out of nowhere: *And all shall be well, and all shall be well, and all manner of thing shall be well.*

I was jarred out of my reverie by a group of boys screaming and chasing each other along the path. They were oblivious to the beauty around them. I made my way back to my car and drove the few miles toward Doolin to check into the bed and breakfast, knowing that I would return to the cliffs later.

Maeve Sullivan greeted me at the door of the Doolin Farmhouse, a two-story pink stucco dwelling with white shutters overlooking the Atlantic Ocean. Maeve, robust with short dark hair and rosy cheeks, and her husband, Brendan, were the fifth generation to farm here. Their three boys, two school-aged and one toddler, lived here too along with a border collie named Murphy. It was a working farm of cattle and horses strewn across many acres along the path to the Cliffs of Moher. The village of Doolin was about a mile up the road and down the hill in the opposite direction. My upstairs room with its twin bed was small and cozy. I settled in and, before drifting off for a short nap, I thought about how grateful I was to be here. I was still feeling the tightness in my body, the nervousness from driving into the unknown. I wasn't accustomed to taking these risks, especially maneuvering a car whose workings were on the opposite side of what I was accustomed to driving, not to mention remembering to keep the car on the other side of the road. I took some deep breaths to quell the butterflies in my stomach and reminded myself that I had succeeded in getting to this point unscathed. Quite an accomplishment for an inexperienced international traveler such as myself. What next, I wondered as I drifted off to sleep.

That evening I drove into Doolin to investigate the pub scene. I had read about the two established pubs before coming here. Both are well-known for hosting the best traditional Celtic musicians. I visited O'Connor's first for dinner. Not being familiar with how to order, I sat at a table in the back and watched the other customers. They were walking up to the counter to place their orders, so I did the same. Waiting for the food to be delivered to my table I struck up a conversation with two college-aged women next to me from Iowa. They were backpacking along part of the western Irish coast known as the Atlantic Way, spending their evenings in pubs and sleeping in hostels.

"That sounds like a great way to travel with your best friend, but not for a middle-aged woman alone," I said.

They agreed. "Yeah, there can be some real creeps out there," said one of them.

I drove to McGann's on the other side of the village. It wasn't as polished as O'Connor's but it had a friendly, more informal feel to it. I ordered an Irish coffee and was invited to join a mother and her college-age daughter from Boston at their table. The mother, Sandy, and her daughter, Lynne, were staying in Doolin and hadn't rented a car. Earlier they had hiked up the coast road in the rain to the little village of Fanore, where Lynne's favorite college professor was from. As they were heading back to Doolin a villager recognized them and offered them a lift back to town. I told them about stopping at an Irish household to ask directions and being invited in for tea. We spent the next several minutes gushing about the generosity of the Irish people while we waited and waited for the trad musicians to set up and get started. I was learning that Irish time isn't my time. The Irish are in no hurry for anything. So nine o'clock my time is roughly ten o'clock their time.

"Hey, you two," said Lynne as she got up from her chair. "I'm going to leave you to yourselves for a while. I see a hunky guy over there I want to introduce myself to."

"Go for it, honey," said Sandy. "Just don't forget that your momma's here."

"No kidding, Mom," Lynne laughed as she left our table.

We sat for a few minutes, nursing our drinks and looking around at the growing crowd.

"So, are you divorced?" asked Sandy.

"Yes," I answered. "Six years ago. And you?"

"Twelve years for me."

We looked at each other with an understanding that divorced women share.

"It does get better," she said.

"I know," I answered, taking a sip of my Irish coffee. "And it is better. It's just hard being solely responsible for my two daughters. They're having a rough time. I worry about them—and me."

"How so?"

"Well, my oldest daughter has dropped out of school and left home. She's living with some friends and working in a pizza place. Hardly the life I raised her for. My other daughter, five years younger, is struggling emotionally. She puts up a strong, stubborn front, but I know she feels abandoned by her father's sudden move to Florida."

"And what about you?"

"Oh God, where do I start? A whole mix of feelings," I said as I brushed my hair back from my damp forehead. "I feel abandoned too, yet I wanted to be free of him. I'm the one who couldn't take it anymore and asked for the divorce. Then I found out about the other woman, and, most likely, there were other women before her. I felt so betrayed and *so* angry. My God, my anger scared me! And I struggle financially, of course. There are always money worries. It's like I'm consumed by all of that when I'm home. That's why this trip is so important to me. Finally, a chance to get away and think and see what I'm capable of on my own." I took another sip of my Irish coffee. "So, Sandy, how did you get through it?"

Sandy put down her beer and played with her long gold necklace. "Well, I was more fortunate than you. My ex and I are on good terms. We're not best friends, mind you, but we respect one another. He's a doting father, and he helps out financially. In fact, he's paying for Lynne's college."

"Wow, that's fantastic!" I said. "That's got to take a big load off your mind." I looked down at my drink, gathering courage, and asked, "Have you dated at all?"

"Some," she answered. "I've dated some wonderful men and a few scumbags, but I haven't met any I would like to be with long-term. What about you?"

"None. I wouldn't even know how to begin dating. I married when I was nineteen, so I don't really have any dating experience. I don't know that I would trust myself anyway. Besides, I'm so busy with my work and my girls that I really don't have any energy left to put into dating."

"As I said, it will get better," Sandy reassured. "As your daughters get older, you'll have more time for yourself. I'm glad you're taking some time now and that we were able to meet in this pub and have this conversation."

"Me too. Are you going to be here awhile?"

"I'm afraid not. We're taking a bus to Dublin in the morning."

"Darn," I answered.

"Yeah," she replied.

I got up to get another Irish coffee. When I came back to the table a New Zealander, who had downed a few too many Guinnesses, offered to take my picture. Reluctantly, I handed my camera over to him hoping that he could get a halfway focused shot. It turned out that he could. When my mother saw the photo of a woman with a big smile, disheveled light-brown hair, wearing a white button-down travel shirt, and raising her Irish coffee in a toast, she exclaimed, "Why, Diane, I don't think I've ever seen you look so happy!"

The trad band began playing around ten o'clock. I wanted to stay, but the light outside was fading, and I wasn't comfortable enough to drive in the dark, even for a short distance. I hugged my newfound friends and carefully drove on the "wrong" side of the road back to Doolin Farmhouse smiling all the way.

CHAPTER FIVE

Inisheer

THE NEXT morning at breakfast Maeve told me about a day trip to Inisheer, the smallest of the three Aran Islands. Since visiting the islands was on my want-to-do list, I was elated. The opportunity to visit one of these magical islands I had read so much about was another dream come true. The boat would leave from Doolin Harbour later in the morning, then let us off at the harbor in Inisheer, where we were free to explore the island for three hours. The trip included a close-up tour of the Cliffs of Moher from the water. The price was right, so I packed my camera equipment and drove to Doolin Harbour.

The weather was perfect, blue skies with puffy white clouds, then those clouds would cover the sun for a while. Lots of different slants of light. Perfect for photography. I concentrated on cleaning and adjusting my camera so that I wouldn't feel seasick on the short ride to Inisheer. I had never ridden in a small boat on the ocean, and I didn't want to take the chance of having to share the one toilet on board with the unlucky passengers whose breakfasts refused to stay in their stomachs.

After we docked, I headed up toward the narrow road leading to the ruins of O'Brien's Castle.

The properties on all three of the Aran Islands were divided with stone walls, making the islands unique from any other place. The view from the harbor made the island look like a hilly sheet cake cut into various-sized squares. Few cars were on the island, and many of the residents got around with donkeys and wagons or bikes. I had never seen anything like it. It was like going back in time one hundred years, yet the place itself felt timeless to me, and the various Celtic crosses in the cemetery brought an ancient spirituality to the place. There was a feeling of being at one with the rugged landscape, but also a deep respect for the land and the sea surrounding it. Living here has always been a life-and-death proposition for its residents, depending on the whims of the wind and the sea. Life's tough and, other than the restaurants and B&Bs for tourists, income has always been hard to come by. But oh, was it beautiful! I felt so fortunate to be there.

I lost myself in my photography and it felt like such a blessing to be so relaxed and engaged with taking both color and black-and-white photos of the Celtic crosses in the cemetery, St. Agnes Church from the 14th century, O'Brien's Castle, and more. I wandered up and down the narrow, hilly roads focusing on anything that looked like a promising image—draft horses in the fields beyond the stone walls, a wrought iron garden gate, a border collie resting in a cottage doorway.

Before long, it was time to head down the hill toward the port. That's when I came upon a boy of about ten on his old black bike.

"Allo, ma'am," he said as he straddled his bike. His short-cropped brown hair, freckled face, and zipped black jacket made him look like photos of my brothers in the 1950s. He looked down at the road with a shy smile.

"Well, hi there! Are you enjoying your bike ride on this beautiful day?"

"Yes, ma'am," he answered, putting his hands in his pockets and looking down at the ground again.

Uh-oh, he's so shy. What can I say to put him at ease? Oh yes, the dog.

"Hey, do you know that dog back there aways?" I asked. "When I tried to take a picture of him, he ran right up to the stone wall like he was going to bite my head off!"

"Ah, yes, that would be the Sullivans' dog, Geordie. He's old and half blind. He don't mean no harm."

"Oh, that's good to know. I don't feel as scared now."

He glanced down at the ground again and then at my camera. "I like your camera, ma'am."

"Thanks. It's like an old friend. I take it everywhere I go. Do you have something like that?"

"Yes, ma'am, me bike," he answered as he pointed proudly to his old black two-wheeler that looked like it had seen better days.

"Wow, that's quite a bike. Do you ride it all around the island?"

"Yes, ma'am. And to school too."

"Good for you! I used to ride my bike to school when I was younger too!"

He laughed and looked down at the ground again.

"Since I have my friend with me," I said, lifting my camera, "do you mind if I take your picture?"

"I don't mind."

"Great! Okay, don't mind me. Just look at the camera and smile."

His shy little smile melted my heart.

"Brilliant," I said as I lowered my camera. "Thank you for posing."

"Yer welcome, ma'am."

"Well," I said, glancing down the hill. "The boat's going to be leaving soon. I'd better get down to the port. I've enjoyed talking with you. Take care and enjoy the rest of this beautiful day."

"And you as well, ma'am."

I walked down the hill and boarded the boat. On the way back the boat stopped beside the cliffs, where we got a close-up look at the waves crashing and gnawing at the shale and sandstone. We were being splashed by the crashing waves, and despite trying to shield it, my camera lens was getting wet. I knew it would be fruitless to try and get a decent shot. So I decided to put my camera away, walk to the boat railing, and let the spray from the rough sea envelop me. I leaned into the mist and told myself that the turbulent sea and the Black Dog would always be with me, determined by my ancestry and my life experiences, but that I would tame them. Along this journey I would become more self-confident and more trusting of my own intuition. Maybe even become more vulnerable too. I would feel renewed, more aware of my purpose in this world. What that purpose was, I didn't really understand, but I knew I was on my way to finding out.

CHAPTER SIX

Turbulence and Grace

A LITTLE BEFORE seven that evening I drove to the cliffs to finish the rest of my black-and-white film. The entrance gate was closing at seven, but the gatekeeper motioned me in without me having to pay. All of the tour buses were gone, and I was thrilled to see that I nearly had the place to myself. I shot the rest of my film rather quickly, taking advantage of the golden light of evening and visualizing the way it would translate to black and white. The crashing sound of the waves hitting the rocks below was mesmerizing. I sat on a bench near the walkway, closed my eyes, and listened. The waves sounded angry, taking me back to a time when I experienced my own anger in its rawest form. I didn't want to go back there, but the angry waves insisted.

I had been married for twenty-two years to a man I had absolutely nothing in common with other than our two beautiful daughters. We had married when we were kids, infused with promises from early '70s pop culture, Kahlil Gibran's *The Prophet*, and the faux poetry of Rod McKuen.

"I can't take it anymore," I told my husband one October evening when the girls were in bed and we were sitting in silence in the family room. "I want a divorce."

He squirmed on the sofa and whined, "But can we afford it?"

What a stupid response to someone you've shared a life with for so long. But what else would I have expected from someone who had always put himself before his family?

"We can't afford not to," I answered.

We agreed that for financial reasons he could stay in the house until December, when the apartment he wanted would become available. I requested that both of us work with a mediator so that we could do what was best for our daughters. He agreed, and we were negotiating quite well, I thought, about shared custody, visitation, and child support. My mom and stepdad drove up from Texas for Thanksgiving but left early because, as Mom told me later, "We could feel the tension and we felt like he was going to explode any minute." As preparations for a very different Christmas were underway, I was on my Apple II computer late one evening adding addresses to my Christmas card list. It was the early days of email when families shared email accounts and surfed the internet via Prodigy. I discovered an email in our shared email account from a woman I didn't know. It was addressed to my husband, but, curious, I opened it anyway. I read in disbelief as she went on and on about how much she missed him and maybe they could meet after work tomorrow for drinks in the bar at the downtown Marriott. She also mentioned that she couldn't wait to get her hands on him. After reading the message several times and letting its meaning sink in, I sat there staring at the screen, absolutely stunned. I was stunned at my husband's betrayal, to be sure. I had always been faithful and expected that he would be too. But I was even more surprised by what turned out to be my own naivete in discovering that he was capable of finding someone to have an affair with! My husband was not known for his social skills, much less his lovemaking skills. He was awkward and self-conscious and vehemently defensive if these shortcomings were brought to his attention. Where in the hell did he find someone who would be stupid enough to have an affair with him, I wondered. And how dare he carry on this charade with the mediators about how the two of us would work in the best interest of our daughters and be friends!

I felt the anger welling up inside me, boiling over like a volcano erupting. My hands were shaking, my arms became weak, and I felt like I was going to throw up. I sat there wondering what to do. Should I respond to the woman stupid enough to send an email to a shared account? Hell yes!

I placed my shaking hands over the keyboard, took a deep breath, and typed a reply to the other woman. (I'll call her Gidget since, surprise, she turned out to be much younger.) I typed that I was so sorry, but that my husband would not be able to join her tomorrow after work due to a previous commitment that he didn't know about yet. I informed her that he would be busy retrieving his belongings from his former home, since he wouldn't have them with him when I kicked his ass to the curb later that night. I didn't wait for her reply. Still in shock, I stomped downstairs and confronted my husband.

What followed was a lot of patronizing "It isn't what you think" remarks, denial after denial of other evidence-based affairs, and the realization that "Gidget" was married too. Despite his protests that he didn't have anywhere to stay, I didn't yield. Why would I feel sorry for someone who lied to me and betrayed me? I kicked him out that night. Angry and sobbing, I then called the mediators to explain what had happened. They didn't seem surprised. Then I called my mom. Though very sympathetic and worried, she didn't seem surprised either. Was it that obvious to everyone but me?

I was furious at him for thinking that I could be so easily replaced. Furious with the lack of respect he demonstrated toward me and our children. Most of all, I was furious with myself for having wasted so many years of my life with him.

How would I be able to pull myself together and go to work in the morning? I had to pull myself together. There was no question that my daughters and I would be relying upon my income to get us through this mess. There was no spousal support in Indiana, with its no-fault divorce law. He would be angry and vindictive about being caught in so many lies. I knew that I could no longer trust him, that his promises were hollow, and that I probably would have to fight for adequate child support and arrange for it to be automatically deducted from his paycheck. But even I was surprised at how low he would go when, a few months later, he told our twelve-year-old daughter that she would have to decide who she wanted to live with because he was moving to Florida. He didn't think I needed to know. His life was none of my business. Apparently, he didn't think that doing emotional harm to our daughter was any of my business either. I was on the phone to my attorney as soon as my daughter came home sobbing and told me the news. Neither my attorney nor his could believe what he was trying to pull. "He just doesn't get it," his attorney told mine. He moved into his parents' vacation home in Florida, but without our daughter. And as I had predicted, child support had to be garnished from his paycheck to ensure that I would receive it.

But all of that was yet to come. I still had to get through that first night. I had to be stronger than I'd ever been. I didn't have the luxury of having a nervous breakdown. I had to be strong and present for my daughters. I spent that night and many nights after that lying in bed staring at the ceiling, falling in and out of a shallow sleep. I did go to work the next morning, but the day after I left to see my doctor about getting a prescription for something that would keep me from breaking into tears in front of my students. He prescribed a low dose of Xanax and, while that didn't prevent me from feeling sad and angry, I was able to control my emotions.

The following months were the most difficult of my life. Although my in-laws lied for their son, I was intent on my daughters maintaining a good relationship with their grandparents. I would make the one-hour trek to their home, drop off the girls, and spend time at the local coffee shop until their visit was over. As for my parents, they wanted to kill him, but they were also relieved that he was out of my life. I never realized how much my family despised him until we divorced. They had seen through his lies and realized right away that he was not good for me.

But my anger was much deeper than theirs and, in time, I realized that it had much more to do with issues of abandonment, rejection, and mistrust in men that dated back to my father's suicide when I was ten years old. I realized that I had married at the age of nineteen the first young man I had dated, who, unfortunately, turned out to be both the worst version of my father (insecure and self-conscious) and the opposite of my father (self-centered and mean).

As I sat at the cliffs absorbed in the beauty of the sea's natural anger, I knew that I was on the road to forgiveness. I had to be. I couldn't begin this new chapter in my life while carrying this angry, bitter monkey on my back. I pictured the anger as flaming red coals bursting from my heart and hurling themselves over the cliff, falling with an extinguishing last hiss into the water below.

I drove back into Doolin hoping to have dinner in one of the pubs and stay for music, but the traffic was ridiculous and the streets were already swarming with tourists. Instead, I made my way back to the coastal road and south to a roadside restaurant called Stonecutters. I loved the name because it reminded me of southern Indiana, where those who carve limestone from its many quarries are referred to as stonecutters. It didn't feel like a coincidence to me that the Burren has limestone deposits too.

Two things happened at Stonecutters. First, I met another angel in the form of a waitress, this time with a young, heart-shaped face, a kind, easy smile, and shoulder-length, light-brown pigtails. Her name was Grace and she was an artist.

"I've lived here since I was a child," she said after she brought my order, "and there's a spiritual connection here that feeds my art. I wouldn't want to live anywhere else."

"What exactly is that spiritual connection to you?" I asked. "Is it Celtic in nature?"

"'Tis, because I focus on nature in my art, most especially the rhythms and colors of nature and how our spirits are renewed by it."

"Wow! That sounds beautiful! What medium do you use in your art?"

"Watercolors mostly, but sometimes I experiment with mixed-media collage."

"Me too," I answered. "I'm a photographer, and I've been doing some digital collage using Photoshop, but I like the down-and-dirty 3D mixed-media collage better."

We both laughed, and then she glanced nervously at the other tables. "I must attend to the other guests," she said, "but I would love to talk with you some more. I'll be back."

"That would be great. I'll be here."

When she returned we talked some more about art, which led to the topic of the unique local landscape, the Burren. She offered some advice about which parts to visit.

"It's really hard," I said, "because I only have a little time left and there's so much to see."

"Well, here," she said as she pulled out a napkin and a pen. "I'll write down a couple of places that would fit well with your schedule. The Burren Centre in Kilfenora is a great introduction to the Burren. There are all kinds of things to see around the center as well. You might also like the abbey at Dysert O'Dea. Not that many tourists know about it, and there's a lovely high cross in the middle of a pasture."

"Have you heard of Brigid's Well?" I asked. "I've been wanting to visit it, but I'm not quite sure where it is."

"Ah, yes, yes, Brigid's Well! Lovely place. Yer in luck, it's just up the rood. I'll draw you a map."

"Oh, thank you, thank you, Grace! I've probably driven past it several times. I really appreciate all your help. You've been so kind. It's been such a pleasure meeting you."

"And you as well, Diane. I wish you were here on holiday longer. We seem to be two peas in a pod, like. There's so much I'd like to show you. Maybe when you come back, then?"

"Oh yes. I'll definitely be back."

"Good, then. Have a safe trip home across the pond," she said as she gave me a hug. I hugged her back. Grateful for having met a kindred spirit.

As I was leaving, the second thing happened. Three older Irish women engaged me in conversation.

"Yer traveling alone, are ye?" one asked.

"Yes, I am," I answered.

"My, yer a brave one!" said another. "Don't ye think she's a brave one, Maura?"

"Indeed," confirmed Maura. "I think it's brilliant, darlin'. Maybe you would fancy moving here someday."

"Yes, maybe she would. Don't you think that would be brilliant, Doris?"

"Right so," answered Doris. "And what about you, dear. Would you fancy living here?"

"Oh, I would love it," I agreed. "But I have a good job back home in Indiana and two teenage daughters. Even though I would like to leave my daughters sometimes, I couldn't leave them behind permanently."

"Oh, teenage daughters! Do tell!" said Maura, throwing her hands in the air.

All of us broke out laughing. Mothers of teenage daughters sharing a universal language.

CHAPTER SEVEN

The Burren Beckons

I WAS ENJOYING my last breakfast at Doolin Farmhouse, and the Sullivan toddler, Finn, was entertaining me by carrying his blankie in his teeth while galloping around the table making horse noises. The other guests had gone upstairs, and I was stalling as Maeve bustled around the table. I didn't want to leave.

"I'm going to miss you and your family, Maeve," I said.

"And we're going to miss you as well, Diane. You've been a wonderful guest. My hope is that you will stay with us again when you return."

"Oh, you know I will, Maeve. I wouldn't want to miss a chance to see how your boys have grown! I've enjoyed them so much."

"Yes, and they're quite taken with you. When will we see you again?"

"Next June, I hope," I answered.

"And you'll plan a longer holiday," stated Maeve. It wasn't a question. "And I'll be certain to have plenty of fresh laundry hanging on the clothesline for yer pictures."

We both laughed and Maeve's rosy cheeks got a little rosier. I had embarrassed her when she first caught me taking photos of the Sullivan laundry flapping in the breeze, until I explained that taking these pictures was "a thing" with me and getting just the right exposure and shutter speed was an art form.

"Let us know when yer ready and Brendan will bring down yer luggage," she said as she wiped down the table. "And, Diane," she paused as she gazed at me with her loving smile, "don't make yerself a stranger here."

I wept as I pulled out of the long drive and onto the coast road. I looked in my rearview mirror and saw their middle son Ronan waving at me as Murphy pranced several feet behind my car, stopping only when he came to the end of the drive. How I was going to miss them. But I had a full day ahead exploring the Burren before checking into my final farmhouse bed and breakfast just outside the town of Ennis with its short drive to Shannon Airport.

Grace's directions to Brigid's Well were good. It was just off the coast road on an unmarked, narrow sideroad overlooking the village of Liscannor, so it was easy to see why I had missed it before. It was raining lightly and the place was deserted. I climbed the steps to a landscaped courtyard with a gate to a cemetery and a small white stucco building with an arched doorway marked "Brigid's Well." Several feet in front of the doorway was a large statue of St. Brigid encased in a plexiglass shield.

St. Brigid is one of Ireland's patron saints, along with St. Patrick and St. Columba. Her roots are pagan, heralding back to Brigit, the goddess of wisdom, poetry, and animals. St. Brigid was a nun and abbess, a contemporary and friend of St. Patrick, who was responsible for founding many monasteries for both women and men. Little is known of her life, but there are many stories and legends about her replenishing large amounts of milk from dairy cows and beer for lepers, giving assistance to women in labor, etc. Hence, she is the patron saint, not only of Ireland, but also of dairy farmers, the sick, midwives, and hearth and home. Her feast day is February 1st, the first day of spring, or Imbolc, in Ireland. There are many wells throughout Ireland bearing her name, the well in Kildare being the most popular, with the well in Liscannor a close second. The Irish are serious about their holy wells, again heralding back to pagan times but Christianized later, and they truly believe in their healing powers.

I thought about all of this as I entered the stucco well enclosure. The stone walls flickered with votive candles, and mementos, photographs, and prayers had been left for loved ones, many attached precariously with string and tape. The smell of dampness and its coolness had a penitential feel to it, and the light sound of water cascading into a trough drew me in. It was like passing through time to a more ancient faith. I could understand why wells like these held such appeal for pagans and continued to hold appeal down the ages for people of faith. The reflecting candlelight, and the light tinkling sound of the water, filled the atmosphere with a prayerful sense of purity and serenity that can only be found in ancient holy places. The inner peace it gave me was so different from the violent beauty of the cliffs. But the healing was the same. I bent down, cupped some water in my hands, and drank its soothing coolness. Hands to mouth, eyes closed, cool, clear water down my throat and into my core, followed by warmth flowing from my core to my extremities. Peace. No anxiety. No depression. A moment of total peace. Overcome with such an unexpected gift, I kneeled in gratitude and thanked God for placing me in this holy place right here, right now.

And all shall be well, and all shall be well, and all manner of thing shall be well.

I wanted to linger at Brigid's Well, but the rain had me pushing toward Kilfenora and The Burren Centre. I was impressed with the modern building of wood and limestone that seemed to blend into the surrounding countryside with Mt. Mullaghmore in the distance. The center had an excellent display and video presentation about the Burren's geological and historical past, and I took advantage of tea and scones in the tearoom. The rain had let up, so I walked through the village, stopping at the magnificent ruins of the circa 1200 Kilfenora Cathedral with its ornate carvings and numerous high crosses. The church's nickname, Church of the Fertile Hillside, reminded me of Luka Bloom's song about the Burren, "Fertile Rock," with its plea to preserve the Burren's unique beauty from development. Kilfenora is also known as the home of ceili (pronounced kaylee) music, traditional Irish music that accompanies a dance. Since I wasn't there in the evening, I didn't have the opportunity to sit in one of the pubs and witness the award-winning Kilfenora Ceili Band. Something I planned to make up for on my next visit.

Instead, I took Grace's advice and made a side trip to the lovely village of Corofin, but I didn't stay long. I simply drove down a few of the main streets admiring the colorful village shops. I was anxious to get on to Dysert O'Dea and eventually I found the one-lane road that led back toward the round tower. There was grass growing in the middle of the road and as I gingerly guided the car along the path without killing the engine, farmers were pausing their work in the fields and smiling to one another as if to say "Here comes another tourist. Let's see if she can stay on the rood." I showed them.

I toured the round tower, even climbing its narrow staircase, and viewed the video that explained its history. Dysert O'Dea originated as a monastery founded by St. Tola in the 8th century, but most of its present structures are from the 12th century. It includes the round tower, the ruins of St. Tola Abbey, St. Tola High Cross, and even the Victorian ruins of Synge's Lodge.

The rain had let up a little, so I took the path to the high cross and the abbey, which was located in the middle of a cow pasture. I was struck by the incongruity of such a treasure being guarded by grazing cows and by how much more commercialized it would be if it were in America. I sidestepped the cow patties while shooting photos of the carvings of the bishops in the stone cross and then climbed over a low stone wall and walked toward the abbey. That's when I met another angel. He was the groundskeeper, and when I first saw him he was busily wielding a noisy Weedwacker around the edges of the abbey. I was silently wishing he would stop disturbing this holy place when I saw him stop to greet his wife, who had brought along their two Jack Russell terriers. They greeted me and we talked while I played with the dogs. When his wife had to leave, taking the dogs with her, he offered to show me around. I was amazed at his knowledge and passion for the place. As we walked around the grounds, he told me even more about the architecture and history of Dysert O'Dea, and he waited patiently as I shot photos. Once he had verified that I was a serious birdwatcher, he told me that he was going to show me something very special. We walked back to a far corner inside the abbey and there, in a little cranny high up on the wall, was a kestrel nest, something I never would have found on my own. I thanked him and told him how helpful he had been and that maybe I could return tomorrow.

"How delightful it would be if ye could do that," he said. "But if ye can't, ye have a wonderful holiday and a safe trip home."

As I walked back across the pasture under the watchful gaze of the cows, I was certain I would return. I was so grateful for meeting this kind man and so sorry that I didn't get his name. I just wanted to spend more time talking with him. I left reluctantly and drove on to Ennis.

What a shock it was to drive into Ennis and discover that it's not a village, but a teeming, noisy, traffic-filled city. The city center is a maze of narrow streets filled with shops and pubs, and the outer, newer section reminded me of an American suburb. The B&B I had reserved was about three kilometers away from Ennis on the road to Killimer. It was a well-kept horse farm, and Maureen, the innkeeper, was very kind and accommodating, but it didn't have the warmth of Doolin.

I drove back into Ennis and managed to find a parking lot close to a pub so that I wouldn't have to parallel park on the street. After dinner, I shopped for souvenirs, but my heart wasn't in it. I grew frustrated trying to walk the maze of narrow streets and still remember how to find my way back to my car. I returned to the B&B around eight thirty fully intending to retrace my path back to Dysert O'Dea in the morning and then on to Galway and Connemara.

Maybe it was delayed jet lag, if there was such a thing, but I felt exhausted. It wasn't that late, but I was ready for bed. It had been a day filled with the excitement of visiting places I had read about and longed to see for so many years coupled with the stress of driving on unfamiliar roads. I was grateful and proud that I had "put myself out there" on the road, explored new places, and met some fascinating people. I looked out the window and saw the horses grazing close to the fence line. Though tired, I didn't want to give up the opportunity to nuzzle with them. Besides, it was the magic hour, the time in the evening when the light is just right.

Bedtime could wait awhile.

CHAPTER EIGHT

The Bogman on the Bus

I WAS TIRED of driving. Tired of having to remember to shift with my left hand, to stay on the left side of the road, that "left is right" when making a turn. The thought of driving from Ennis to Galway and on to Connemara exhausted me and made my stomach churn. I needed to rest.

I expressed my concern to Maureen at breakfast. "Poor dear," she said as she poured a cup of tea. Handing me the delicate white cup and saucer, she stepped back and ran her long fingers through her short red hair in deep concentration. "Ah, yes. I know! Perhaps ye might be interested in taking a guided day trip on a short bus. There's one that leaves the car park behind the visitor center later this mornin' and returns late afternoon. I can call and make the arrangements if you'd like."

"Oh, gosh, yes. That would be wonderful."

A few hours later that morning, I drove the narrow streets of Ennis and found a parking spot in the same parking lot as the bus, but I couldn't figure out how to use the parking meter. An older man approached and said, "Here luv, let me help. How long will you be here?"

"Oh, probably eight hours or so."

"Not a problem," he said as he pulled out some euros and inserted them into the machine. The machine spit out a ticket. "Here," he said, handing the ticket to me. "Now, put this inside your car window and ye can be on yer way."

"Thank you! Please let me pay you for the ticket."

"No, luv. Glad to help," he answered as he walked away.

I love the Irish! I love the Irish!

The short white bus was ready and waiting behind the visitor center. I gave my name to a middle-aged woman with a clipboard, and she welcomed me as I boarded the bus and found a seat midway back. The black vinyl seats were comfortable enough and the bus was filled with an assortment of ages, mostly couples but a few singles like me. It was pretty quiet. A little too quiet for a tour bus, I thought. Even though I had vowed that I would never take one of those bus tours where the tourists disembark at various scenic points to snap a few pictures and then board the bus again to do the same thing a few miles down the road, I had to admit that I was so relieved to turn the driving over to someone else while I simply sat and took in the view.

The middle-aged woman introduced herself as Carol and her husband, Michael, was the driver. She explained that we would head northwest, stop for a snack and shopping in Gort. (I love that name. It rhymes with snort.) We would proceed along the coast of Galway Bay, on to the town of Spiddal, and make our way along the edge of the Connemara region. We would then stop in Galway City for a few hours to have lunch and do some sightseeing on our own before making our way back to Ennis. Sounded like a great plan to me.

I loved the town of Gort, despite its name. It's a bustling little town with a square filled with all sorts of shops. I stopped at Michael Kennedy Ceramics—he's one of the leading ceramic artists in Ireland—where I bought a unique votive candle holder glazed in shades of sky blue and green. I watched his apprentices work for a while and marveled at their talent at the potter's wheel. I had tried the wheel a few years earlier and all I had to show for my artistic ability was a ceramic pancake with a lopsided rim. I met up with three fellow bus riders, and we decided to have tea and a Danish at a small café on the square. I enjoyed talking with the two teenage girls from Austria and a young woman from Vermont. We two Americans laughed when the two Austrians remarked on the difference in our accents. Moving toward Spiddal, we drove past the Salthill area along Galway Bay. As Carol talked on and on about the wonderful recreational activities at Salthill, I was reminded of the Florida Gulf Coast with its crowded sandy beaches and new high-rises under construction. To top off the gaudy scene, a giant Ferris wheel emerged from the other side of the walkway.

As we motored to Spiddal, Carol explained that the town was well-known as the place where The Waterboys made their groundbreaking album, "Fisherman's Blues," back in the 1980s. The album was one of the first to mix trad music and rock. Being a fan of The Waterboys, I already knew about this, and I felt some excitement about going there, even though the studio was gone and The Waterboys definitely wouldn't be there. Snippets of the title song played in my head.

Spiddal was a charming little town with a town center full of shops with prices much more reasonable than in Ennis.

We took about thirty minutes to look around, and I bought a candy bar in a storefront grocery as an excuse to engage in conversation with the locals.

"Look at ye. Traveling all by yerself! Brilliant! Enjoy yer holiday!"

Next, we stopped along the roadside to explore a field filled with bog cotton. I had heard of it but had not seen it yet. The Irish take it for granted just as Americans take beavers and cardinals for granted. But I found it beautiful and put my camera's micro lens to work and took several shots of its fluffy, downy white tufts.

Carol walked over and said, "Our ancestors used it to stuff pillows and mattresses."

"Really?" I got up off the ground, brushed off my hiking pants, and said, "Wow, that would take a lot of bog cotton to fill a mattress. If we did it with our cotton in America at least it wouldn't take as much since the cotton's bigger. Not that I would like the mattress either way."

"Everything's bigger in America," she remarked in a snooty tone as she spun on her heel and stomped away.

Well, Ms. Snooty, apparently some bog cotton got up your smarty arse. Sheesh, who do you think you're earning your living from anyway?

Afraid that I might express these thoughts out loud, I didn't look at her as I boarded the bus.

Ms. Snooty picked up her little microphone and attempted to make a joke.

"Our next stop will be Galway City. You are free to explore for two hours. Please be on time getting back to the bus. If you are the least little bit late you will be required to stand at the front of the bus and sing a song." Everyone except me laughed heartily. I snickered to myself because I was hatching a plan to get one up on Ms. Snooty on our return trip to Ennis that would surprise the heck out of her.

I felt some culture shock from coming out of bog country into a large, overcrowded, and traffic-jammed city. There was one place I was dying to see though. Kennys Bookshop is legendary for its huge variety of new, used, and rare books. The Kenny family has been at it for over seventy-five years and now provide a very successful online service. Every author who is any author has been there for a book signing. I found the shop on High Street. I took a deep anticipatory breath and entered. It was tall and narrow, books everywhere, but not particularly crowded. I enjoyed walking around the shop perusing the books about Ireland and admiring the art on the walls.

Remember, Diane, you can't buy a bunch of books here. Your suitcase won't hold them, and no way would you want to take them on the plane. Stifle the urge, Ms. Librarian. Write down some titles and order them when you get home if you just have to have them.

I purchased two books and two small art prints then stopped at a gourmet coffee shop for a sandwich and an iced mocha, but they didn't have iced mochas. I was disappointed that a so-called gourmet coffee shop didn't have iced mochas but, then again, Ireland didn't have iced anything. I was quick to catch on that if I wanted a glass of iced tea (and I did because I was addicted to it) I had to order hot tea with a glass of ice, and the Irish are pretty stingy with ice.

Before I knew it, the time had come to board the bus. I wasn't late, but that didn't affect my plan. About fifteen minutes into our trip back to Ennis, I stood up and made my way to the front of the bus. Although I wasn't accustomed to performing in front of a crowd, I gathered what courage I had. This was going to be fun.

"Hi everyone! Even though I wasn't late, I thought you all might want to join me in a song. Here's the part you will join in on: First stomp your foot twice and then clap your hands twice. Let's practice that first. Stomp, stomp. Clap, clap. Stomp, stomp. Clap, clap. Great! Keep repeating as you sing this: 'I'm a Bogman, deep down. That's where I come from.' Okay, is everyone game?"

"Yeah," clapped everyone on the bus. Everyone except Ms. Snooty. She just stared at me with her mouth open as she realized that she had just lost control of her bus.

"Okay. Everyone keep stomping and clapping while I sing the first verse. Well, not sing exactly, it's more like a rap. You'll get the idea. Anyway, here we go!"

Stomp, stomp. Clap, clap. Stomp, stomp. Clap, clap . . .

"'Everybody looks at the bog as a place that just lies dead. Nothing to do with the body. Nothing to do with the head. Take me where the heather and the moss grow. The earth lies row and row out there in the sun to dry. I breathe it in when I pedal on by. With the kids and the dogs mucking together, bringing in the turf, no matter what the weather.' Okay, everybody sing!"

"I'm a Bogman, deep down. That's where I come from."

"Again!"

"I'm a Bogman, deep down. That's where I come from."

"One more time!"

"I'm a Bogman, deep down. That's where I come from."

"Wow! You guys were fantastic! That's just a little song that Luka Bloom wrote for his brother Christy Moore. Thanks so much for helping me out!"

Cheers of "Well Done, Brilliant, Fair Play to Ye luv" guided me back to my seat. I stopped long enough to give Ms. Snooty a big smile. She glared back.

I enjoyed getting back at Ms. Snooty while providing some fun for the passengers. And it was especially worth it to see an elegant, older English couple, he dressed in a shirt and tie with a tweed jacket and cap, and she dressed in a gray skirt and jacket with a pearl necklace, clapping and stomping joyously and singing at the top of their lungs:

"I'm a Bogman, deep down. That's where I come from."

CHAPTER NINE

Missing Anne

WHEN I arrived back at the B&B Maureen came out with a message for me to call Anne Rynne. I had been trying to reach Anne since I arrived in Ireland. We had met on a fan site for Luka Bloom, where her handle was "Anne from West Clare." That's why I wanted to get to know her. I wanted to correspond with someone who lived in West Clare. We emailed back and forth for a few months, and I was impressed with her knowledge of anything and everything about Clare. She seemed to know everyone, including Luka. Also, she was kind. She reached out to me when she didn't have to. Shortly before my trip she had confirmed something I had expected from hints in her emails: She is Luka's sister. One of her other brothers is the even more famous Christy Moore, the legendary folk-singer-songwriter, an icon throughout Ireland and Great Britain. I didn't let her brothers' fame influence my attitude toward Anne. I wanted to meet her and be her friend because I was interested in her. We had agreed to meet when I came over, and I was frustrated that I hadn't been able to reach her. She told Maureen that she had my dates confused and had just returned from Scotland. Great. She gets back the night before I leave. I used my calling card and dialed the number that Anne had given me but, once again, I got her answering machine.

"Maybe at least you can talk to her before you leave tomorrow," said Maureen.

"Yes, I hope so," I answered.

"So, how do you know Christy Moore's family?" asked Maureen.

"Oh, it's a long story and who knows where it's going to lead." I laughed. "I met her on her brother Luka's fan site. I didn't know that she was Luka and Christy's sister. We've corresponded ever since, and we were supposed to meet up."

"Well, I do hope ye get to meet her, dear."

"Thanks, Maureen. And thanks for taking the message. I think I'll go to my room and get ready for dinner now. Does the restaurant just up the road have good food?"

"Ah, yes," she said. "The best and very reasonable."

"Good," I said. "That means I won't have to drive back to Ennis."

Maureen laughed. "Enjoy your dinner, dear."

After returning from a delicious dinner, I used my calling card to check in with each of my daughters, hoping I could reach them this time. My eldest was living in Cleveland with her husband and waitressing in an Italian restaurant: "Mom, I can't believe how busy we are! Between waitressing and working on the play I'm writing, there's just no time. And, uh, we're short on money for the rent. Could we borrow a few hundred dollars?"

"I won't be able to answer that until I get home and look over my finances," I said, then biting my tongue so I wouldn't say what I wanted to say. *Why didn't you stay in school and go on to college the way you should have? Of course you're short on money, and you will be as long as you're stuck working menial jobs!* But it would have been pointless to argue with her with an ocean between us. "Well, I guess I'd better go now," I said. "I don't know how many minutes I have left on this calling card, and I still have to call your sister."

"Oh yeah, how is Ireland?" she asked as if it just occurred to her that maybe she should inquire about me.

"I'm having a wonderful time exploring new places, but the driving can be nerve-racking. It's so beautiful here though."

"Cool," she said.

"I'll talk to you soon, honey. I'll be home soon. I love you."

"Love you too, Mom. Bye."

I took a breath, let out a long sigh, and dialed the number where my youngest was staying. Her best friend's mother answered the phone.

"Hi, Kathy, how's it going?"

"Well, hi there, world traveler!" Kathy laughed. "I'm sorry we missed your calls. The girls are doing fine and having a great time. She misses you though, and I can tell that she's nervous about you being over there."

"I miss her too, but I'll be home soon," I said.

"I'll remind her of that. Unfortunately, she's not here right now. They're over at the softball field watching a game. She's going to hate missing your call."

"Darn, I know," I said. "Tell her I love her, and if I don't talk to her before then, I'll see her soon."

We talked some more about my travel, and I filled her in on a few of my adventures, leaving out the hazards of driving.

My daughter is a worrier. I didn't want her to get wind of anything risky I might be doing and obsess about it. Once, when I took a leisurely sightseeing raft trip down the Snake River, she pictured me drowning in a white-river rafting accident.

After the phone call, I headed to my room to pack my suitcase for tomorrow's journey home.

CHAPTER TEN

Heading Home

THE MORNING was cloudy with another soft rain. After breakfast, I went out to photograph and pet the two chestnut mares in the front pasture before I packed the car and shifted with my left hand one last time on the trip to Shannon Airport. I didn't want to leave. I wanted to spend the whole day at Dysert O'Dea and then go back to the Doolin Farmhouse and blend right in with the Sullivan family. Instead, I called Anne from the airport and finally reached her. We talked about what a shame it was that she had misunderstood the dates and that we couldn't meet up, but that we would definitely make up for it next time. I loved hearing her voice, but her accent was harder to understand on the busy airport payphone. I was embarrassed to have to ask her to repeat herself several times. We laughed about that too, and I promised to send an account of my trip with photos.

The flight home was extremely long due to the strong headwinds, but it left me with plenty of time to reflect on my journey. Despite it feeling like a long day already and my brain feeling numb from too much sitting, eating, and fatigue, I was conscious of how life-changing this week-long trip was for me. I had accomplished much this week and conquered many demons while putting others into perspective.

This journey of self-discovery had forced me to travel outside my comfort zone. I had felt fear, especially the fear of driving, and driven anyway. I had discovered wellsprings of strength that surprised me. I hadn't caved in. I hadn't given up. Even the decision to forgo driving to take a one-day bus trip had turned out to be a wise decision. Where else could I have led a crowd in a rousing rendition of "I'm a Bogman"?

Clearly some emotional and spiritual healing had taken place. My experiences at the beehive huts, Brigid's Well, and the Cliffs of Moher attested to that. I felt lighter, less angry, less depressed. There was still work to do, but I felt thankful for everything I had experienced in Ireland, even the terrifying things. They had made me stronger, more self-confident. I had experienced so much in such a short time. I knew that though I missed my daughters, my friends, and my greyhounds, making the transition to being home would be difficult. I would need to remind myself to wrestle the Black Dog, to stand my ground, to love unconditionally, to forgive others, to forgive myself. And most of all that . . .

All shall be well, and all shall be well, and all manner of thing shall be well.

PART TWO
Synchronicity

What motion of the sun or stream
Or eyelid shot the gleam
That pierced my body through?
What made me live like these that seem
Self-born, born anew?

W. B. Yeats

CHAPTER ELEVEN

Shift to Automatic

I SLEPT FOR two hours on the plane, tops, arriving from Indianapolis at Shannon Airport in the west of Ireland at 8:30 a.m. to a sunny June sky filled with fluffy clouds. I was back a year later, still without the teacher creativity fellowship, but this time I allowed myself two weeks to get away from the stress of teaching and single parenting and to revel in a place that, for now at least, felt more like home. My stomach was expressing the usual jitters about driving, but nothing like last year. I had enough sense this time to pay the difference and rent an automatic transmission car, being aware that I would need to accommodate its larger size to the narrow Irish roads. I taped my directions to the dashboard and headed toward Doolin via Ennis and Ennistymon.

The drive was so much easier and less exhausting, since I didn't have to downshift all the time, but, just as in my first trip, I continued to have problems with my passenger side mirror scraping anything that was on that side of the road, usually a stone wall. There was already a dent on that side that I hoped I wasn't responsible for. I still couldn't believe how the Irish just turn the tourists loose on their narrow, winding roads. At least I knew how to handle the roundabouts this time. No more "Yer going the wrong way, woman!" being shouted at me. At least for now. I had been driving almost an hour. I was famished, and I wanted to stop in Ennis to take a break, center myself, get something to eat, and "top off" the Irish mobile phone a new friend had lent me. I found a parking spot next to a cramped, but friendly, bistro. They didn't have the soup and soda bread I craved, so I ordered vegetable quiche and a side salad consisting of coleslaw, tomatoes, and corn. I slid into a seat in the corner away from the other customers. I was jetlagged and not feeling up to engaging in small talk. My brain was in that strange schizoid state where my senses were magnified, yet I felt tired and sluggish. I just wanted to sit, eat, observe, and think.

I thought about how much synchronicity had been at play this past year. "Synchronicity" is a term coined by the brilliant psychoanalyst, Carl Jung, referring to "a meaningful coincidence of two or more events, where something other than the probability of chance is involved." Think about the "coincidence" of Lennon meeting McCartney at that church picnic in Liverpool in 1957 or the likelihood that Emerson, Thoreau, Hawthorne, and Alcott would all be living in the little village of Concord, Massachusetts, at the same time. In other words, a lot of "signs" were pointing me back to Ireland, and I knew in my gut that they were more than coincidences.

Through my cousin, a bestselling author, I had met Patricia Monaghan, a prolific writer and educator who travels to Ireland frequently and retains dual Irish/American citizenship. Patricia introduced me via email to Jessie Lendennie, owner of Salmon Poetry Publishing in County Clare, just up the road from Doolin. In an act of true kindness, Pat also entrusted me with her Irish cell phone, for which I will be eternally grateful. My email friendship with Anne Rynne also continued to grow. We shot frequent emails across the pond about everything from Irish music and politics and favorite books to personal family stories. Her son Niall was working as his Uncle Luka Bloom's tour manager. I had met up with him before Luka's concert in Chicago a month before my return to Ireland, and we caught me up on all the latest family matters, including Anne's recent gall bladder surgery. Afterward, I met Luka, who was genuinely kind and very interested in my friendship with Anne. He said he hoped we could meet up at Anne's when I returned to Clare the following month. I told him I hoped so too.

This trip would be different. I would have friends to visit. Friends whom for the most part I hadn't met yet, but it was as if I knew we would become good friends. I could feel the ancient pull of anam cara (soul friends) at work, and though I didn't necessarily believe in reincarnation, I was intrigued with Carl Jung's concept of the collective unconscious, which incorporates déjà vu—the feeling of having known someone before or having been to a place before. I was confused by all of this and questioned what it was all about and where it would lead, but, despite my pleas and prayers, no answers were forthcoming. All I was hearing was, *All shall be well, and all shall be well, and all manner of thing shall be well.*

My yearning to return to Ireland had been the same as the year before only it had intensified upon returning home and entertaining friends, family, and acquaintances with story after story of my adventures. I gave slideshow talks to my colleagues, teacher retiree groups, photography clubs, even at my annual family reunion, complete with home-baked scones for refreshments. I relived every moment of that short, one-week trip, knowing all along that I wouldn't be satisfied until I returned for a longer visit. I was like a child who had been given one piece of exquisitely delicious chocolate candy. I wanted more.

I needed a respite from parenting. Both of my daughters were over eighteen and had left home. Despite my wishes, neither had attended college. Instead, they lived with friends and worked menial jobs while taking classes at the School of Hard Knocks. I loved them and worried about them constantly. They were capable of so much more, and I wanted them to be happy and self-sufficient. Why couldn't they see that? Even though I'd married young, I had realized the importance of getting a college education in order to be able to support myself. I was frustrated that they weren't recognizing their potential and knew that farther down the road they would regret some of the choices they were making. It was hard not to intervene, but I knew from my own experience that my daughters wouldn't grow unless they were allowed to learn from their mistakes.

I was nearing my twenty-fifth year as a school librarian too and, though I loved my work, I was weary of the administrative politics and the never-ending battle of feeling like I had to justify my worth. Teachers, librarians, and counselors were increasingly being observed and evaluated using archaic, meaningless standards that bore no resemblance whatsoever to reality. I wished that I could retire, find a cottage in County Clare, move to Ireland, and leave my frustrating life behind.

As it was, I was lucky to manage two weeks away. The cost to board my two greyhounds was enormous, but they adored the Greyhound Resort, and I knew that I wouldn't need to worry about them. Airfare wasn't cheap and neither was the car rental with farmhouse bed and breakfast vouchers. Still, I charged what I had to my credit card and went for it. As my cousin often reminded me, "Ireland is your destiny!"

I patted my napkin around my mouth and dropped it on my empty plate as the sound across the room of a dish crashing startled me out of my reverie. I left the bistro and drove toward Ennistymon. I missed the turn to Lahinch, known for its famous golf course, and ended up in Lisdoonvarna, the matchmaking capital of Ireland. I got out of there as fast as I could and took Corkscrew Hill (a very apt description of the road) toward Doolin. About two miles up the road on the right I saw four Clare farmers, adorned in wool sweaters, boots, and caps, who had blocked the road to coax three reluctant donkeys out of a small black trailer, through an opened gate, and into a field. I saw the tail end of the transaction, so to speak, with a view of the donkeys' butts scurrying into the field. Quite a deal must have been struck because, after securing the gate, the farmers spent some time enthusiastically shaking hands. I didn't mind the delay. I was enjoying the sunny day and the beautiful landscape spread out before me. I rolled down my window, waved to the startled men, and yelled, "Brilliant day! Fair play to you all!" I caught the farmers in my rearview mirror smiling and waving back as I pulled around the trailer and drove down the hill toward Doolin.

CHAPTER TWELVE

Singing to the Cows Along the Cliffs

I SPOTTED THE familiar driveway and drove up to the pink house. Out came Maeve in her light-blue blouse and denim skirt. "Ahh, Diane, it's so good to see ye," she said as she embraced me with her strong arms.

"It's so good to be back," I said, hugging her back. Her arms felt as welcoming as Ireland itself.

"I just hung some laundry on the line for ye," she said with a wink.

"Oh, great! Let me get my camera!" I laughed. I was so happy she remembered our little joke.

Murphy, the border collie, came bounding around the corner from the backyard followed closely by little Finn, only Finn wasn't so little anymore.

"Oh my gosh, Finn, you've grown so much, little man! Look at you!" I stooped down and gave him a hug. He giggled and pulled away. Murphy gave me a sloppy kiss on my cheek.

"Ronan and Rory are out in the fields with their dad," said Maeve. "They'll be along in a bit. Come with me, and I'll show ye to yer room."

I spent the rest of the afternoon in my upstairs room catnapping, trying to figure out the mysteries of Pat's Irish cell phone, and, finally, calling Jessie and Anne to arrange times to meet. Jessie surprised me by sounding depressed and alluding to financial matters at Salmon Publishing being very bad. She told me it wasn't doing well, and she didn't know if she could spare much time, but she agreed that I could stop by late tomorrow morning. Well, so much for our plans to explore the Burren. Why would she sound so excited in her recent emails and now sound so reluctant to meet? Fortunately, Anne sounded positively happy to hear from me. However, today and tomorrow she was busy. She wanted me to call her on Saturday morning!

Now it was my turn to feel depressed. A lot of it was the fatigue, I suppose, and also the fact that the weather had turned cloudy, cold, and very windy, making me wonder if I had packed the right clothes. I had tried so hard to make this trip more about spending time with new friends and less about spending time alone, and now it was looking as if I would be exploring the Burren by myself. I began to heap on the negatives and the "what-ifs," feeling more and more depressed, but then I caught myself.

Well, here you are again, Diane. Sitting here on your bed feeling sorry for yourself. You already know the choices: you can stay here and wallow in your pity party or you can get up off yer arse and go do something. What's it going to be?

I got up off my arse and headed toward my two sanctuaries: the Cliffs of Moher and Brigid's Well.

I awoke the next morning in my comfortable double bed with the sun streaming through the lavender-and-white striped curtains. I got up, opened the window, and felt revived by the warm breeze. Despite it being Friday the 13th, it proved to be a lucky day. After breakfast, I decided to take advantage of the good weather and attempt to hike the four-mile coast trail to the Cliffs of Moher that began behind the Sullivans' farm. Laden with my camera and tripod, I started down the hill and turned left onto the path. Murphy ran down the hill ahead of me, seeming eager to show me the way. We hadn't gone far when I saw Brendan Sullivan along the fence, tending the cattle. He waved at me and walked over to talk.

"Ah, Diane, out for a wee hike are ye?" he asked. He looked like a younger, leaner version of the Clare farmers I'd seen yesterday, only he sported a red sock cap over his prematurely balding head, a navy-blue fleece jacket, and blue jeans with waterproof hiking boots instead of the traditional wool sweater, cap, and rubber boots. His hazel eyes glinted with kindness and humor as he pulled off his work gloves and leaned against the fence post.

"Good morning, Brendan! Yes, I thought I'd give this 'wee hike' as you call it a try." I rested my camera gear on the ground beside me and placed my sunglasses on top of my head. "I'm not sure how far I'll get with this camera equipment though." I laughed nervously, pointing to the camera bag and tripod.

"No worries. Ye might come upon some brooks here and there and maybe some barbed wire with a sign about a bull but pay it no mind."

"Pay it no mind, huh?" I shifted my feet and gave him a doubtful look.

"Ye know," he went on, "I've been on a committee for many years now to upgrade the trail so that it's easier to walk to the cliffs. We still have aways to go, but it's getting much better. Ye shouldn't have any problem, ye know. It will be lovely. You can take yer photos, rest along the way if ye like, and then enjoy a cuppa tea at the visitor center."

"What about getting back?" I asked.

"Oh that," he said, putting his elbow on the fence post and resting his palm against his chin. "Well, ye can either take the trail back the way ye came or, easier still, you can walk back on the coast road."

"Well, I'll give it a try and see how far I get."

"There ye go now. So, Diane, how long are ye stayin' this time?"

"I'll be here until Monday. Then I'm heading north to County Sligo for a while and then maybe on to Donegal before I head south again. I'm not really sure. Two weeks total. I know I'll end up in Clare again before I leave."

"That sounds like a good, busy holiday," he said as he laughingly pushed a cow away that was nudging him.

"So Brendan," I continued, "you said you've been working on this trail for many years. How much of this land is yours?"

"All of it," he answered, gently waving his arm in all directions. "All the way to the cliffs and back to the road that runs alongside Doolin Castle. It's been in the family for generations."

"Wow! That's amazing, Brendan, and so different from what we have in the States now, where family farms are going under and being bought by developers who build look-alike subdivisions. Your farm must be a lot of responsibility though."

"'Tis," he answered. "But, Diane, I wouldn't want to do anything else. We keep the bed and breakfast for some liquid funds and that's good, especially when farm prices are down, but my heart is in the land."

"I hope you realize," I said, "there aren't too many farmers who can stand on their own land at the bottom of a cow pasture overlooking the Atlantic Ocean. I can honestly say I've never seen anything more beautiful in my life."

"Oh, that it is. I never tire of looking at it and its many moods, and I'm forever grateful for it." We stood for a while in silence gazing out at the sea, taking in the view of the Aran Islands in the distance.

"Brendan, do you know the musician Luka Bloom?" I asked, stooping down to pet Murphy, who was begging for more behind-the-ear scratches.

"Luka Bloom? Oh yes, I know Luka Bloom. He and his brother Christy Moore used to visit my next-door neighbor, Micho Russell, frequently."

"Micho Russell was your next-door neighbor?" I asked. I couldn't believe it! Micho Russell was the Doolin farmer and musician who was famous for introducing trad music to a much wider audience. He put the little village of Doolin on the map, and he is the reason that trad musicians and tourists flock here. "Well, Luka wrote a beautiful song about Micho called 'Hands of a Farmer.' It has a gorgeous verse about how Micho used to sing in Doolin and how now, out over the limestone, his sweet words still ring."

"Oh, lovely," said Brendan. "I don't know that song, but I would love to hear it. He and Christy are fine men. So talented. And they thought the world of Micho." He picked some grass off his sleeve, deep in thought. "You know, I remember as a child, Micho and his brother, Gussie, would have sessions in our kitchen and we would dance. One time, oh I guess I was about five or six, I got up on the table and danced and me ma didn't even scold me for it! Ah, there were so many good times like that. Gussie Russell still lives in the house, ye know. He spends a lot of time telling stories to the tourists at O'Connor's. I'm fairly certain they pay him for it. He rides his bike back and forth."

"Oh, I've seen him," I said. "He was entertaining a group of tourists at a corner table and later I saw him peddling his bike on the coast road."

"That's Gussie," said Patrick.

"I know that Micho died tragically," I said, "but I don't know the details."

"Oh, yes," answered Brendan. "A young woman was giving him a lift home from Galway after a gig and the car crashed. He was killed straightaway."

"Oh God, that's awful."

"Yes, it was a tremendous loss for all of us."

We stood by the fence a little longer as the cows milled about and two Connemara ponies gazed down at us from the adjoining hilltop. Brendan talked about how his boys helped out on the farm and his hopes for their futures.

"You know, Diane, it won't be too many years before Rory goes to university. He wants to study environmental biology and organic farming. Ye know, something that will benefit him when he takes over the farm." He pulled his hat down over his ears and smiled. "Well, I'd best be going, like. I have some business to do in Ennis, and I'm keeping ye from yer wee hike."

"Oh, no problem, Brendan. I've enjoyed talking with you," I said as I hoisted my tripod onto my shoulder.

"And I as well, Diane. Enjoy yer holiday. Bye now." He started toward his truck and then turned back around and shouted, "Don't be alarmed if the cows follow ye most of the way. They seem to have taken a fancy to ye."

I laughed. "They'll be good company!" I shouted back.

I watched him start up the small red truck, and I waved until he pulled onto the road beside Doolin Castle, thinking what a privilege it was to spend time with such a kind man.

"Well, cows, we might as well get going. Murphy, are you coming with us?" Murphy looked at me for a moment as if he was seriously considering it, then he turned, gave me one last fleeting glance, and sprinted up the hill toward the farmhouse.

"Okay, Murphy, we'll miss you. Right, cows?" I headed south on the dirt path, followed by the herd of a half dozen or so cattle plodding along beside me with heads lowered making occasional snorts and moos and other soft cow sounds against the mild ocean breeze.

I was so pleased to have their company that I decided to entertain them by singing the Irish folk tune "I'll Tell Me Ma."

"I'll tell me ma when I get home
The boys won't leave the girls alone.
They pull my hair, they stole my comb,
But that's all right til I get home.
She is handsome, she is pretty.
She is the Belle of Belfast City
She is a-courtin' one two three
Pray won't you tell me who is she."

I went on to sing all three verses and repeated them several times until we came to an incline where, at the top, standing perfectly still and staring down at us in a not-so-friendly manner were three cows, one white and two brown and white. *Maybe they don't like my singing,* I thought, though the herd who came with me didn't seem to mind. All of us stopped and I pulled out my zoom lens, attached it to my camera, and quickly set up my tripod. I figured if I occupied myself and ignored them, I would pose no threat and they would ignore me. It worked. I took shot after shot of cows in the pasture, cows overlooking the ocean, cows looking straight at me from the top of the path until I had my fill of shooting cows.

"Okay guys. I'm heading on through." I picked up my camera gear and walked up the path. The cows parted like they were opening the gateway to paradise, the white one gently nudging me along. The herd must have decided they'd had enough of this strange woman who sang slightly off-key and carried this metal-and-glass thing around her neck that she kept holding up to her face, so they stayed behind. I spotted the two Connemara ponies halfway up the hill on the left. They were a beautiful pale white, heads bent down to the ground, gently nibbling the grass. I set up my tripod again and lost myself in the scene through my viewfinder. I took shot after shot of the grazing ponies. I was in the moment, feeling the warmth of the sun overhead, the wind whistling off the water, the sound of crashing waves below. *Adjust the tripod, compose, check exposure, focus, press the shutter button, repeat.* My mantra. I walked some more and stopped to take more photos. Walked and stopped. Until I saw the WARNING! BULL! sign to my left. "Pay it no mind," Brendan had said. It was hard to ignore, but I trudged on, nervously glancing around as the path veered in toward the farmland and out again toward the cliffs.

My gear was getting more and more heavy. I was wearing a large camera waist pack, with my camera around my neck and my tripod hoisted on my shoulder. The wind was picking up and I was walking into it. Then I came upon a line of barbed wire running horizontally in front of me with a brook just beyond it. Should I go under the barbed wire and across the brook? It was doable, but I might risk tearing my clothes and, worse still, getting my camera gear wet. Where the heck was I anyway? How far to the visitor center? I figured I had at least another mile and a half to go, and it was already past ten o'clock. I needed to get back to the Sullivans', get ready, and be at Jessie's at eleven thirty. I decided to take the path to the main road and walk back north to Doolin. So much for that "wee hike"!

My legs were tired from the hike, but I felt centered and refreshed. I sang to myself all the way back, striding alongside the curve of the winding road as the cars sped by and the welcoming sight of the Sullivans' house slowly came into view.

CHAPTER THIRTEEN

Jessie

I MANAGED TO keep the bigger-than-I-should-have-been-driving rental car on the left side of the road as I rounded another curve toward the Cliffs of Moher. Only this time, I was looking for a drive on the left that would lead up a hill toward Jessie's house. I started to slow down, but a car was on my tail and, before I knew it, I had missed the turn.

Damn! I was already nervous about meeting Jessie, and I didn't want to mess it up by being late. I drove ahead to where I could make a U-turn and tried again, this time almost landing in the ditch from overcompensating on the turn.

Sheesh! *And all shall be well . . .*

Jessie Lendennie, the founder and managing editor of Salmon Poetry, is one of the most important publishers in the Irish literary world and recently has gained some much-deserved international recognition. Jessie founded Salmon in Galway City in 1981, later moving its offices to her home near the Cliffs of Moher. There, she and Siobhan Hutson, the head of production and administration and the partner of Jessie's son, Tim, publish high-quality books of poetry from both emerging and established poets from Ireland, Great Britain, and the United States. Poets as diverse as Adrienne Rich, Rita Ann Higgins, Joyce Sutphen, and Joan McBreen.

Through the synchronicity I mentioned earlier, I was introduced to Jessie through Patricia Monaghan, a friend of my cousin, author Charlene Ann Baumbich. Pat, a professor at DePaul University and a multi-genre author, had published a book of poetry, *Dancing With Chaos*, with Salmon. Pat had a "hunch" that Jessie and I could become "great friends." While I trusted her hunch, I felt a bit out of my league. The inner critic rose from the depths once again:

Who are you to be meeting someone so important? Why would she be interested in you anyway? You're just a school librarian from Indiana. You're not a poet. Sure, you've written some, but you haven't published any of it, and it's probably not that good anyway.

And so it went as I drove up the dirt road past a few cottages searching for the green house that was Jessie's. The house came into view and so did a variety of mixed border collies bounding out the front door and barking in greeting as I pulled into the drive. I quit counting at four, but I think there were five. They were followed by a tall, robust middle-aged woman dressed in an oversized sweatshirt, blue jeans, and sneakers. Her long blond hair and bangs were unkempt and she wore no makeup. I relaxed a little. She obviously loved dogs, and she certainly wasn't dressed like a high-power publisher.

"Diane," she shouted as she came toward the car, the dogs beating her to it. "It's so good to see you! Zeke, Big Jack, Freck, Shannon, Zena . . . C'mon, give her some room now."

I opened the car door and the dogs, yes, there were five of them, jumped up in turns to give me kisses.

"Hi guys," I said, laughing and trying to push my way out of the car. They moved back at Jessie's command.

"Hi, Jessie," I said. "It's good to see you too. Much better than email." We gave each other a hug, and I felt immediately drawn to her, like I knew her already. It was a strange feeling but one I was learning to trust.

"What a beautiful place you have here! And the view! My God, how do you get anything done?" I moved in a slow-motion circle taking in the view of green hills and pastureland on one side and Liscannor Bay in the valley below.

"Isn't it a gorgeous view of Liscannor Bay?" Jessie folded her arms, smiled, and let out a sigh. "It's my sanctuary, my peace, this view. I never tire of it." We crossed the road and walked partway down the hill to have a closer look. We stood in silence for a few minutes except for a few "Oohs" and "Ahhs." I watched the clouds changing shapes and the light shifting and slanting, imagining what settings I would have used on my camera if I hadn't left it in the car.

"Let me show you what's behind the house," Jessie said, breaking my photography daydream. I was trying to make sense of Jessie's accent. It was an interesting mixture of all the places she had lived: Arkansas, California, Alaska, New York, England, and Ireland.

We walked around the house to a fenced-in area where we were greeted by the hee-haws of a light-gray donkey and an aloof brown horse in the distance.

"Oh my!" I gushed as I went toward the fence as fast as I could without spooking the animals. "This is Clint," Jessie said, putting out both hands to cuddle the donkey. "He's a lover. And that's Hilly." She pointed to the horse in the distance. "She's a little shy."

I looked at wary Hilly, her mane blowing in the wind. She was beautiful. Just then Clint put his big, adorable face between Jessie's arms and nuzzled up to her chest making loud, almost pathetic, hee-haw noises.

"Oh, Clint, you're adorable," I gushed again. Jessie stepped back and Clint moved over to me for more cuddles, which I gladly gave him. "What a sweetheart. I really must take some pictures of you before I leave. Is that okay with you?"

"Hee-haw," he answered.

"Well, we could stay out here all day, but let's go in and have some tea, shall we?"

"Sounds good."

We took the longer way back along the cow pasture and entered the house through the front door. The downstairs was a mixture of pine and white walls with matching light hardwood floors and lots of windows taking in the gorgeous views. The furniture and accent rugs were simple and colorful, reminding me of a modern Scandinavian vibe. The couch and chairs were covered with blankets and afghans for their protection and the dogs' comfort.

We made our way to the cluttered, homey kitchen followed by the dogs. "Okay, guys," said Jessie with mock resignation as she picked up a tin can from the counter and opened the lid. "A treat for each of you. Here Zeke, here Big Jack, here Shannon . . ." As its name was called each dog came forward and Jessie placed a biscuit in its mouth like a priest giving a communion wafer during the Eucharist. Then each of them scurried off to their favorite spot to savor their treat.

"Ahh, Diane," Jessie said as she filled the kettle with water and placed it on the gas stove. "It's been a rough time. Finances aren't good and I'm trying to keep Salmon afloat. There's never enough, never enough." She pulled a couple of mugs from the open shelves and placed teabags from a box on the counter into each mug. "Ahh, I don't know . . ."

"Well, how bad is it, Jessie? I mean, do you feel like Salmon is close to going under or is this just a bad patch that will pass in time?"

"We've been close to going under several times, but somehow we manage to keep it together. Maybe this time won't be any different, but I worry. I worry so much." She poured the steaming water into our mugs. "Do you take milk or sugar?"

"Just a little milk. Thanks."

"Now," she said as she placed the milk back in the refrigerator, "let's go into the front room, and I'll show you the office and introduce you to Siobhan."

We entered a large room full of bookcases and windows with two desks placed on opposite ends of the room and a long oak table and chairs in the middle. Sitting at the desk on the far end was a stunning young woman, thirtyish, with long, light-brown hair and large dark eyes. She was dressed casually in jeans and a long red cardigan. I felt myself relax as she rose from her desk with a big smile and said, "Diane, it's so good to meet ye. Jessie's told me so much about ye." She came around the desk and hugged me. "So this is yer second trip here by yerself, eh? My, yer a brave one."

"Oh, not really," I answered. Evading any more talk about that tired subject, I quickly went on, "It's nice to meet you, Siobhan. Jessie has spoken highly of you. She told me that you keep everything organized and running. You do a great job with the website, and I love the graphic designs you do for the book covers."

"Oh, yer too kind, Diane," said Siobhan.

"It's true!" said Jessie. "She handles everything that I can't or won't handle, and she does it so much better than I could. She's a gem, and I'm so lucky to have her."

"Oh, you two," said Siobhan with a wave of her hand as she sat back down at her desk and looked at her computer screen.

I perused the titles in the bookcases while Jessie and Siobhan sat at their desks talking across the room and conducting business at their computers. I already owned some of the titles, but many more were new to me. I wanted all of them.

"I contacted Joan McBreen about meeting her when I'm in Tuam next week, but I never heard back from her," I said.

"Joan can be . . . how should I put this . . . private," said Jessie. "She's not one much for meeting fans."

"I assumed as much," I said as I placed one of her books back on the shelf and pulled out another one farther down. "And that's fine. I don't want to be intrusive. She's a fine poet and I just wanted to . . ." I trailed off as I stared at the slim book in my hand. "Ray Bradbury? He wrote a book of poetry? And you published it?" My mouth must have fallen to the floor because both Jessie and Siobhan were exchanging glances and stifling laughs.

"Yes, it's true," laughed Jessie. "Ray loved Ireland. He was in poor health by then and in a wheelchair, but he and his wife came over for the book launch in Galway. It couldn't have been easy for them, but they were both so kind and gracious. Ray still had some spitfire in him, and he could argue passionately about things he felt strongly about, you know, the misuse of technology, the urgency for space exploration. So much more. He was curious about everything and impatient with those who weren't. I loved working with him on *I Live By the Invisible*. It's not his best work, but so what? It's Ray Bradbury, and there are some poems where his brilliance clearly shines through."

"Wow, what a story. I love his work. I taught *Fahreneit 451* and some of his short stories when I did my student teaching in high school English. Well, I definitely want a copy of that, and of Joan McBreen's latest . . ."

Jessie joined me at the bookcase. "You might like Mary Dorcey. She's known for writing short stories, but she's an amazing poet too. And Mary O'Malley's *Asylum Road*. Very contemporary. A mix of Irish history and our response to the recent immigration issue. Oh, and here's a new one by Paul Perry."

"Jessie, you know I'd like to take one of each, but I'd be broke for the rest of my trip, and I wouldn't be able to get all of them on the plane anyway." I laughed, pulling another book from the shelf. "Oh look here. *Daughter and Other Poems* by Jessie Lendennie. I hear this one's sorta good." I glanced up at her with my you-know-I-am-joking look.

"Yeah, it's okay," she smiled.

"Seriously, Jessie, it's wonderful. You write about your experience with your parents with such simplicity yet so eloquently. That is so hard to do! I'd love to talk to you about it in more detail sometime."

"Why don't I finish up a few things here, and then we can have a long late lunch at Stonecutters just down the road?" said Jessie.

"I love Stonecutters! I hope Grace, the waitress I met last year, is still working there. Here, I'll make a stack of books I want and add them up while you and Siobhan finish up. And lunch is on me. Siobhan, would you like to join us?"

"Oh no, but thank ye," said Siobhan. "Tim will be home from teaching in Ballyvaughan soon, so I'll finish up here and head back to the cottage."

"Do you want me to drive?" I asked Jessie as we walked out front.

"No, I'll drive. I'm going to take the dogs. I don't like to leave them by themselves."

"Oh." My head was swimming. I knew that Jessie was eccentric when it came to her dogs, but all five of them in the car? Where was I going to sit? "So what will they do while we're in the restaurant?" I asked.

"No worries," she answered as if it wasn't a problem at all. "We'll park close to the building and get a table by the window where we can see them. If I roll down the windows, they should be fine. There's a little fenced-in play area where we can let them out when we're finished."

"Okay. Let's do it," I said with more confidence than I was feeling at the moment. We walked toward Jessie's compact navy-blue car with the dogs in hot pursuit.

Somehow, we fit. The dogs piling into the back with the backseat folded down and happily panting down my neck. Me with my seat up as far as it would go to give the dogs more room. And Jessie shifting the manual transmission with her left hand like a pro, acting like this was a natural everyday occurrence because it probably was for her. With the windows down and the dogs jockeying for the cool breeze, including the window just over my shoulder, off we went to Stonecutters.

The lunch crowd was gone, so we easily found a table by the window. The dogs had worked out their pecking order and were snoozing in the car. I gathered that they were accustomed to this arrangement, though I wondered if they wouldn't have been happier at home. Jessie kept a watchful eye on them, but she was relaxed and talkative. She talked about how much weight she had gained while she ate and ate, topping her meal off with a banana split and half of my banoffee pie.

Don't judge, Diane. Remember how much weight you put on after the divorce. She's under a lot of stress, just as you were.

"So, Jessie," I began, digging my fork into what was left of my banoffee pie, "how did you get from Arkansas to here?"

"Oh, that's a long, convoluted story," she said, laughing uncomfortably and taking another bite of her pie. "Let's skip over all of the Arkansas stuff now and just say that I ended up in New York City and had Tim. Then I took Tim to London, attended King's College, and got married. Then we moved to Galway and started the Salmon Literary Journal. My husband and I parted ways, and I remained with Salmon, moved here, and turned Salmon into what it is today."

"That's amazing!" I said, though I wondered why she had wanted to skip over Arkansas. "Have you ever thought about writing a memoir?"

"Oh, I think about it a lot," she laughed. "But there's never any time to sit down and do it. Maybe someday."

"Yeah, I have a lot of 'maybe somedays' too. Some of them I can't do until I retire."

"Such as?" Jessie asked.

"Oh, like the writing. I do a little now, but I just don't have the energy it takes to devote to my career and then write. And that doesn't count all of the other things, like managing the house, my two greyhounds, helping my daughters . . . you know, all the other life stuff."

"Yeah, I guess that's why my memoir is still a blank page," Jessie said, before taking a last bite of her sandwich. "That and the fact that I don't want to revisit some of the things that I would have to put into it."

"You mean some of the childhood things you alluded to in *Daughter?*"

"Yeah." She gazed out the window for a few moments, lost in thought. "I had to get out of Arkansas. I never fit in there. And you know from reading my book how dysfunctional my parents were. My dad drank and my mom was bipolar. Both were abusive."

"Yes, I'm sorry. I can't imagine the pain you must have gone through."

"Yeah, well, what I put in the poems isn't the half of it," she said, flicking her hand in the air as if to dismiss all of it. "There were things, horrible things . . ."

She went on to tell me incidents during her childhood, and especially during her teenage years not necessarily involving her parents, that were painful to hear. Abuse, assault, abandonment, and more. More than anyone, much less a child, should have to bear. I sat there at that table by the window and listened, nodding now and then, tears brimming in my eyes as she poured out her story in horrific detail. Holy Jesus! How did she ever survive this, much less become the successful literary woman she is today? I had no idea, but I wanted to find out.

"Why am I telling you this?" she asked as she blew her nose loudly into a tissue. "Hell, I haven't even told my therapist these things." She laughed.

"I don't know." I placed my fork on my plate of half-eaten pie and pushed it to the side. I folded my hands on the table and looked into her sorrow-filled eyes. "But I think it's good that you're getting all of this out, and though it's painful to hear, I'm honored that you've shared these painful memories with me. You know you can trust me, Jessie."

"I sensed as much, so that must have been why I opened up. I meet so many people who seem to want something from me. You know, to look at their work or to introduce them to someone who's influential in the literary world. I meet very few who don't want anything. I'm sure there must be others, but, really, only you and Pat Monaghan come to mind." She paused and looked at my plate. "Are you going to eat the rest of that banoffee pie?"

"No, do you want it?"

"Sure," she said as she eagerly scooted the piece onto her plate. "God, I'm so hungry."

We talked awhile longer about her neighbors, some of whom I knew as being well-known musicians; her writer friends, including Thomas Lynch, the writer, poet, and Michigan undertaker who would later become internationally known for his 2007 award-winning book and documentary, *The Undertaking*; and the bodhran player with a drinking problem next door.

"Oh, yeah," I said. "He must have been the guy standing outside in his boxer shorts and wellies. He waved to me when I drove by."

"Oh my God! How embarrassing." Jessie sighed.

I hadn't seen Grace our entire time in the restaurant, so as we were leaving, I asked our waitress about her. "Oh, Grace," she said. "She met some lad late last summer, got married straightaway, and moved with him to London. We haven't heard from her since."

"Oh, I'm sorry to hear that," I answered, feeling totally confused as to why this young girl who loved the Burren so much would suddenly marry a Londoner and leave.

"Yah, let me tell ye, we were sorry too. She was a good worker, she was, and none of us were too keen about that lad she fell for."

"Wow," I said to Jessie as we were heading toward the car.

"Yeah, the folly of young love," Jessie agreed.

The dogs were eager to see us, and, as promised, we let them pile out of the car and coaxed them into the enclosed play area. They chased each other, frolicked, buzzed past us, and then frolicked some more before we herded them back into the car and headed back to the house.

"Why don't I fix some more tea and we can sit outside?" Jessie said as we led the dogs inside for their dinner.

"That sounds good. I'll get my camera gear from the car and take some pictures of Clint while you're getting things ready if that's okay?"

"Lovely," she said, going to the refrigerator. "Here, take him a carrot. He'll like that. Hilly will be too shy to come to the fence but snap the carrot in half in case she does."

It was a beautiful evening with just the right amount of clouds in a blue sky and the sun lowering over the hills to the west. Clint was overjoyed to see me, and hee-hawed and nuzzled several times to prove it. I lost myself in taking pictures of his lonesome, lovely face. I tried coaxing Hilly to the fence, but she wasn't having it. Then I heard Jessie calling me for tea.

We sat in lawn chairs drinking our tea, talking, and gazing at the beauty of Liscannor Bay. I kept reminding myself over and over how fortunate I was to be sitting here enjoying the company of this new friend whom I had met through synchronous circumstances. How different it was from this time last year when I didn't know anyone.

When I left Jessie's place, we agreed that I would come for dinner on Sunday.

"Tim is a great cook," Jessie said. "I'm not sure what he'll fix, but I know it will be good. Just give me a call when you get back from whatever you're doing that day."

"I'll do that," I promised. "Thanks again for everything, Jessie."

"Oh, thank you for lunch, my new friend. I'm so glad we finally got to spend some time together."

"Me too," I said, giving her a big hug. "Bye, guys!" I said to the dog parade standing beside my car, waiting to see me off. "See you Sunday!"

I drove down the winding road, past Jessie's neighbor's cottage, who, thankfully, was not outside in his boxer shorts, and maneuvered the right-hand turn (remember, right is left) onto the coast road back to Doolin Farmhouse. There were hours of daylight left, and I thought about touring the Burren, but I was exhausted. I had to face the fact that I'm an introvert who was putting myself "out there" and, as any introvert knows, it takes everything out of you. This morning's talk with Brendan, the morning hike, meeting Jessie and Siobhan, being a listening ear to Jessie's horrific story. I was zonked, exhilarated, and filled with questions. What was the purpose of my being here? What was all of this about? Where was this journey leading me? So many experiences had been packed into these few days. So different from my life in Indiana, and yet I felt so at home here. And I was just getting started! There was so much to process. I decided to go for a "thinking walk" along the cliff trail again. I took my camera gear so that, later, I could capture the sun setting over the Aran Islands. But mostly I walked, then sat, walked, then sat. And the evening calmed, the sea birds flew out over the water toward the setting sun, and I knew . . .

And all shall be well, and all shall be well, and all manner of thing shall be well.

CHAPTER FOURTEEN

Limestone and Sheela-Na-Gigs

I KNEW THAT it would be pointless to ask Jessie to go with me on a tour of the Burren. She wouldn't want to leave her dogs and, though I loved her dogs, them panting down my neck from the back seat for several hours wasn't something I wanted to experience. Anne wasn't available this weekend, but I was meeting her on Monday morning at Spanish Point, south of the cliffs near the town of Miltown Malbay. So, I went exploring alone. I left right after another leisurely breakfast with great conversation, or *craic* as the Irish call it, with the other guests, a young French woman and her eight-year-old son and a married couple from Maine who were on their way to visit the Hill of Tara in eastern Ireland. I wanted to visit it too, but I wasn't sure if it would be worth the drive across Ireland. They took my phone number and promised to call and give me a report. The French woman was excited about visiting the ancient church ruins of Clonmacnoise in nearby County Offaly.

I played with Finn, Ronan, and Murphy in the front yard before heading again toward the town of Kilfenora, home of The Burren Centre. There, I learned about the geology of this area, with its limestone features similar to those found in southern Indiana—the underground rivers, caves, swallow holes, and closed depressions. But the Burren is unlike anywhere else on earth. Its glacial erratics, karst limestone pavements, and dry lakes give a moonscape impression, while the flora consists of different ecological species growing side by side. There isn't anywhere else in Europe where alpine and Mediterranean plants grow together in such a way. This combination of a lunar landscape with colorful flowers growing out of the deep cracks in the rocks with the ever-changing light and cloud formations makes the Burren a photographer's dream. And that doesn't include the fact that it's dotted with ancient ruins and, in the more remote areas, feral goats. It's no wonder that this living limestone landscape is known as the Fertile Rock.

I couldn't wait to get out and explore, but I wanted to take advantage of everything The Burren Centre had to offer. It is a medium-sized, modern building housing a visitor center, exhibition and audiovisual space, meeting rooms, and, of course, a tearoom. I watched the video presentation about the Burren's geologic and historical record and enjoyed the lifelike displays from prehistoric to current times. After I had seen everything in The Burren Centre and taste-tested the tea and scones in its café (they were excellent), I walked next door to revisit the Kilfenora Cathedral and its high crosses.

The 12th-century cathedral was built on the site of a 6th-century monastery. It's massive, in partial ruin, and roofless—the original roof rumored to have been made of oak.

Since the building has been added to over the centuries, it's a mishmash of architectural styles. My favorites were the 15th-century Gothic carvings around the doorways and windows similar to those at Dysert O'Dea. In fact, I felt the same sense of peace when I entered Kilfenora's nave through its arched doorway. I couldn't explain it. Maybe it was the mixture of shadows from the walls and sunlight beaming through the roofless building, combined with the ancient history of this sacred space. Having the place to myself, I stood there in silent contemplation for some time letting the sacredness soak in. It felt good to be enveloped in such peace. Then I could have sworn I heard the ancient voices of the singing monks. They sounded similar to the monks I'd heard so often at the Abbey of Gethsemane in Kentucky, only older and farther away.

I snapped back into the present when a small group of tourists entered the room. I took some photos of the carvings over the archway and went outside to see the high crosses.

There were three complete crosses and three shafts scattered about the grounds, some surrounded by graves and all exposed to the elements. The most ornate was the Doorty Cross with carvings of three different croziers on one side and a scene of Jesus entering Jerusalem on the other. I wouldn't have known this except for the informative signs throughout, since all of the crosses were quite weathered and badly in need of restoration. I took photos of the crosses and some of the graves in the bright sun, but I was eager to move on to experience something Patricia Monaghan, artist Fiona Marron, and I had discussed at length a month earlier in a little café back in Chicago—the Killinaboy Sheela-na-gig.

I took the road out of Kilfenora about five kilometers east to the tiny village of Killinaboy, where another 12th-century church ruin stood. But this one was different. Instead of carvings of bishop heads and Celtic crosses above the arched entrance, there was a mysterious single carving known as a Sheela-na-gig, an ancient image of a naked woman in a squatting position with her hands boldly exposing her vulva. Sheela-na-gig is a generic name coined by a Tipperary farmer describing one he found in the 1840s, and it's safe to say that you won't find any information about them on the Irish Tourist Board website.

I first read about Sheela-na-gigs in Patricia Monaghan's book, *The Red-Haired Girl from the Bog: the Landscape of Celtic Myth and Spirit*. The carvings, often etched into churches and cathedrals, are found throughout Ireland. Some, such as the Sheela in Killinaboy, are still in place, but most have been removed and banished to the basement of the Dublin National Museum by male archaeologists who, until recently, debated their origins but agreed that they depicted evil women and gave them names such as evil-eye stone, devil stone, and witch on the wall. One overly zealous male scholar described them as "the pornography of our ancestors." Fortunately, an increasing number of scientists entered the field with a more open-minded view, including many feminists who understood the role of the goddess in ancient Celtic mythology and spirituality and who held a passion for reintroducing the goddess to our present-day society. Though the origin and purpose of Sheela-na-gigs remains a mystery, it's generally agreed that they represent an ancient goddess connected to female power, energy, and transformation, not just limited to fertility and reproduction. With the goddess's powerful stance, one Sheela scholar, Starr Goode, says she is "the perfect antidote to the war on women." With her aging appearance and sagging breasts, others see her as the Cailleach, or hag, wise woman,

Great Mother, the old woman who gave birth to all the races. Patricia Monaghan, however, believes that she is ageless. Still others think the carvings were meant to protect and ward off evil. For Irish artist Fiona Marron, Sheela-na-gigs represent transformative feminine energy.

Fiona is one of the few nonaccredited people allowed to view and eventually hold and photograph the many Sheelas in the Dublin National Museum's basement in preparation for an artistic project to portray the authentic spirit of different Sheela-na-gigs through paintings and mixed-media sculptures. Just as Fiona had the right connections and was in the right place at the right time to view the Sheelas, so I had been when I had the opportunity to meet her.

I was in Chicago to attend a Luka Bloom concert. I was excited about seeing him and meeting his tour manager, Niall—Anne's son and Luka's nephew. But I had also arranged to meet up with Patricia Monaghan, with whom I had been corresponding all year. Pat lived in an old Victorian house in a downtown neighborhood not far from my hotel. As we were deciding where and when to meet, she told me that her artist friend from Ireland was in town for the opening reception of her Sheela-na-gig exhibition at a gallery in Old Towne. Would I mind meeting both of them in Andersonville, the Swedish neighborhood in Chicago, for brunch, since, unfortunately, the opening was the same night as the concert?

"Do you mean Fiona?" I asked. Pat had written about Fiona in her book, and I was fascinated with her story as well as with the Sheela-na-gigs.

"Why, yes. Do you know Fiona?"

"No, Pat, but you wrote about her in your book, remember? So I feel like I know her. And she's doing an exhibition of Sheela-na-gigs! What are the chances of that? Oh, I'm so excited! I can't wait to meet her . . . and to see you too, of course!"

Pat laughed. "Oh, I can tell right now, this is going to be fun."

I found them in a booth in the back. Pat looked striking in her red hair and colorful scarf, and Fiona's long, full brown hair was pulled back with a beautiful green barrette, making her look younger than her forty or so years. Both stood up and gave me hugs.

As an introvert, I was nervous about meeting new people. Though it was hard to discern on the outside, my stomach was always tied in knots. I was hoping they wouldn't regret taking time out of their busy schedules to meet me. I needn't have worried. We talked about Sheela-na-gigs a lot, with Fiona giving me more details about what it was like being in the basement of the Dublin National Museum with the Sheelas.

"They were quite restrictive with me the first time I visited," she said. "I couldn't touch them, a guard was watching me the whole time, and as soon as the short time was up, I had to leave. I hardly had time to do any sketches. When I was finally allowed to go back, I could stay for a longer time and the guard moved about. I had snuck in a small camera, and I managed to get some shots when the guard wasn't around, although I had a close call when the film rewound, making this whirling noise, like. I don't know if the guard noticed or if he even cared, but I wasn't taking any chances. I could hold the Sheelas then too, and I swear, Diane, I heard this buzzing sound and felt this almost electric-like energy. It was such an amazing experience."

"Wow. You actually heard and felt them buzzing?"

"Yes, I swear I did."

"Isn't that amazing?" said Pat.

"Definitely," I agreed. "Were you able to use the photos as models for your art?"

"Indeed. They were very helpful, especially with the 3D figures."

"I'm so glad they turned out." I took a sip of tea while Fiona and Pat finished their salads. I was too wound up to eat. "So will the gallery be open this afternoon?" I asked. "I thought I might walk over there before I get ready for the concert tonight."

"Oooh, I don't know. You could give it a go." Fiona placed her finished salad plate to the side and took a sip of tea. "I'd love for you to see the Sheelas."

Pat saw someone she knew at another table, excused herself, and went over to chat.

"So, yer going to see Luka Bloom tonight, eh?" asked Fiona.

"Yes, do you know him?"

"I do," she answered. "We're both from Kildare. I've known Barry since we were children. Such a kind person. Always has been. And fame hasn't changed him, unlike his older brother Christy. I'd love to go with you and surprise him. Wouldn't that be fun!"

"I wish you could," I answered. "It would be so great to go with someone else for a change."

"Do you always go to concerts alone?" asked Fiona. "Ouch! I didn't mean for it to sound like that! Sorry! I think it's great that you are willing to drive here and go by yourself, but it's a bit . . ."

"Unusual?" I answered for her. By now I was accustomed to this curiosity about my lone adventures.

"Uh, yes. I guess so."

"No, I don't always go alone. My cousin went with me the last time he was here, but she's on a book tour now and no one else was available. Besides, I would rather go by myself than go with someone who doesn't appreciate his music."

By that time Pat had rejoined us and picked up the conversation. "Oh, Fi, you would never have to worry about that happening at one of Brian's concerts, would you?"

"Oh, never!" laughed Fiona.

Pat saw the puzzled look on my face and said, "Why, I don't think Diane knows who your husband is, Fi. Should we tell her?"

"You might know him, and you might not. He's Brian Dunning and he's the flautist in the band Nightnoise."

My mouth must have fallen open because both Pat and Fiona stared at me with a maybe-we-shouldn't-have-told-her-because-she's-going-to-go-fan-crazy-on-us look.

"No, it's not that," I said, reading their expressions. "I mean, I am a fan of Nightnoise. They're one of my favorite Windham Hill groups. But it's just that all of these connections to Ireland keep happening to me, and it creeps me out sometimes."

"Brian and I lived in Oregon for several years when he was with Nightnoise," explained Fiona. "It's only been in the last few years that we've moved back to Ireland. During that time in Oregon, I became friends with a shaman named Vicki Noble. She shared an interest in Sheela-na-gigs too, but she would say, and I agree, that these connections, or 'coincidences,' you're experiencing just show that your soul has become receptive to the spiritual realm. You're on a journey. It's all good, Diane."

"Your goddess energy is guiding you," added Pat.

"Well, who am I to doubt you two, and I'll take any kind of energy I can get! Thanks for meeting up with me today. I really appreciate it."

We talked and talked some more about art, Pat's teaching job at DePaul University, her gardens, her grief over her husband's sudden death a few years earlier, Fiona and Pat's friendship, and so on. As we were leaving, Pat suggested that we explore some of the Swedish shops, so we spent another fun hour on a beautiful sunny day enjoying each other's company. We laughed as we tried to beat the crosswalk signals, Fiona almost losing her beige bucket hat and me falling out of one sandal. Meanwhile, Pat raced past us, her voluptuous body bouncing and her scarf blowing in the breeze.

As we were saying our goodbyes, Fiona scrawled out her phone number and shoved it into my hand. "Here's my number. Give me a call when you get to Ireland. Maybe we can meet up."

I had walked to the gallery to see Fiona's exhibit that afternoon, but it was closed. However, it was a storefront, so I could get a good view of most of it through the windows. I had been amazed at how powerful the paintings and figures were, so different from her serene landscape paintings for which she's known. Her Sheela-na-gigs expressed a transformative feminine energy in all its power. They were strong, angry, menacing, mysterious, and uniquely beautiful.

I was thinking about this as I drove up to the church in Killinaboy. I parked along the side of the road, grabbed my camera gear, and walked up the steep little hill to the roofless church ruin. I unlatched the black metal gate, walked forward to about twenty feet in front of the arched entrance, and looked up. Shielding my eyes from the bright sun, I stood there waiting until my eyes were able to focus on the gray stone just above the arch. She was surrounded by ivy that had been cut back, but there she was in all her glory, the Killinaboy Sheela-na-gig, known in Irish as Inghean Bhaoith. That is the name of the abbess of the ancient monastery that used to reside here, an intriguing name because it translates to "daughter of madness." And I had to admit that the Killinaboy Sheela did look a little crazy. Not only was she contorted in the usual squatting, vulva-revealing position, but she appeared to be laughing and having a jolly time. *Fair play to her,* I thought. I stood there for a long time just staring at her, taking in the details of the carving on gray granite that had been there for nine centuries. I set up my tripod and attached my zoom lens so that I could get as close as possible. I took shot after shot from different angles and then set the timer and took shots of myself standing under the arch with the Sheela above me. I felt so excited and longed to share my experience with someone. And then I remembered that Fiona had given me her number. I ran over to my backpack, retrieved my phone, and dialed her number.

"Hi, Fiona, this is Diane."

"Well, hello, Diane. How are you?"

"I'm doing great. Guess where I'm calling you from?"

"Hmmm. Well, I assume it's somewhere in Ireland."

"I'm standing under the Sheela in Killinaboy."

"You're not!"

"Oh yes, I am!"

"Well, how is the old girl doing today?"

"She's looking good. All of the ivy has been cut away."

"That's good, because the last time I was there it hadn't been, and Brian had to hoist me up on his shoulders while I pulled it away."

"Oooh, that's no fun."

"Let me tell ye, no it wasn't."

"I hear a lot of noise in the background. I hope I haven't caught you at a bad time."

"I'm working an art fair in Carlow. I hate to rush off, but it is rather busy."

"Hey, no problem. I just wanted to let you know where I was."

"I'm so glad you did . . . Hey, Diane."

"Yes."

"Before you leave there, try lying down on the ground under the arch for a while. See if anything happens."

"Did you say 'lie on the ground'?"

"Yes, it's important to lie down, not sit or stand."

"Okay, Fiona, I'll do that."

"Good, and have a lovely holiday. Are you planning to get over to Kildare?"

"I don't think so, but I'll let you know if anything changes."

"Oh, do. It was wonderful hearing from you, Diane. Take care now."

I put the phone away and looked to see if anyone else was around. The place was empty, so I lay down on the weathered stone under the arch and closed my eyes. The sun was bright and warm on my face, and the breeze ruffled my bangs. The swallows and sparrows were chirping, and I could hear what sounded like a lark in the distance. I felt sleepy and was about ready to doze off when I heard a low buzzing sound much deeper in tone than an insect. I opened my eyes and looked around. The buzzing stopped. *That's weird.* I relaxed again and closed my eyes. The buzzing started up again, only louder. I sat up and looked around. It stopped. *What the hell?* The sound seemed to be coming from overhead, and the only thing overhead was the Sheela. I felt a little spooked, but I was intrigued. I lay down one more time and closed my eyes. Before long the buzzing started up again and grew in intensity. This time I didn't open my eyes. Although it reminded me of the Emily Dickinson poem that begins "I heard a fly buzz when I died," I didn't feel like I was dying, and I wasn't afraid. Instead, I felt a low, calming, buzz-like vibration throughout my entire body. It felt amazingly soothing, like an internal massage. I instinctively knew that some type of healing energy was emanating from the Sheela. I knew that it didn't make any sense and yet it seemed perfectly natural and normal, so I decided to go with it. I lay there a little longer until I heard a car pull up and car doors slam. I got up slowly, not sure if my legs would feel wobbly, but I was fine. In fact, I felt invigorated. Grabbing my things, I blew a kiss to the Sheela and walked to my car still marveling at this new experience. *This is all so strange,* I thought, *but I'm loving it.*

CHAPTER FIFTEEN

Goodbye Jessie, Hello Anne

I STOPPED BY Dysert O'Dea after visiting the Sheela to see if the groundskeeper I had met last summer was there. The narrow road back to the tower was worse than I remembered, and I was thankful that I didn't encounter any oncoming cars. The map I had bought last year wasn't clear about what was where, and the groundskeeper was nowhere in sight. I took photos of the crosses and the cows in the field. I watched an American woman with her husband on their honeymoon try to scale the stone wall in her high heels. And I marveled at the mystery of there not being any Sheela-na-gigs here, yet the Killinaboy Sheela-na-gig was less than five miles away.

I walked back to the tower where the visitor center was located and asked the older woman behind the desk about the groundskeeper.

"Oh, you mean, John Ryan," she answered, busily unpacking a box of tourist brochures and placing them in a revolving rack by the desk. "He finished his scheme."

"I'm sorry," I said. "I don't understand what that means."

"It means," she paused to adjust her brown-framed glasses and brush a wisp of salt-and-pepper hair from her face, "he doesn't work here anymore. He finished his time and now a young, lazy lad has taken his place. That's how the scheme works these days, I'm afraid."

I thanked her and walked to my car, sad that I wasn't feeling the magic from my visit last summer. John Ryan, God bless him, must have taken the magic with him.

My last evening at Jessie's wasn't quite what I had thought it would be either. Tim and Siobhan had gone out with friends, so Tim would not be cooking for us after all. And I realized after suggesting a few restaurants that Jessie didn't want to leave her dogs. She made a big salad for us instead. I did get to meet Tim, a tall handsome man, when he and Siobhan stopped by briefly after dinner, and I said a heartfelt goodbye to Siobhan. Freck had developed a fungal infection and her mucus was giving off an obnoxious stench, so Jessie suggested that we fix Coke floats and sit outside. We sat in chairs overlooking Liscannor Bay and talked for a few hours until the sun began to set. I told her about a teacher creativity grant I had been trying to get for years that would pay my way to Ireland, and she offered to write a letter of recommendation for me. She continued to obsess and fret about her business and politics, especially about the war in Iraq. She talked of moving to a farm in Sligo or possibly Maine. I was hoping that her talk of relocating was just talk.

I hated to say goodbye. Despite her eccentricities, she was a good and kind woman who had opened up her heart and her home to me. We had become friends, and I wanted to live closer to this new friend who meant so much to me. Who knew when I would ever return or if she would still be here when I did.

She and the dogs, along with the lone cat, gave me a great sendoff. I had quite an audience as I backed out of the drive with barks and kisses blown in both directions. As I ventured down her road, there stood her neighbor in front of his cottage clad only in striped boxer shorts and wellies. I couldn't resist this unique Kodak moment. I rolled down my window and asked if I could snap his picture. "Oh, be my guest luv!" he laughed as he flexed his muscles and struck a pose.

Saying goodbye to the Sullivans was difficult too for the same reasons. I had grown closer to all of them and watching the boys grow was such a joy. Maeve was busy inside, so I gave her a quick hug.

"Thanks again for everything, Maeve," I said. "I'll miss you."

"And I'll miss ye as well, Diane."

"I'll be back," I said. "I just don't know when."

"I know ye will, and it won't be soon enough."

I loaded my luggage in the car and took photos of Rory and Ronan as they waited for the school bus. Finn insisted that I take some of him too as he sat nearby playing with his truck. Murphy entertained all of us by running on top of the stone wall along the driveway. He barked as the bus approached. The boys got on board and waved to me from their seats. I gave Finn a final hug and Murphy a final pat on the head before starting the car and heading down the coast road to meet Anne at Spanish Point.

I was nervous about meeting Anne. We had corresponded for over a year, talked on the phone when I was here last summer, but we had never met in person. What if she didn't like me? What if she thought I was using her to get to her brother? What if we ran out of things to talk about? What if . . .

What if you just shut up and keep driving. If she didn't like you or if she thought you were just using her, she wouldn't have agreed to meet you at Spanish Point. Give her some credit for having the ability to discern between a potential friend and a cuckoo, would ya?

I pulled into the parking lot of the Armada Hotel next to Spanish Point and ran inside to use the restroom. Anne would be meeting me in the parking lot in a few minutes. I saw a small blue car pull in when I exited the hotel. It was making the *vroom* noise of a manual transmission, and an older woman with short, straight gray hair was driving. Assuming it was Anne, I waited until she parked and then walked toward the car.

"Anne?" I asked when she opened the car door.

"Diane! So happy to meet ye!" She fumbled with her car door, pulled herself out, and gave me a big hug. "Finally, together at last!"

"Yes," I said, hugging her back. "I was beginning to think it was never going to happen."

"Me too," she said, taking my face in both of her hands and gazing at me with a kind look that filtered through her glasses. "But I'm so glad that we have this morning together, and I regret that Davoc and I must leave for Donegal this afternoon."

"Well, I appreciate you taking time from your schedule to meet with me. I know you must be busy getting ready for your trip," I replied, secretly wishing that she hadn't planned a holiday trip during my visit but reminding myself that I was lucky she wanted to meet with me at all.

"Come, get in and I'll drive into Miltown. We can go for tea," she said as she fastened her seatbelt and turned over the engine. I climbed in and off we went, as Anne expertly shifted her way across the parking lot and onto the main road toward her town of Miltown Malbay, a few miles down the road.

If I'd had any fears that Anne would be filled with pretense at being a member of one of the best-known musical families in Ireland, I needn't have worried. She drove a well-worn, basic-model car without floor mats, sounding like it was only a thousand miles or so away from the junkyard. Dressed in jeans, a maroon top, and a navy-blue jacket covering her large frame, Anne herself didn't appear to be out to impress anyone. Everything about her exuded a warm, genuine attitude. "She's the salt o' the earth, Diane," her brother Luka Bloom had proudly told me when I had met him in Chicago a few weeks earlier, "the salt o' the earth."

Luka was right. I felt comfortable with her immediately, like I was reconnecting with a long-lost friend. We talked about things in general as she drove into town and found a parking spot, each of us treading carefully, I suspect, measuring our compatibility.

"So have ye been here before, Diane?" Anne asked as she parked the car.

"Only an hour or so last year, when I stood on a street corner asking any woman about your age who looked like a local if she was you," I replied.

"You didn't!" she laughed.

"Yes, I did. Somehow, I had it in my head that we were supposed to meet in Miltown Malbay that afternoon. I couldn't reach you on your phone, so I stood outside the busiest pub I could find in the center of town and asked several women until I gave up and drove back to Doolin. The women I asked were very polite, but they assured me that they weren't named Anne."

"Ha," Anne said. "I wonder what ye would have done if one of them was named Anne?"

"Oh, we would have had quite a conversation, I'm sure," I replied.

Miltown Malbay is a bustling tourist town of about one thousand along the Clare coast. With its main industry being tourism, it's full of pubs, shops, and B&Bs. It's most famous for its Willie Clancy Summer School and Festival, named in honor of the late uilleann piper, where thousands jam into the little town every July to take classes and perform traditional Irish music. Anne and her husband, who live on the edge of town, have participated in the festival for many years.

We walked the block or so to the tearoom and Anne engaged in "Hellos" and "How ye beens?" with several people. She seemed to know everyone, and everyone seemed happy to know her. She engaged in a kind, short conversation with a bag-carrying older woman who was muttering to herself. "Poor soul, we have the same conversation every time," she said as we entered the bright, crowded shop. A casually well-dressed, middle-aged couple waved to Anne and motioned for us to join them at their table by the window. Introductions were made and we settled in for a chat with Sakura and Charlie Turner, a retired couple from Seattle who spend their summers in County Clare.

"So, how long have you known Anne?" I asked.

"Oh my, I think going on ten years now," answered Sakura. Charlie nodded his head in agreement.

"We've been coming here for that long," he said, before taking a sip of his tea. "We found a great summer home here when we retired five years ago, and we split our time between here and Seattle."

"My sister lives in Port Orchard, just outside Seattle, with her husband and daughter. I haven't been there yet, but I would love to go there for a visit," I said.

"Oh, you must do that, Diane," Sakura said. "Shouldn't she, Anne?"

"Right so," Anne agreed.

And so the conversation went with Anne catching up on the latest news with Sakura and Charlie, whom she seemed to know well, and me feigning an interest in their talk of real estate and world travel and realizing that the Turners must be millionaires. They were very friendly and did not give off a whiff of superiority, but I was out of their league financially and not knowing any Miltown Malbay town gossip, I couldn't really contribute much to the conversation. I concentrated on smiling, drinking my tea, eating my delicious pastry, and nodding my head at the appropriate moments. That seemed to do the trick and, saying our goodbyes, Sakura and Charlie invited me to stop by whenever I'm in the Seattle area.

Anne motioned to me as were leaving the tearoom. "Look," she said. "Here comes Donnacha!"

A bespeckled man with dark curly hair approached in a motorized wheelchair. Donnacha is one of Anne's four sons and Niall's twin. In his thirties now, he was born six weeks premature, resulting in some motor and speech impairment. To make matters worse he was diagnosed with MS about ten years ago and now uses a wheelchair. Though he lives in his own apartment, he requires round-the-clock care, a situation that will only intensify with time.

"Hello, Donnacha!" said Anne, walking over to him to give him a hug. "So, ye are out and about this fine mornin', eh?"

"Hi, Mam," Donnacha answered in a slow, measured voice. "And ye have a new friend?"

"Indeed, I do. This is Diane. She's visiting from the States, and she's a fan of Luka's too."

"Hello, Donnacha," I said, extending my hand to take his limp one in mine. "I'm happy to meet you. Your mother is an amazing woman. We've emailed each other a lot, but this is the first time we've actually met."

"Mam is amazing," he drawled out with some difficulty. "She looks out for me."

"Yes, that's what your Uncle Luka said," I offered, not quite knowing how much conversation I should engage him in, since talking was so difficult for him.

"Luka, he's a good man," he said. "He listens to me."

"That shows how much he loves you," I answered.

Donnacha nodded his head in agreement.

"So, Donnacha luv, are ye doing some errands this mornin'?" asked Anne.

"Yes, Mam. Then I will go home so that Michael can torture me again."

I shot a quizzical look toward Anne.

"He means working with his physical therapist." She laughed.

I laughed too and said, "You're quite the joker, Donnacha. You had me going there for a minute."

He looked at me with a gleam in his eyes and replied, "I'm a real barrel of laughs."

It took him even longer to get that sentence out. I could tell that he was getting tired. Anne seemed to agree because she lovingly brushed her hand across his forehead and softly said, "Indeed you are my luv. Now, go about your errands and I'll see you a bit later."

"Bye, Mam," he said as he turned his wheelchair and headed off in the opposite direction.

"Bye, Donnacha," we both replied as we turned away and walked to Anne's car.

"Ahh, Diane," Anne said with a sigh, opening her car door and tossing her purse into the back seat. "It's so hard sometimes. He's not getting better, and he won't be." We got in the car. "Seems like every time I see him," she continued, "I notice something else—he's speaking with more difficulty or he can't raise his arm as high . . ." She trailed off and put her hand over her eyes, trying to fend off tears.

"I can't imagine how painful this must be for you," I said, placing my hand on her arm. "It must be devastating for him too. He seems like such a wise soul and to be unable to communicate very well . . ." I trailed off too, not knowing what else to say. We sat in silence for a moment, each dabbing tissues to our eyes. Finally Anne said, "Enough of this, let's drive back to Spanish Point. We can gab all the way back." She started the engine, jerked the stick shift into gear, and pulled out of the parking lot.

"Sounds like a good plan," I replied, relieved that she had changed the subject but feeling so much admiration for her patience and love in such a tragic situation.

As we rounded the first of many curves Anne surprised me by saying, "Oh, I meant to tell ye, Luka is doing a show in Lisdoonvarna next Monday night. Might you be able to go? I should be back from Donegal by then, so I'll be there as well."

I sat there in disbelief. So, Luka happens to be doing a show in nearby Lisdoonvarna during my stay in Ireland. What are the chances of that? Again, the synchronicity was too obvious.

"He's doing a show next Monday night?" I asked. I wanted to be sure I hadn't misheard her.

"Yes. At the Spa Hotel," she answered.

Oh my God! Oh my God! Am I lucky or what! I can't believe this! I get to see Luka Bloom in concert again and *in his own country! Wow! I mustn't act too excited though. I don't want Anne to think I'm looney. Let's see, I'll need to change my itinerary around, but it's doable. I'll just have to switch things around a little. Probably won't have time to drive as far north into Donegal. I wonder how I can get a ticket. Oh my God! I'm so excited! Is this really happening?*

"How do I get a ticket?" I asked, sounding excited but trying not to sound too excited.

"Oh, don't worry about that." She reached over and patted my leg. "I'll have Niall put you on the guest list."

"The guest list?" I asked.

"That's right. Just tell them your name at the door. We'll all sit together. It will be fun. Luka is looking forward to it."

"So am I," I assured her. "Thank you, Anne." Now it was my turn to reach over and pat her.

"Yer so welcome, Diane. I'm glad we'll get to spend more time together after all."

She steered the car into the Armada Hotel parking lot, and I pointed out my car. She pulled up next to it, and we talked some more about the details for next Monday. I still couldn't believe it. I told her that I would arrange to stay at a B&B in Lisdoonvarna that night and thanked her again for putting me on the guest list. We hugged, and I watched her vroom out of the parking lot.

"Yes! Yes! Yes!" I shouted, jumping up and down with my fist in the air. "I'm going to see Luka Bloom! I'm going to see Luka Bloom!" I sang as I skipped to my car.

And all shall be well . . .

CHAPTER SIXTEEN

I Useta Love 'em—The Saw Doctors

DRIVING NORTH on the N17, I was singing along at the top of my lungs with the song named for this highway by the Irish rock band The Saw Doctors—the familiar refrain about green grass and stone walls blaring from my car's speakers.

I was headed toward the town of Tuam (pronounced choom) in County Galway, home of The Saw Doctors. Their songs are filled with references to the town and its landmarks, and I was excited about taking a look at some of these places myself—the church with the two towers mentioned in the song "Same Oul' Town," Sugars, the pub mentioned in "Villains," and, and . . . well, come to think of it, there probably aren't that many landmarks in Tuam itself. Most of the songs are set in the landscape outside of Tuam: the hayfields, back roads, parades, and pubs of County Galway, and the beauty of Clare Island and Clew Bay in County Mayo.

The core members of The Saw Doctors are scruffy blond lead singer Davy Carton and bespectacled nerdy guitarist Leo Moran. Since their formation in the late '80s and their smash hit "I Useta Lover" in the early '90s, they've had a revolving door of drummers and bassists, but when I became familiar with them, baby-faced bass player Pearse Doherty was writing brilliant songs along with Carton and Moran, and former Waterboys saxophonist and multi-instrumentalist Anthony Thistlethwaite was adding his musical genius to the group. Their records are well received in Ireland, the UK, and among their small, but fervent, US fanbase, but they are best known for their rollicking concert performances where their fans sing along and perform hand motions and dance steps to such Saw Doctor staples as "Hay Wrap" and "Tommy K the Dee Jay."

It's no surprise that synchronicity brought me to The Saw Doctors. I didn't know anything about them on my first trip to Ireland, but shortly after getting home I called my friends Bill and Judy to tell them that an Irish rock band was scheduled to perform the following weekend at a small club in Indianapolis. They're always up for a good time, so I asked if they wanted to go with me.

"Of course, we'll go with you. You weren't planning on going by yourself, were you?" Judy asked, in that ever-protective concern-for-her-single-friend's-safety voice.

"Hey, don't worry about it, Judy, if you and Bill don't really want to go. I'll be fine. I'm used to—"

"We're going and that's final," Judy interrupted. "Besides, it will be fun. We're looking forward to it. We'll pick you up at six thirty."

We sat at a small bar table toward the front of the half-full club, watching the all-ages crowd and viewing the band's hodgepodge slideshow of tour shots and candid family photos while waiting for the band to appear. Finally, they strolled out onto the stage, smiling and waving while donning their instruments—five middle-aged fun-loving lads dressed in well-worn T-shirts and Gaelic football jerseys, displaying no rock star pretense whatsoever, ready to play their hearts out, tell stories with their thick western Irish accents, and sing their own songs. Songs about Irish football, corrupt Irish parish priests, small-town life, ceili bands, Irish emigrants, unrequited love, and western Ireland's natural beauty. Davy Carton's voice, one of the most versatile and underappreciated in rock, moved easily from smooth romantic ballads to rough and rowdy rock anthems, while cute Leo Moran's little-boy voice was especially poignant on ballads like "Clare Island" and "Galway and Mayo."

I was hooked on their catchy, well-honed tunes and their exhilarating party atmosphere stage performance. I became an ardent fan. I bought all of their records, knew most of the lyrics to their songs, and promoted them ad nauseum to my friends and family. Suddenly, it seemed as though I was hearing their music everywhere: Bands covered their songs at every Irish fest I attended, their music poured out of the speakers at every "Irish pub" where I dined. I joined their active online fan site and corresponded some with Leo Moran about his well-written tour reports. I appreciated his ability to gently poke fun at American customs, such as our insistence on closing swimming pools right after Labor Day no matter how hot the weather. "We Irish would kill to swim in your post–Labor Day pools," he wrote.

So there I was, the following summer, driving to Tuam on the N17, with plans to spend two days exploring the "landmarks" of The Saw Doctors songs. As for the Docs themselves, they were touring in the US. I knew I wouldn't be running into them, but their office manager had invited me to stop by at their office in Galway City, and who knew who else I might run into in Tuam itself? I was up for an adventure.

Driving past the gentle, rolling landscape filled with farms and old stone houses, I began to question what kind of adventure I was expecting. I reminded myself that Tuam is a small, nondescript town. There were only so many adventures that would fall within my moral compass. It wasn't as if I would have been willing to hang out in the pubs and meet someone to go home with. That's just not me. I'm the kind of woman who would require a deep connection and relationship with a man before having a sexual relationship. Some might see that as being old-fashioned, but I see it as a way of protecting my vulnerability, safety, and emotional well-being. Maybe I would meet a family who would take me in the way the Sullivans had. Maybe I would meet another traveler who would be willing to take in the sights with me. Then the inner critic chimed in. *Maybe you're too old to be chasing an Irish rock band. Maybe you should have made this trip a real religious pilgrimage instead. Visit Iona or Knock or . . .*

"Oh, shut up," I said out loud. "Just cut the chatter and leave me alone." I turned up the music and continued on toward Tuam.

I was unable to reserve a room at my first-choice farmhouse B&B, but my second choice didn't sound too bad and it did have the word "Farmhouse" in its name. Still, as I drove past it heading toward Tuam, I thought, *Hmm, where's the farm and why is the house so close to the busy and noisy N17?* But I was excited at the prospect of exploring Tuam's town center, so I didn't pay it much mind at the time. After finding a parking space in what turned out to be a grocery store parking lot (darn, I didn't mean to park there!), I made my way toward the town center feeling disoriented and beginning to wonder why I was making this journey. What was I hoping to find anyway? The warm nostalgia I felt when listening to their songs was in stark contrast to what I was seeing here in this small, working-class Irish town. None of the landmarks The Saw Doctors mentioned in their songs were within sight except for the two church towers in the center of town they sang about in "Same Oul' Town." And, again, I reminded myself that there weren't that many actual landmarks. Lots of narrow streets and alleys led off the town square, none of them signposted very well. I wandered aimlessly for a while, hoping I wouldn't get lost and be unable to locate my car. Lots of people moved about with other things on their minds besides helping a frazzled-looking woman wandering the streets. They didn't mistake me for a tourist, because it was obvious that Tuam wasn't exactly a hotbed for tourists. Case in point, when I finally located the Tourist Information Centre there was a CLOSED FOR THE SEASON sign on the door. *Huh?* Summer was *the* tourist season. I did manage to obtain a map from a place next door called "Corrib Country"—as in nearby Lough Corrib. The map had apparently been made for some past gathering of an unknown nature that was to meet in the car park by the launderette. Needless to say, it was incomplete and pretty worthless to me, though it did show the Purcell Stockwell Road and Tuam Stadium, which The Saw Doctors mention in their songs, but so what? When I made it back to my car, I stopped a woman and her teenage son to get alternative directions out of Tuam and thus avoid the town center traffic. They cheerfully complied, though they spent what seemed like an eternity arguing about the best route, with the teenage son winning the argument. Since it was five thirty by then, I decided to get settled in at the B&B and come back to town for dinner. Perhaps Mrs. Fogarty at the B&B would give me some helpful information about touring Tuam. The room was adequate, but I decided right then that two nights in Tuam would be too many. I was accustomed to my large room at the Doolin Farmhouse with its scenic view of the Clare coast—not a small, nondescript room on the main floor facing a busy highway.

In the meantime, Mrs. Fogarty suggested that I could get some excellent pub food at The Brogue (formerly Sugars). That was confusing too as there are two Brogues, The Brogue and The New Brogue. Was there some kind of small-town cutthroat competition happening here? They looked to be the same age to me. Maybe I should have discussed this with the phantom Tuam Tourist Information Centre.

A few months after The Saw Doctors' show in Indianapolis, at the urging of friends and fellow fans on the fan site, I had driven to Chicago alone to see them at the Celtic Fest in Grant Park. I had checked into the Congress Street Hotel, where, from my upper room, I had a clear view of Grant Park just across the road. I was excited about seeing the band perform in a much larger venue, and I was confident that I would meet some of the fans I had corresponded with on the fan site. Still, here I was, alone again. *Oh, screw it, Diane. You're here. Quit moping and look at it as an adventure.* So I did.

The festival grounds were crowded, but not overly so. I was able to visit several booths peddling everything from Scottish shortbread to Irish turf pellets complete with a ceramic thatched cottage burner. *Wow, this is more of a tourist trap than the Irish Fest in Indianapolis!* That's when I glanced down the row to my left and saw Davy Carton and Pearse Doherty sitting at a folding table signing autographs. *Hot dog, there they are but, darn, where's Leo Moran?* I made my way toward the table and stood in line.

Okay, I need to take my camera out of my bag and act like I know what I'm doing. That's right. Make sure the autofocus is set and set the aperture on auto too because I won't have time to mess around with manual settings. I hope my hair isn't too messed up. Damn! Why didn't I put on more lipstick? Keep cool, and don't say anything stupid.

"Look, Davy," said Pearse as I stepped up to the table."She has a fancy camera, like. Ye better behave yerself now."

"Ha," answered Davy, as he leaned toward Pearse to pose for my raised camera."And may the fairies fly up yer arse if I'm ever caught behaving meself!"

I cracked up and so did the others around me.

"Hey, c'mon back here and strike a pose with us," said Pearse, motioning to me to stand between them. "Give yer camera to this kind lad and he'll snap our picture, won't ye, Ronnie?"

I recognized Ronnie as one of their roadies.

"Oh, yeah," said Ronnie with a mischievous smile."Then, I'll keep yer camera."

"Oh no you won't!" I laughed, grabbing for the camera.

"Hey, luv, didn't we see you at a gig not long ago?" asked Davy.

"Yeah, in Indianapolis."

"Yes, yes. Small club but the crowd was brilliant. We hadn't played in Indianapolis in years, but it was most fun."

Pearse nodded his head in agreement.

"That was my first time seeing you, and I'm a big fan now. You'll have to come back. I'll bring a bunch of my friends and family next time."

"Right so, luv," said Pearse. "It was lovely to see you. Will you be in the crowd tonight?"

"Sure thing. I drove from Indianapolis to see you."

"Brilliant! Take care now, luv."

At the concert that evening in the huge Grant Park outdoor venue, I managed to find an aisle seat in the second row. I introduced myself to a couple next to me, and they quickly recognized me as "that woman from Indianapolis on the fan site." So did the woman in front of me, a second-grade teacher from Evanston, and the couple behind me. It was such a relief to have people I could talk to and who were willing to hold my seat for me so that I could wander around between acts. The crowd was huge compared to the crowd at the club, at least 2,000, and the clear September evening was crisp and cool. Just right for a big party of singing and dancing with an Irish band. Finally, as darkness was descending The Saw Doctors took the stage and the crowd roared. Clearly, they were more popular than I had assumed. My new friends and I had a great time doing all of the dance moves together to their songs. The stage lighting against the dark sky was perfect for taking photos, and I was able to shoot several close-ups of the band.

During the song "Macnas Parade" one of my new friends, Amy, and I decided that we could dance as well as the Irish dancer onstage with the lads, so we brazenly made our way toward the stage, dancing all the way. Unfortunately, a security guard with no sense of humor thought otherwise, and we were ushered back to our seats with a stern warning that if we tried that again, we would be ushered off the premises. Some of the audience members booed at the guard, but as I waved to Davy and he waved back with a big smile, I couldn't help but notice that the security guard was smiling too, a much smaller smile that he was trying to hide, but, still, a smile. Far too soon they were ending the show with a rousing rendition of "Hay Wrap."

I exchanged email addresses with my new friends so that I could send them some photos, and we said goodnight, promising that we would meet up again at a future Saw Doctors concert. As I headed toward the exit gate, I came upon a tent where a small informal group of musicians were sitting in a circle singing Luka Bloom's "City of Chicago." I went inside and listened for a moment, taking a few pictures of the group to send to Anne. How fitting that such a perfect night should end with a classic Luka Bloom song about an Irishman in Chicago pining for his homeland. And here I was, a woman from Indiana, in Chicago pining for Ireland, her spiritual homeland.

I stuck close to others as I left the festival grounds and walked back to the hotel, wanting to stop at a café along the way but knowing that it wouldn't be safe to do so. I felt grateful that I had made the journey here, but sad about returning home in the morning to my humdrum life. What I really longed for was to return to the "stone walls and the grasses green" in County Clare.

Back in Tuam, I found the car park on the main road just past the Shell petrol station. Much better, though I wondered why the parking lot was so empty compared to its full state an hour or so earlier. I felt a sudden sense of foreboding coming on. Suddenly, I remembered the verse from "Same Oul' Town" that begins "Same oul Monday, closed all day." *Oh, shit! It's Monday.* By the time I found The Brogue, I realized that everything in Tuam was closed! A young man standing in front of The Brogue informed me with much sadness that "every other pub is closed as well." When I told this story to Leo Moran months later, he leaned in and whispered, "Ye jes didn't find de right pub."

So much for my plans for a night out in Tuam. I walked the deserted streets all the while wondering how on earth this place inspired The Saw Doctors to write such wonderful songs. It's just a small, working-class town, much like my hometown in Indiana. Nothing special at all. The young people I encountered hanging out in town looked like they would rather be somewhere else, and the streets, well let's face it, it's unlikely that Tuam will ever stand a chance of winning Ireland's Tidy Town Award. Tuam reminded me of Ennis without any of the amenities, such as good restaurants and great music. And Ennis didn't close down on Monday nights!

I drove south toward the B&B and did find a restaurant on the edge of town (I think it used to be a steak house, or so the old sign said). Though no hours were posted, it appeared to be closing, but the waitress took pity on me, and I ate a quick meal of "blended" vegetable soup and brown bread. When I returned to the B&B and told Mrs. Fogarty what had transpired, she was surprised and said, "Oh, I guess I should get their (The Brogue's) hours." I doubt that Mrs. Fogarty will be a top contender for the B&B Proprietor of the Year Award.

After a night of trying to sleep through the noise and bright lights of the traffic just outside my window, I checked out after breakfast the next morning and stopped in Tuam for gas. A young man working there gave me the directions to Sun Studio, where The Saw Doctors record.

"I know Kenny Ralph, their producer," he said as he wiped a rag across my windshield. "I can give ye his phone number if ye like."

"That's very kind of you, but I don't want to bother him," I answered.

"It's no bother, ma'am," he said, handing me my change. "I'm sure he'd like to meet ye."

"Thanks, but I really need to get to Sligo, so maybe next time." *And if I do ever come back, it won't be on a Monday!*

The Saw Doctors were off touring in America, and what would I say to Kenny Ralph anyway without seeming intrusive or, worse yet, a groupie? This entire trip to Tuam was a disappointment. First, I had hoped to meet the poet Joan McBreen, but she hadn't responded to my emails. And maybe if I'd had another Saw Doctor fan with me, I would have enjoyed touring Tuam, but its charm, so obvious to The Saw Doctors, just wasn't there for me. So, after driving past the studio, I took a side trip on the back roads to Boyle, thus avoiding the traffic in the pilgrimage town of Knock, and proceeded on my way to Drumcliff in County Sligo, the burial place of William Butler Yeats.

But driving on, I couldn't resist popping *The Best of The Saw Doctors* back into the CD player and cranking up "Hay Wrap," with Leo Moran rapping about how he'd kill for a pint of porter while wrapping hay in the heat of summer.

CHAPTER SEVENTEEN

Into the Twilight

I WAS BUSY maneuvering the roundabouts on N15 coming into Sligo, being sure to go clockwise this time. I wanted to get a good look at the beautiful, bustling town full of shops, statues, and even stoplights, but I could barely lift my eyes off the road and there weren't any easy parking spots to be found. Besides, it was already midafternoon, and I was anxious to get to the B&B in Drumcliff. I continued north on the narrow, rough two-laned highway, dodging the trucks in the oncoming lane by veering to the left and praying I wouldn't snap off my side mirror on some low branches.

I was using Drumcliff as a base for my visit to Sister Hilda the following day, who lived east of there in the middle of nowhere. It wasn't until I had driven past the church on my way to the Mountain View B&B that I realized I was in Yeats Country. I saw the signs, Yeats Tavern and Yeats this and Yeats that and I realized, *That's right, he's buried here, and Ben Bulben is right over there!* Sometimes I'm a little slow. It's a good thing that synchronicity didn't require my memory to work. I was so excited about the prospect of spending two nights in this area. Yeats spent his boyhood summers here and turned those experiences into timeless poems such as "The Lake Isle of Innisfree" and "The Song of Wandering Aengus." I had memorized those poems and many others during my college days and held them close to my heart.

Yeats himself was an enigma, his views ever-changing and often contradictory. He was an Irish Nationalist, but not enough of one to consider participating in the 1916 Rising. He served in the Irish parliament, but he admired fascist rulers like Mussolini. He was a master at writing traditional forms of poetry, yet those poems were infused with elements of spiritualism and Irish folklore not seen in modern Irish poetry. Still, his genius is unsurpassed and shines on in his poetry, plays, and other writings. With his friend Lady Gregory, he was responsible for the creation of Dublin's Abbey Theatre and for bringing the Irish Literary Revival to the forefront when he received the Nobel Prize in Literature in 1923.

Yeats's last wish was to be laid to rest "under Ben Bulben," the flat-topped mountain of his childhood summers. He died in France in 1939 and was buried there, but his remains were later moved to the cemetery at St. Columba's Church, Drumcliff, under the gaze of Ben Bulben. His simple grave marker contains the infamous epitaph he wrote:

> Cast a cold Eye
> On Life, on Death,
> Horseman, pass by!

Like the Horseman, I decided to pass his grave by, since it was swarming with busloads of tourists. I retrieved my camera equipment from the car and carried it to the less crowded opposite end of the cemetery to photograph the Celtic cross gravestones and the 10th-century high cross, which was smack in the center of the two-laned N18. Drumcliff is odd that way. The highway splits the historic section straight down the middle and, with no bypass, all of the traffic between Sligo and Donegal noisily snakes past what should be a sacred area for meditation and contemplation.

I tried wading out to the center of the road to get a few close-up shots of the carved details on the high cross and of the ruined high tower in the distance, but the traffic kept me at bay. I retreated back to the roadside and used my zoom lens. The cemetery itself was more promising. There were lots of marble crosses and one wooden one, its white paint peeling, revealing the worn gray wood underneath. I concentrated on it, setting my tripod low. Kneeling, practically lying on the ground, I looked through the viewfinder and focused. I liked the way the cross was in the forefront, the gray-white clouds above and behind, and the background blurred just as it should be. Wiggling and squirming around to get the right angle, I took several shots until I was satisfied. After getting up and folding my tripod, a thin, graying bearded man approached. He was wearing khakis and hiking boots like me with a travel vest to match.

"So, are you a professional photographer?" he asked. His accent surprised me—I had taken him for a tourist but he had a Dublin accent, less pronounced than the accent in western and southern Ireland.

"Oh no," I laughed, fitting my camera into its bag and zipping it shut. "It's a hobby. I took it up again a few years ago after being away from it for several years."

"Why were you away from it?"

"Oh, you know, this thing called working and raising a family. It doesn't leave much time for anything else." I lifted my tripod and slung it onto my shoulder.

"Ahh, I tend to forget about these things," he laughed, his hand nervously brushing his vest, "not having a family myself."

I stood there, not knowing how to respond. Sensing the awkwardness, he added, "I teach at Trinity College, Irish literature. You might say that the students and faculty are my family."

So I was right! He's a Dublin man!

"Wow! Teaching at Trinity! That must be wonderful! Do you research and publish as well?"

"I do," he answered. "Truthfully, that takes more of my time than teaching."

"It's similar in the States," I said.

"So do you teach at university?"

"No, I'm a librarian and teacher in the public schools—in Indiana."

"Ahh, lovely. I carry the utmost respect for librarians. Brilliant, they are, and most helpful."

"Being a librarian at Trinity College would be my dream job," I couldn't help but gush.

"Have you been there as yet on your tour?" he asked.

"No," I answered, "I'm afraid not, and I doubt that I'll get to Dublin this trip. Maybe next time though."

"You won't want to miss it," he said. "For the library if nothing else. It has its share of tourists, but it's not a tourist trap like this." He gestured toward the parking lot with the tour buses. "Since I study Yeats I've been coming over here now and again for years. It's changed, it has. It used to be so simple—just the church, the high cross, and Yeats's grave.

Now they have this bloody new tearoom. Anything to attract the tourists!" He threw up his hands in disgust.

"I understand that it must be upsetting," I offered, "but Ireland has faced some very hard economic times, especially here in the west. Tourism is its bread and butter. I haven't been inside it yet, but at least the tearoom looks like it's been tastefully done, don't you think?"

"Aye, I just don't see the need for it. It takes away from the purpose and meaning of the place," he answered, looking down at the ground and poking the gravel with his foot.

"You may be right but think about what it would be like in the States. Well, first of all, it wouldn't be anything special in the States because Americans generally don't hold writers in high regard the way the Irish do. Americans worship athletes. But if they did worship writers, this would be a theme park. There would be the Flying Yeats Roller Coaster, the Wandering Aengus Ferris Wheel . . ."

"Innisfree Treasure Island!" he added, laughing.

"Yes! You see what I mean? It could be worse!"

We laughed and talked a little more about Yeats and Trinity College. He looked at his watch and indicated that he needed to be getting back to Dublin.

"Before I go," he said with a twinkle in his eye, "you know there's a lot of evidence that the bones in Yeats's grave aren't his. That they got mixed up with someone else's when they were removed from the grave in France."

"Really?" Somehow, I hadn't heard about it and I mentally placed it in the same trash can as the "Shakespeare's plays weren't written by Shakespeare" theory.

"Indeed. So, all of these people coming here to pay their respects and he's not even here!"

"It doesn't matter," I said. "People are coming here to pay their respects to the work, not the man, and certainly not to his bones! The work is what's sacred. There could be a monument to Yeats anywhere and people would come. But it's here, in a place that was sacred to him, and that's all that matters."

"Oh, begob, she gets it!" he shouted raising a fist to the sky.

I was beginning to wonder about this professor going nutty on me. He must have read the thought on my face. "That was a test, you see?" he laughed. "I wanted to know if you would understand the sacredness of the work and you do!"

"So, I passed the test?" I asked, bemused.

"With flying colors," he answered. "It's been a pleasure talking with you. If you do make your way to Trinity, look me up." He dug into his vest pocket, pulled out a small gold case, and opened it. "Here's my card." He placed the card in my palm and smiled. "Goodbye now. Safe travels."

I watched him walk to his car and waved as he pulled out of the parking lot.

I walked into the "bloody new tearoom" and found the tea and scone delightful. Its modern but cozy interior filled with light wood and lots of windows did nothing to subtract from the ancient Drumcliff churchyard, and I enjoyed having a spot in a quiet booth to collect my thoughts.

The professor was an interesting, if somewhat eccentric man. I wished we could have gone to dinner to continue our talk about Irish literature. Not long ago I would have imagined he was hitting on me, but I'd had enough experience by now with numerous chance encounters with Irish men to know better. The Irish, men and women, tend to be friendly to strangers—especially to tourists. At least, that's been my experience as a solo middle-aged woman traveler.

I was proud of myself for making it all the way from Tuam to Drumcliff safely. I was getting better with driving but, still, it was anything but relaxing. My stomach still churned, and the stress was exhausting. I wanted to stop by Yeats's grave, but as I left the tearoom, I noticed a group of tourists, fresh off the bus, making their way in that direction. I decided to drive back to the B&B, rest for a while, and return after dinner.

With Ben Bulben in full view, I made the ten-minute drive back to Mountain View B&B, a large, modern, two-story home with dormers and, as the name implies, outstanding views of Ben Bulben. Sitting high on a hill, it was expensively decorated with immaculate gardens of foxglove, azaleas, and cala lilies. It's owner, Mrs. Murphy—tall, slim, dressed in a casual but stylish pantsuit—appeared to be closer to my age. Her short reddish hair looked professionally styled and her warm smile and easy manner made me feel right at home. What a saving grace it was to be here after my time in terrible Tuam!

"Would you like a cuppa tea, Diane?" asked Mrs. Murphy.

"No, thank you. I had a cup at the tearoom in Drumcliff. I think I'll rest in my room for a while before going to dinner. Do you have any suggestions?"

"I have a list of nearby places in the hallway, but I think you would like The Yeats Tavern. It carries a good selection and the prices are reasonable."

"Yes, I saw it across the road from Drumcliff Cemetery. I planned to go back there this evening anyway, so that's perfect."

"Lovely, then. You go up to your room and rest. You must be exhausted. We can visit later. Let me know if you need anything at all."

I climbed the stairs to my room, one of the dormers, with a clear view of Ben Bulben. The large room was papered in muted florals in shades of pink and light green, and the double bed with a matching spread looked so comfortable that I wanted to take a nap right away. But the green upholstered chair by the window called to me, and I sat there watching the light change over Ben Bulben for the longest time, lost in my thoughts.

I felt that I could spend the rest of my trip right here and not regret it. *Why does this area move me so deeply? I'm sitting here with tears in my eyes. What's this about? I came here because it's a good stayover spot between Sister Hilda's place and Donegal. Since I'm going back to Clare for Luka's concert, I'm not going to Donegal now. And this Sister Hilda visit . . . everyone thinks I'm crazy for driving out in the middle of nowhere to see a woman I don't know. What if I just stayed here instead? I could read Yeats's poetry, play with Charly, the Murphy's springer spaniel, and hang out at Yeats Tavern.* It didn't sound too bad, really. I stepped over to the bed and was out cold the moment my head hit the pillow.

When I awoke two hours later, I felt rested and ready for dinner and a visit to Yeats's grave. The sky had cleared, and Charly gave me a quick goodbye lick before jumping up onto the stone wall, his eyes fixed on the long driveway, waiting for Mr. Murphy to come home.

The Yeats Tavern was as good as Mrs. Murphy said it would be. Dark wood throughout—the woodwork, tables, and chairs—lots of small windows, and a huge stone fireplace gave the place a cozy cottage feel. I sat at a table by the window eating soup and the best brown bread ever. I reread the section of Pat Monaghan's book about nearby Knocknarea, the limestone hill with Neolithic burial sites and the large cairn on top that is, according to Irish folklore, Queen Maeve's tomb. I was looking forward to exploring the site in a few days on the way to County Mayo.

After dinner, I walked across the street and into Drumcliff Cemetery. The tour buses were gone, the tearoom closed, the parking lot nearly empty. It was a gorgeous, warm June evening. I checked my watch. 8:30. The sun wouldn't set for another two hours. I walked straight to Yeats's gravesite and sat down next to it. The only others there were a man and what appeared to be his approximately ten-year-old daughter. They talked in hushed whispers and smiled at me. I smiled back. Soon they left, and I was alone with what may or may not have been the remains of William Butler Yeats.

I sat there in what is called the golden hour—that time in the evening when the setting sun casts a golden glow over everything. It felt magical. I recalled the first stanza of my favorite Yeats poem, "Into the Twilight," which seemed so appropriate to where my life was right at that moment.

"Out-worn heart, in a time out-worn,
Come clear of the nets of wrong and right;
Laugh, heart, again in the grey twilight,
Sigh, heart, again in the dew of morn."

It's true that my heart was worn out from being broken. My expectations of meeting someone after my divorce who would be my true love seemed to be a fleeting dream. "It's not in the cards," I told my mother. "Honey, never say never," she answered. But time was wearing out too. I was getting older, and I wasn't sure what I wanted or what I should be doing. "Forget about wrong and right, should and should not," Yeats seemed to be saying. "Go with your heart."

If I went with my heart, I would leave my home and my career, stay in Ireland, find a job and a place to live somewhere near the Clare coast, and write. Of course, I would continue to love my daughters and make regular visits, but I wouldn't be defined by them. Their dramas would not become my dramas. It was a grand plan, but a far too risky one for someone as practical as me, and I couldn't do that to my daughters. Their father had basically abandoned them by moving to Florida. Would I abandon them like my father had abandoned me? No way. I was their rock, and they needed me. Truth be told, I needed them too. They were, after all, my babies. But my heart had brought me here. I was sure of it. I felt so much at home here, and it seemed natural to be sitting here on this magical evening next to the resting place of this great Irish poet.

For the first time I was aware of the sound of running water, and I realized that I was next to the Drumcliff River. It flowed along and behind the church. I felt that it was calling me, so I stood up and followed the sound until I came to the riverbank. I followed the wooded path that meandered along the river until I came upon a small footbridge and crossed over the river. It felt like an enchanted fairy tale. Downstream, a few anglers were fishing for trout. Otherwise, no one else was around. I sat by the bridge and took it all in—the golden light, punctuated by the sound of the running river and the occasional splash of a fish jumping or a kingfisher diving. I wept at the beauty of it all, and at that moment I heard these words in the brogue of a male Irish voice:

"Julian told you that all shall be well. And I tell you that your heart, your muse, brought you here."

How strange to hear these words so clearly, yet it seemed so natural. And I knew from hearing recordings of his voice that it was Yeats's. There's no mistaking that high, sing-song voice of his. I continued to sit there, thinking about how uncanny it was that I'd made plans to stay in Drumcliff because of my visit to Sister Hilda, not because it is the burial place of William Butler Yeats. Yet clearly, feeling gobsmacked, I knew something out of the ordinary was happening here.

I arose and followed the path back across the bridge, past the church and Yeats's grave toward my car, feeling strangely at peace and not at all concerned about who had spoken or how it had happened. As I returned to Mountain View before dark, I felt that whatever had happened seemed as natural as getting ready for tomorrow's journey, writing out the directions to Sister Hilda's place and taping them to my dashboard.

CHAPTER EIGHTEEN

The Risky Road

MY DAY to meet Sister Hilda had arrived, so I gulped down an early breakfast at Mountain View and prepared for a day trip into the back roads of County Sligo and County Leitrim to visit this nun I had connected with on the internet. A month earlier, a woman in a contemplative prayer group I belonged to had contacted me to tell me about a new member in Ireland who was a hermit nun. That's how I first heard of Sister Hilda. She gave me her website address in case I wanted to check it out. Yes, the hermit nun had a website. I was intrigued and explored her site, which was filled with photos of abbey ruins, cottages, and cattle amid the beautiful Irish countryside. I emailed her to tell her about my upcoming visit to Ireland and to inquire about the possibility of meeting her. With her being a hermit and all, I wasn't expecting a response, but much to my surprise she agreed to my visit. She sent detailed directions to her hermitage along with her phone number. I was to call her after I arrived in Ireland, and we would arrange a day to meet.

So here I was, directions in hand heading toward Lough Allen, knowing that finding her place would be an adventure in itself. I drove into the most remote area of Ireland I had encountered thus far, stopping in several tiny villages along the way, mainly to be certain that I was on the correct road, where I encountered lots of old men sporting well-worn caps and wool sweaters. I had been told by my friend Pat Monaghan that these friendly men give the best directions and they usually part with a "God bless ye." I was not disappointed.

Sister Hilda's directions were great until I tried to locate the dirt lane that was to take me up, and I do mean up, to her place. I took the wrong path not once, but twice. The first path dead-ended at the top of the hill. At the very end there was nothing but a bunch of sheep staring warily at me like I was an alien who had invaded their pastoral planet. With great difficulty, I pulled forward then backward, turning the wheel sharply so that I didn't end up in the ditch. Then repeated as needed until the car was pointed in the right direction and headed back down the hill.

The second path was even narrower and hillier than the first. I was feeling pretty desolate by then when, much to my relief, there appeared out of nowhere the much-needed old man in a cap and wool sweater, this time sporting a cane and a faithful border collie.

"Ah, she's a nun, is she? Nah, I don't know anything about that," he said as his dog jumped up, rested his paws on my opened car window, and licked my face.

"What about Paddy O'Connor, do you know him?"

"Paddy O'Connor. Ah, yes. He lives just down the rood aways and up the next hill." (Thankfully, she had told me his name earlier in case I got lost.) "Ye should ask him."

I scribbled down the man's directions and thanked him.

"No trouble. God bless ye."

He and the dog supervised my attempt to turn my much-too-large-for-the-dirt-path rental car around. What seemed like an hour later, off I went back down the steep hill in search of the correct dirt lane. As I glanced in my rearview mirror, the kind man was waving me off, cane in hand, no doubt quite surprised at encountering a wayward American woman on his very remote road. I imagined him increasing his pace a bit as he made his way down the hill, eager to get to the local pub to share his story.

Finally, finding the next, and I hoped the last, dirt path, I drove all the way up, passing by what I hoped was Paddy O'Connor's place. He wasn't home. He was probably being entertained at the pub with a story about a lost American woman looking for a nun. Then I spotted the battered metal mailbox and, just beyond it, the closed farm gate. I pulled onto the grass and gazed down the hill just beyond the gate. That's when I saw her running up the hill toward me: a tall, thin, old lady, her gray Sisters of Clare habit flapping in the wind, her right arm waving excitedly as if she were flagging down a race car at the finish line. I breathed a sigh of relief and went to greet her.

"Ah, Diane, it's good to see you. Did you have any trouble finding it?"

"A little," I said, lying. "A gentleman gave me directions to Paddy O'Connor's place."

"Good enough," she said as she hugged me. "Let's go on down the hill and I'll show you the place."

I watched her as we maneuvered down the hill toward her cottage. Her traditional Sisters of Clare habit was considerably out of date. Now, the fashion for most nuns in all orders was polyester knit tops and slacks with elastic waistbands. Sister Hilda's face, framed by the white trim of her habit, was long, thin, devoid of makeup, and lined with experience. Her bulbous nose, prominent on her framed face, overpowered eyes that, on deeper inspection, were a penetrating steel blue, like turquoise mixed with granite. The short gray hairs protruding from her chin gave her a crone-like appearance, reminding me a bit of the witch in Hansel and Gretel. But unlike the witch, her warm smile seemed genuine, not rehearsed.

"I hope I haven't kept you waiting too long. I did get a little sidetracked," I admitted.

"Not at all."

We stepped inside the whitewashed cottage. It was dark inside and, in true hermit decorating style, contained only the bare essentials: a hand-me-down sofa and two white plastic chairs in the living room, a small sparse kitchen, and a closet-sized bathroom with elaborate instructions taped to the wall about how to flush the toilet. There was a bedroom, too, but the door was closed, and she told me she preferred to keep it private. Oh yes, and the computer on a small table shoved against the kitchen wall.

"So, how long have you lived here?" I asked.

"Oh, about two years, I suppose."

I waited for her to add to her story, but she was silent as she offered me a seat on the worn sofa. I knew from reading an interview she had given to an obscure hermit quarterly, though, that she had flown here after facing a "drastic, but necessary" move from her home with nothing but one of her three cats (that's all she was allowed to bring on the plane), a rucksack, her laptop, her Bible, and her breviary. She went on to say that her car "laden with essentials—like my two other cats—followed later." I was confused about how her car and her two other cats had managed to arrive here, not to mention where she came from, and I wanted to ask her about it, but she said, "Come, Diane, let me give you a tour of the cottage. When I bought it, the paint was peeling, plaster flaking, there was no water, plumbing, or bathroom. Two months later, it was transformed into a two-roomed hermitage with a kitchen and bathroom and a water supply based on rainwater running off the high peat bogs."

"Is the water drinkable?" I asked as I tagged along behind her.

"Heavens, no," she laughed. "Most of the time it's dark brown. I bring drinking water in. Of course, I use it for cooking too." She didn't mention bathing, and I didn't ask.

As we made the short walk around the cottage, I felt a little depressed, but I chalked it up to being tired from the long drive. Sister Hilda must have noticed something in my expression.

"Are you feeling a bit sad?" she asked.

"I'm just a little tired from the drive from Sligo," I answered.

"No, that's not it. You're feeling the ghost of a young woman who committed suicide here. You'll feel better soon enough," she added.

"What? When was that?"

"Oh, many years ago. Her father abused her, and she couldn't take it any longer. Poor thing, she couldn't see any other way out."

"That's so sad. How did you hear about that?"

"Oh, I've been doing research on the history of this place. Her brother stopped by one day and told me."

Strangely enough, the feeling did lift after a while, but I had another feeling of the nagging kind. Something wasn't quite right, and I didn't think it had anything to do with a ghost.

"Before we have lunch, let's sit and talk awhile. Would you like a cup of tea?"

"Yes, that would be wonderful."

It wasn't difficult to engage Sister Hilda in conversation. In fact, I had a difficult time getting a word in edgewise as we sat in her living room with her chatting away in her English accent while she obsessed over her three cats—two Siamese and one tabby. I'm not a cat person, but I understood the comfort they must have provided. I felt the same way about my two rescued greyhounds.

"So, where did you live before you came here?" I ventured.

"I stayed at a friend's house in Sligo, but it was too close to the tourists, you know, so I ended up here. It's a lovely place, don't you think?"

"Yes, the view of the hills is very peaceful." *Hmm. What about where you lived before that? But I guess you're not going to tell me.*

"Yes, it would be a shame if I would have to leave it behind."

"What? Are you thinking about leaving?"

"Well, Paddy is wanting to sell another cottage he owns just down the road, and if he does, I will have to move because I would be afraid to have others living that close to me."

"Why is that? I mean, Paddy lives close to you, right?"

"Yes, yes, but that's different. I know Paddy and I trust him. I help him with the lambing, and he helps me. Having strangers living close by would be different." She paused. "They might hurt me."

Before I could comment, she hurriedly said, "Let's go to the table now. Lunch is ready."

It was clear that she had gone to a lot of trouble for my brief visit, preparing a lunch of salad, homemade bread, vegetable soup, and tea served on English china, one of the few material luxuries she had. I wondered if that was one of the "essentials" she had brought over in her car. We talked about lighter subjects at lunch—food, her cats, and anything else that was not about her.

Later, she offered to take me around her property, and after I had borrowed an extra pair of her wellies, we walked along the muddy fence line. She pointed out the flora and fauna as we gazed at Paddy's sheep grazing in the adjacent field. I could see why she loved this peaceful place. We came upon an old cottage ruin complete with a hearth and rusted iron kitchen utensils.

"Wow, this stuff is amazing!" I said.

"Do you think these antiques are worth anything?" she asked.

"I don't know. You should check it out on eBay."

"Grand idea. I'll do that."

We went back into the cottage and continued our conversation, me on the sofa and her in her rocking chair with her cats.

We talked about theology for a while. She had complex, mostly negative views of the Catholic Church, of which I was a member, and she was currently "looking into" the Orthodox Church.

"But what about your Sisters of Charity vows?" I asked.

"Oh, my dear, I'm not a Sister of Charity. What makes you think that?"

"Well, you wear the habit and you say that you are on your website."

"Oh, that. Well, I put that on my website so that people will think I am. That way people will open up to me, and I can spread the love of Jesus to all. I always wear my habit when I visit the nearby villages, because the people feel more comfortable confiding in a nun who wears one. Not like today's nuns in their street clothes, you know. I help them with their problems, and the local clergy, Anglican and Catholic, don't like me. I'm afraid they are jealous of the fact that local people prefer to talk to me."

"How often do you visit the local villages?"

"Oh, I drive down every few weeks to stock up on supplies. Jesus has blessed me with a reliable car. I call it the 'Nunmobile' so that I can do this and minister to the people."

"Do you attend Mass when you go?"

"No, I wouldn't be welcomed, since I'm not Catholic. I have my own Mass here."

"Oh."

At this point I was totally confused, not to mention wondering what I had gotten myself into. I was visiting with a woman who presented herself as a Catholic nun but wasn't. Who claimed to be a hermit but drove her own car to the local villages and was active on the internet.

I'm so naïve. What was I thinking? That I was going to meet a modern-day Julian of Norwich? That she was going to see into my soul and tell me that "All shall be well"?

And there was more. Much more. I filled in some of the blanks during our conversation and came up with the following scenario: She's originally an Anglican from Sussex who has had a very troubled past including being, at some point, institutionalized in a facility for the mentally ill. For example, she mentioned an Anglican priest who had "misunderstood" her intentions when she visited him unannounced late one rainy night in an agitated state to ask him some "important" questions, and he had called the police on her. Her voice broke and she sounded hurt and angry, but she assured me that she didn't hold anything against him and that she had forgiven all who had mistreated her. She had been abused by her father and "hid" from him until she had learned recently of his death. She had lived as a hermit on one of the Orkney Islands but had been harassed and run off by the locals. Apparently she then returned to Sussex, I don't know for how long, sold her belongings, packed up her cats, and flew to Ireland, living for a short time at a "friend's" house in County Sligo before buying her current home. I never did find out how her car and other two cats made it to Sligo. She's considered disabled (due, she said, to her chronic fatigue-like "affliction") and she receives free medical care and utilities; that's how she could afford electricity and a phone line for her computer. She wasn't a member of the contemplative prayer group either; she had just visited our online chat room. She made some extra income by using, as she says on her website, "handskills of many kinds" to make rosaries, cards, and other gifts that she sells to "feed the hungry and clothe the naked in the Name of Jesus, all for Him and His people." I purchased a few cards and a small St. Brigid's cross, feeling a little betrayed and yet pitying her at the same time.

At her "usual time" of two o'clock, we followed along with a tape of an authoritative-sounding woman saying the rosary and praying for the lives of unborn and aborted babies. I sat there keeping my pro-choice views to myself. Then she handed me a piece of paper with her handwritten directions for a full tour around nearby Lough Allen. She apologized that her "condition" prevented her from accompanying me, although it was obvious by her detailed notes on her topographic map and her description of the area that she had done a lot of exploring herself.

We moved the white plastic chairs outside after that and enjoyed the stunning view of the hills and valleys, listening to the cuckoos in the distance. The weather was perfect: warm and sunny with a light breeze. I took a few photos of her with her cats, and, using her tiny digital camera, she took pictures of me with the cats. I left shortly after, telling her that I would explore Lough Allen before driving back to Drumcliff. I thanked her for letting me visit and for providing a delicious lunch.

"Ah, Diane," she said as she hugged me. "I so enjoyed meeting you today. God bless you, and I'll continue to pray for you."

As I drove away, I thought about how she seemed sincere about what she was doing, except for the fact that she had lied about being a nun and insinuating that she was Catholic. Still, I felt that something was "off" and, though I was glad I had made the visit, I knew I wouldn't want to do it again. She wasn't like Julian of Norwich at all. She was just a lonely woman hiding her mental health condition behind the mask of being a hermit nun. I'm aware that all of us at one time or another balance precariously on the tightrope between sanity and insanity. Anyone who has been visited by the hungry ghost of depression or addiction can attest to this. Our sense of reality, of what is most important, changes over time. And today's miracle pharmaceuticals, though helpful, do not guarantee a sane, happy life. All I know is that for one day she graciously welcomed me, a stranger she had met on the internet, into her home for a meal, conversation, and companionship. Who was I to judge her eccentricity?

"Please God," I prayed as I drove down her narrow lane, "watch over her and comfort her. Keep her from harming herself or others. Grant her peace."

I didn't stop at Lough Allen. It was late afternoon, and I was exhausted from the visit. Instead, I followed her directions to the next village, pulled over, and plotted a less confusing way back to Drumcliff, one that took me through some picturesque villages proudly displaying TIDY TOWN WINNER signs and onto the main road toward Sligo. When I arrived at Mountain View, Mrs. Murphy was waiting for me.

"Come, let's sit down and have a chat," she said. She led me into her lovely living room, and I sat on her cream brocade sofa hoping that the seat of my pants wasn't dirty.

"So, how was yer visit?" she asked, sitting in the chair across from me, her hands folded on her lap.

I explained about the drive to the remote location and how the woman wasn't who she claimed to be. "I'm not sorry I went," I explained. "It does make for a great story, but it's not something I would want to do again."

"I'm glad to hear you say that, Diane." Mrs. Murphy's eyes and voice revealed a level of concern that surprised me. "I was worried about you traveling over there by yerself, and I've been thinking about ye all day. I almost called your mobile to see how ye were getting on, but then I thought, *Don't be daft, Martina. She knows how to take care of herself.*"

"I appreciate your concern, Mrs. Murphy, I really do. You don't have to worry about me visiting any more hermit nuns, at least not on this trip!"

"Well, bless God for that!" she laughed.

"You have such a lovely home, and I've enjoyed my stay here so much. I can't believe I'm leaving tomorrow. I wish I could stay in this peaceful place forever," I said, sighing.

"You know you're welcome to stay on," she said quietly. "I can't say forever, but I, for one, am glad to have some more days, maybe some more years, here."

"What do you mean?" I asked.

"Ye see, I'm a breast cancer survivor and there's a seventy percent possibility that it will return, so I am grateful for every day I have. Maybe that's why I was so concerned about you taking this risky visit. Life is so precious." She paused. "Well look at me now, your last evening here and I'm getting all teary-eyed."

"So am I." We laughed, stood up, and gave each other a hug.

"You go on now," she said, "and enjoy yerself on yer last evening."

"I will. After I get cleaned up I'm going back to Yeats Tavern and then over to the cemetery one last time. Thank you again, Mrs. Murphy. I'll see you at breakfast."

Putting her hand to her eyes and turning toward the kitchen she said, "Good evening, luv."

CHAPTER NINETEEN

The Woman on the Bog Drives into the Mystic

MY STAY in Drumcliff and the trip to visit Sister Hilda were more than I could have hoped for. I continued to be astonished by the variety of Ireland's beautiful landscapes. The picturesque villages, Ben Bulben, Innisfree, holy wells along the roadside, newly planted pine forests. Though driving kept me from giving my full attention to the landscape, the quick images registered in my brain and made their way straight to my heart. I could live here. I knew it was pointless to think about living on the western coast because I couldn't afford it, but this interior landscape not far from the coast might fit my pocketbook. I let the dreamy thought drift away as I headed southwest along the border of Sligo and Mayo and then south along the western coast of the Nephin Beg mountain range in County Mayo. The halfway point of my two-week stay in Ireland was already upon me.

Midway points of any trip can be difficult and tiring, but my loneliness, coupled with the dreary weather, caused the Big Questions to rear their ugly heads: *What are you doing here? What do you hope to gain from driving Ireland's perilous roads by yourself? Aren't you tired of being alone?*

I ignored the pesky inner critic and kept driving.

I stopped at Knocknarea: the 1,000-foot-tall limestone hill topped with a Neolithic cairn said to be that of Queen Medb from Irish folklore. I had read about Medb and Knocknarea in Pat Monaghan's book, *The Red-Haired Girl from the Bog*. I was intrigued by her story originally told in *The Tain*, the Irish equivalent of *The Iliad*, where Medb is portrayed as not only a woman who started a war, but one who drew up the battle plans for it! She is portrayed as a devious, unscrupulous manipulator. Pat didn't like her because she was bloodthirsty and irresponsible, but other women disagreed. I remember hearing the Irish poet Nuala Ni Dhomhnaill read a poem about Medb at Butler University in Indianapolis and declare her be a "feminist declaring merciless war on any man who insults her dignity." That description of her sounded best to me, without the violence.

My plan was to climb up to the top of Knocknarea, but the climb would have been treacherous in the rain, so I decided to explore the nearby Carrowmore megalithic monuments instead. The site contains thirty remaining Neolithic passage tombs over several acres. Many of the tombs had only been properly excavated and researched in the past thirty years, and some, such as the Listoghil, the largest passage tomb, were in the process of being reconstructed. I would have found all of this extremely interesting had the rain not started pouring down. I sloshed around the grounds in my drenched hiking boots and poncho, lost my sense of direction in the middle of a field, collapsed onto the muddy turf, and pondered those Big Questions.

I'm looking to heal from the devastating failure of my marriage. I'm looking to conquer fear—fear of being vulnerable, fear of appearing stupid, fear of rejection, fear of failure. I'm looking for love in its truest form. Agape. Anam cara. Have I found answers? Yes, some. I'm more confident. I am conquering some fears. I'm here, alone, driving, meeting new people, putting myself in new situations. But there are more answers to find.

No answers were forthcoming here. The ancient voices from the mound gravesites were silent. Eventually, I got my bearings and slogged across the boggy field to the parking lot. I went back to my car, dried off as best I could, and kept driving.

The sun came out later that morning and I put my hiking boots and wool socks in the rear window to dry. I approached the town center of Ballina and got caught in a traffic jam due to road construction or, as the Irish say, "major roadworks." (Major roadwork, by the way, is not major at all. It usually consists of a few portly looking middle-aged men holding shovels, standing beside a dump truck acting as if they're engaged in a serious discussion when, in fact, they're probably arguing over the latest football match between Mayo and Galway.) Ballina is a beautiful place to be stuck in traffic though. It's a bustling old cathedral town with quaint shops around the town square and the River Moy running straight through it. Emerging from the traffic, I continued to drive north past Killala Bay. I began talking into my tape recorder to keep myself company, attempting to describe the wild, windblown beauty of Downpatrick Head, a tiny green peninsula jutting out into the North Atlantic. Getting out for a moment to photograph the vast expanse of bogland and sea, I had to lean against the car to keep from being blown over. Just up the road was Ceide Fields, an ancient Neolithic farming community now covered with blanket bog. Underneath the bog are the oldest known stonewalled fences in the world, nearly 6,000 years old, discovered by the local school master in the 1930s and later excavated by his archaeologist son. Its modern visitor center, with its striking glass, oak, and sandstone pyramid form, fit right into the wild landscape. The interior was equally stunning. I was amazed to see a 4,000-year-old pine tree, unearthed from nearby bogland, standing tall in the middle of the foyer. I took the tour around the grounds and tried to stay upright on the windy paths as the interpreter shouted his rehearsed spiel. It felt good to get back inside and rest while enjoying a warm lunch in the cafeteria with one of the young interpreters. She wasn't familiar with Pat's book, so I pulled it from my backpack, and she browsed through it as I finished my soup.

"So, she covers geological areas of interest throughout Ireland, but it's not really scientific, is it?" she said with a smug, know-it-all authority that I found irritatingly familiar in her just-out-of-college generation.

"Well, as the subtitle says, her discussion of the landscape is based upon Celtic myth and spirit, not science," I answered, trying not to return her patronizing tone.

"Fair play to her then, but I've never had much need for the myth and spirit stuff." She slammed the book shut as if that closed the discussion.

"Then why are you here?" I blurted out.

She looked at me, surprised. "What do ye mean? I'm doing my graduate study in archaeology."

"Yes, and this is an ideal place for archaeological study, but it's also a place of myth and spirit. Don't you feel it?" I went on without giving her a chance to answer. "Why, this place inspired Seamus Heaney, you know, the Irish poet who won the Nobel Prize, to write a famous poem about it called 'Belderg.' Even your boss says on the Ceide Fields website that there is 'magic' here. That she sees skies and cloud formations that defy belief and 'seem almost unreal sometimes.' You can still love the science and appreciate the mystical beauty of the place too."

"Indeed," she admitted. "That's something to think about, I suppose." She collected her tray and rose from the table. "It's been lovely talking with ye, but I must return to work now. Are ye staying in the area?"

"No, I'm driving down the coast to Croagh Patrick. I plan to climb it tomorrow."

"Brilliant. The coast road is very scenic. Watch for the turn south onto N59 before Belmullet or yer likely to miss it. Well, best of luck then and safe travels."

"Thanks for the advice. Best wishes to you and your studies too." I watched her as she returned her tray and walked toward the office, not looking quite as self-assured as she had before.

I was reluctant to leave Ceide Fields behind, but I needed to keep to my schedule of checking into the B&B in Murrisk near the foot of Croagh Patrick by late afternoon. I marveled at the wild beauty of the northern coast as I successfully maneuvered the turn just before Belmullet onto N59, which would take me along the western coast of County Mayo. The national road was a narrow one-and-a-half-lane upward spiral. Fortunately, the sun had reappeared and the wind had let up a little. Other than the ubiquitous herds of sheep standing in the middle of road every couple of miles, I pretty much had the road to myself. This part of Ireland was so rugged and sparsely populated that it was only every so often that an isolated farmhouse came into view, never mind a one-pub village. I decided that this is where the photographers must come when they take the postcard pictures of Ireland.

I turned on my tape recorder and talked about how beautiful it all was until I grew tired of hearing myself talk. Then I inserted Van Morrison's *Beautiful Vision* CD into the car's player. "I'm a dweller on the threshold," he sang. The combination of Van Morrison's poetic words coupled with the ethereal sounds of the uilleann pipes was enough to stir my emotions toward the spiritual splendor so appropriate to the Celtic landscape and to my own feelings of being a "dweller on the threshold." As I rounded curve after upward curve with the green-shadowed mountains on the left and, to the right, a pure-blue sky with an endless, white-capped sea far below, I experienced what Henry David Thoreau describes as "a moment of an azure hue." A numinous moment of such unexpected beauty and clarity that one is both aware of the gift of grace and made humble by how undeserved such a gift is. It's a transcendent moment when the past, present, and future become one, all that ever matters can be seen, and God's grandeur, in all its glory, is revealed. One moment. Here. Then gone. Just like that.

I was in tears. Tears of astonishment at experiencing such beauty. Tears of gratitude at feeling both at one with the landscape and with the spirit of my Irishness. Tears of happiness that this moment had happened, and tears of sadness that it wouldn't last forever.

All of my senses were firing at once. I was beyond feeling gobsmacked. But through it all, the calm sound of Julian of Norwich's words was running through my soul: "And all shall be well, and all shall be well, and all manner of thing shall be well."

I knew then that the rest of my trip would be different. That the rest of my life would be different, and that I would use this moment as a touchstone to remind myself of what truly matters and of what doesn't matter at all. I would continue this journey with a sense of peace and a desire to confidently immerse myself in the many adventures to come. I knew that it wouldn't be easy. That within the circuit of this plodding life (as Thoreau says in the poem of the same name) there would also be moments of pain, confusion, and despair. But I could hold on to that moment when the veils of time were lifted, when I crossed over into what the Irish call that "thin place" and caught a glimpse of eternity.

CHAPTER TWENTY

Halfway Up the Holy Mountain

I NEARLY DROVE off the narrow coastal road when I caught my first glimpse of Croagh Patrick, Ireland's Holy Mountain. I had dreamed of this day since first reading about it years ago, and my desire to climb it only increased as I read accounts of others who had done it. I came to understand how its imposing presence could lure pilgrims throughout the ages to its summit. The numerous pictures I had seen of the majestic mountain didn't do it justice. As I got closer, I found a spot to pull over and shoot a few photos of a pastoral scene with sheep on a green hillside and Croagh Patrick's bare conical shape watching over it in the distance.

I arrived at a B&B outside of Murrisk at the foot of Croagh Patrick. The accommodations reminded me of a 1950s-style motel, nothing like the beautiful Mountain View, but it was clean. And the owner, Mrs. Foley, was friendly, so I couldn't complain. I settled in for the night with the intention, weather permitting, of climbing Croagh Patrick the next day.

Croagh Patrick rises 2,500 feet up from the bogland surrounding Clew Bay in County Mayo. It's said that St. Patrick climbed it in AD 441, rang his bell from the summit, and drove the snakes and demons out of Ireland. Never mind that there weren't any snakes in Ireland, though I suppose one could argue about demons. St. Patrick was symbolically banishing the pagan religion of harvest gods and mother goddesses and replacing it with Christianity. He succeeded to a large degree, but, more importantly, Christianity merged with the pagan practices, creating a unique blend of Celtic spirituality. This blending made it perfectly logical, among other things, for the Irish to be Christians and still believe in fairies. The harvest celebration known as Lughnasa, where the multitudes would make a pilgrimage to the foot of the mountain to make merry in late July, has been replaced by Reek Sunday, where thousands of penitents climb the mountain (some barefoot) to honor the saint.

I wanted to experience the spirituality of the place, both Christian and pagan, believing that such sites as the Reek are, indeed, sacred for all of us regardless of our religious beliefs. Thousands of years of rituals are bound to leave spiritual energy unique to such places. It was a healing place, and I wanted to be healed of the anger and resentment that was still plaguing me years after my divorce. I was so sick of it. Maybe planting my feet into this holy ground would provide some healing. Maybe. It was worth a try.

The next morning, instead of the gray, misty mornings I had come to expect in Ireland, I awoke to the sun streaming through the lace curtains at my bedroom window. I hurriedly ate some breakfast, donned my hiking boots, and set off for the mountain.

Strangely enough, my first impression upon arriving at the foot of Croagh Patrick was how big and modern the parking lot was. Next to it was a new visitor center complete with a tearoom. I smiled at this reminder of my conversation with the professor at Drumcliff, and I imagined how disgusted he would be about this new tourist attraction. Maybe I would send him a postcard announcing this along with the forthcoming Drive Out the Snakes with St. Patrick Tram attraction. Or maybe not.

After parking my car, I walked past the imposing white statue of a stern-looking St. Patrick at the trail head and meandered up the paved path, not intending to start up, but to gauge what I was up against. The mountain was straight up with minimal, if any, switchbacks. I realized that I would need a walking stick. They rented them in the gift shop. And I would need a hat too. Not that it was that cold, but it was windy, the kind of wind that makes your ears ache. So into the gift shop I went to purchase a wool stocking hat and rent a walking stick just my size.

A woman working in the gift shop said, "It will take ye near two and a half hours to reach the summit and 'tis a little rough with some climbing of rocks at the end."

"That shouldn't be a problem," I replied. "I'm in pretty good shape, and I've hiked in the Grand Tetons."

"Whatever you say, luv. Enjoy yer climb."

Hmmm. She's being a bit snippy about this. I wonder if she's related to Ms. Snooty-Tone-Tour-Guide from Ennis. Oh well. I'll show her!

Of course, I wanted to document this occasion. I was alone, and the folks back home might not believe that I actually hiked up. So, I crammed my 35 mm camera with detachable zoom lens into my large waist pack. I knew I would get thirsty too, so I packed two bottles of water. The sun was still shining; I felt great and ready to begin the ascent. I passed the statue again and with a nod to Saint Patrick, started up.

The paved trail soon gave way to dirt. It wasn't crowded, but, still, there were plenty of people around—people of all ages, mostly couples and families with older children. Some, clutching rosaries or wearing crucifixes, seemed to be on a spiritual quest. Others seemed to be out for a morning walk. Many were wearing sneakers, not hiking boots like me, and way too many were without walking sticks. I found myself gloating at how unprepared they were compared to me and how sorry they would be once they reached the midway point.

It wasn't long before the people in sneakers were passing me like I was walking in slow motion. And then I realized that I *was* walking in slow motion and that I was out of breath. *It's just the altitude,* I thought. These people must be from mountainous areas like Colorado or Switzerland where they're accustomed to the thin air. My waist pack felt like an anchor, practically pulling me to my knees, which, while making me look very holy, wouldn't help me reach the summit. *Maybe I shouldn't have packed so much stuff. No, it will get better.*

It didn't get better, and as the dirt trail turned into loose rock, I realized that I had totally underestimated the sheer magnitude of what I had undertaken. I knew that at this rate it would take me all day to reach the summit and another half day to get back down. Then I made the mistake of turning around to take in the view of Clew Bay. My knees went soft as I was enveloped in a wave of dizziness and nausea. I leaned against a boulder along the side of the trail to steady myself. I had forgotten about my fear of heights. Well, maybe not forgotten, but I had figured that with my being so focused on this spiritual quest and all, I wouldn't notice it. Just like the boat ride to the Aran Islands a week earlier when I concentrated on cleaning every part of my camera in order to keep from getting seasick. Determined to see this through, knowing that it would probably be my one and only opportunity, I plowed upward, stopping now and then to catch my breath and take pictures of the gorgeous bay far below. Each time I stopped, I leaned against a boulder and prayed I wouldn't throw up.

As I continued wobbling up the trail, I made it a point to engage in small talk with some of the people around me, err passing me, so that in the event that I did lose my footing and tumble off the side, there would be witnesses.

"Excuse me," I asked a young couple just ahead of me. "Would you mind taking my picture?"

"Of course," the woman answered in an American accent. As she reached out for my camera she asked, "Are you alone?"

"Yes, I am."

"Wow! You're brave!" Her companion nodded in agreement.

I started to use the "brave or stupid" response but stopped myself. That joke was getting old.

"Thanks. Where are you guys from?"

"Colorado Springs. And you?"

"Indiana."

"It's kinda flat there isn't it?" the young man asked.

"Yes, in the central and northern part. The southern part has some beautiful hilly areas, but nothing like this. You're probably used to this, right?"

"Yes," answered the woman. "But this is pretty steep. No switchbacks, just straight up."

"You're telling me! Thanks for taking my photo."

"Hey, no problem. Enjoy the rest of your trip."

They left me in the dust as I plugged along.

The photo turned out to be an interesting shot of a petrified-looking woman sporting a blue windbreaker and striped wool hat clinging onto a walking stick for dear life. There's a frozen smile on her face with a stunning view of Clew Bay in the background.

The problem was that, although I made it a point to stay close to others, I was climbing alone with no one to encourage me onward. And any seasoned hiker will tell you that the buddy system works wonders when taking on a challenging trek. I could have kept going, but I knew the ascent wasn't going to get any easier (I didn't even want to think about the strenuous part just before reaching the summit) and it occurred to me that if I banged up my knee or twisted an ankle the remaining week of my vacation would be shot. What was I trying to prove anyway? And to whom? I had no idea. This was ridiculous! I didn't need to prove anything to anyone, least of all myself. The folks back home already thought I was nuts for wanting to travel around Ireland by myself, let alone climb a pyramidal mountain, and even the gentle-natured Mrs. Foley at the B&B had blurted out, "Good God, girl, why would ye want to go and do that?"

So, when I reached the halfway mark, I made the difficult, but necessary, decision to turn back. I wouldn't have the satisfaction of reaching the top and saying a prayer of thanks at the church on the summit, but I felt a huge sense of relief and an immediate settling in my stomach. Going down wouldn't be tough at all, I reasoned. I put my rented walking stick to good use, but my knees still took a beating going down, and I had a couple of close calls when the scree flew out from under my boots and I nearly lost my balance. I stopped several times to take in the view, and, though nothing like what I had experienced on the coast road the previous day, I did feel the spiritual energy. I felt both exhilarated and peaceful at the same time. I felt like I belonged there. I even tried to reach one of my friends back in the States on my cell phone to share this momentous experience with someone who would appreciate it. She wasn't home, so I left a message on her answering machine.

"Hey, Angie. I'm climbing Croagh Patrick, but I forgot I'm afraid of heights, so I'm going down now. But hey, it is so beautiful up here! I wish you could see it. There's a gorgeous bay down below. I'd love to look at it more but it makes me feel like I'm going to throw up. I feel so alive up here though. So wonderfully alive . . ."

She told me later that I sounded like an ecstatic drunk.

Most hikers passing me on the way down had clearly made it to the summit. I could tell by the satisfied smiles on their weary faces. One of them, a man who eerily resembled my hero, the late Trappist monk and writer Thomas Merton, paused and turned my way to give me a brief but penetrating look of kindness before spreading his arms wide and gazing upward as if in thanksgiving before continuing his descent. Was Thomas Merton, author of the autobiographical spiritual classic *The Seven Storey Mountain*, trying to tell me that making it halfway up the mountain was good enough? Was he trying to tell me that I had nothing to prove? That just being here was enough? I've loved that man since my college days when I first read his autobiography. I've been reading his work ever since, and I've felt his presence on my many trips to the Abbey of Gethsemane, where he lived until his untimely death in 1968. Now I was feeling his presence here. What a gift! I continued down the trail with tears of gratitude.

Later, happy to be sitting in the touristy tearoom relishing a bowl of hot soup and nursing my sore knees, I thought about St. Patrick and the earlier pagan worshippers who came here to pray, and I said my own prayer of thanks for being given the opportunity to be here on this Holy Mountain at this time, this halfway point in my life. St. Patrick had climbed this mountain during what was probably the halfway point in his life too, but, unlike me, he must have been one helluva hiker.

I hobbled to my car and drove back to the B&B. I spent the rest of the afternoon walking on the rocky beach along Clew Bay just down the lane from the B&B. I had the place to myself, which was a good thing, since I'm sure my stiff, uneven gait resembled someone who was drunk. My knees were sore, but I was too busy taking in the beauty of my surroundings to care. The beach was filled with the most perfectly shaped, colorful rocks I had ever seen in shades of blue and red. Just the right size to fit into my palm or skip across the water. The sun provided sidelight to Croagh Patrick across the bay, and Clare Island shimmered in the distance. I took a lot of photos and enjoyed the solitude and the chance to rest. Walking the beach calmed and revived me. I couldn't help staring longingly at Clare Island and thinking of The Saw Doctors' song of the same name with its first line: "Will you meet me on Clare Island when summer stars are in the sky?" *How romantic it would be to meet someone on Clare Island . . . Oh, c'mon, get a grip, Diane.*

I drove to Murrisk to see the Famine Memorial sculpture created by John Behan in 1997. This huge bronze sculpture across the road from Croagh Patrick is a stunning work of art. It depicts a coffin ship with skeletal figures in the rigging to symbolize the one million Irish who died during the Famine of 1845–1852. The sculpture also serves as an effective reminder of the horrors of the coffin ships who betrayed their purpose of providing a safe escape to a better life. I zoomed in with my camera lens, fascinated with the details of the skeletal figures, especially the outstretched hands and looks of terror on their faces. That feeling of horror and loss touched my soul. Had my ancestors experienced this horror? I didn't know much about my Irish ancestry, but from what I had been able to gather, it appeared that they had emigrated long before the Famine. Still, the Irish were poor even then because of British rule.

I had a good dinner that night at a place called The Tavern and ordered an Irish coffee for dessert. Then, wanting to walk off my dessert before driving back to the B&B, I wandered around the Murrisk Abbey ruins across the road. Founded in 1457 by Augustinian friars, the abbey is believed to stand over the same site as the church that St. Patrick built. Save for the main aisle and a few walls, there wasn't much left of the church, but the cemetery was still in use by the locals. I surveyed the younger and older grave markers, marveling once again at the respect the Irish demonstrate toward their departed loved ones. The well-kept graves were adorned with flowers, small statues, candles, and photos. I witnessed this in every cemetery I visited during my travels. I thought about my own father's grave. Although it's less than two hours from my home, I visit it once a year at the most. I saw a grave marker with the words Treasured Memories of a Loving Husband and Dad, and I felt ashamed.

I knew the melancholy that was coming over me was simply fatigue. It had been a long day coupled with a long day of driving yesterday. I traveled back to the B&B and prepared for the next day's adventure: a visit to Connemara National Park and then south to the town of Clifden in County Galway.

In bed that night, I stared into the darkness, thinking

about all that I had done so far on this trip. So many adventures and so different from last year's short trip, when I spent the majority of my time with my stomach clenched in awful fear of driving. Though I still felt that fear, it wasn't as bad, and I was feeling more and more comfortable behind the wheel. Still nervous and wary, but more comfortable.

My mind wandered to Luka's upcoming concert. What would it be like? Would I have a chance to visit with him? *Don't be a starstruck idiot,* I told myself. *Just be yourself and what will happen will happen. After all, he's always put you at ease when you've talked to him before. Just relax and try to enjoy yourself for a change.*

I fell asleep recalling my walk along Clew Bay. The colors of the wet rocks—red, blue, and brown—sparkled in the bright sunlight, and the azure blue waves gently kissed the shore again and again.

CHAPTER TWENTY-ONE

Confusion in Clifden

THE ROAD to Connemara was hilly, rough, and full of curves, but the scenery was from a picture book. Green hills, flowing streams full of trout, cottages and inns dotting the landscape. Historically, it was a famine road, and staked amid the gorgeous green hills were memorial plaques commemorating specific occasions when starving hundreds had walked this road for countless miles in hopes of receiving food and possible passage to America. Instead, they were turned back by British authorities and died along the roadside. There are famine roads all over Ireland, especially along the coasts. It's like the Native American Trail of Tears, only magnified a thousand times. Every conqueror believes in its superiority over the natives. That's how they can justify such inhumanity. I felt so hopeless standing outside the village of Delphi reading this plaque, and I knew why. Along with Carl Jung's work, there are numerous studies confirming the idea of ancestral memory being carried in our DNA. I was feeling the hopelessness and despair of my ancestors. Maybe some of them had emigrated before the Famine, but there were others left behind who would be among those destined for starvation. Though I had no genealogical evidence at that time, I felt sure of it.

Farther along, at Connemara National Park, the day was perfect for a good hike and after my morning on the famine road, I was ready for it. The park didn't have the rugged beauty of north Mayo, but it was spectacular enough, and I enjoyed photographing the Connemara ponies mingling among the hills. I also discovered that the Diamond Mountain Luka Bloom sings about in his wonderful song of the same name is located here, although it has the less majestic name of Diamond Hill. I wanted to climb it, but it was off-limits due to erosion. I made a mental note to tell him about the closure on the off chance that he would want to climb it anytime soon.

I drove on to the picturesque market town of Clifden in County Galway, where I had reserved two nights at the Connemara Farm B&B. When I arrived, I was disappointed to discover that it was located on a hilly street at the edge of town. The house was one of the ubiquitous modern one-story suburban stucco structures prevalent throughout Ireland—new, clean, and sterile. Other than a gray donkey standing forlornly in a fenced-in area in the side yard, there was no evidence of a farm in sight.

Oh well, at least I don't have to drive as far to get into town. Since the roads in Clifden, unlike the rest of Ireland I had seen thus far, were laid out in a somewhat predictable pattern, I was looking forward to exploring the pubs and shops "downtown" without the usual prospect of getting lost.

Mrs. O'Malley, a short, thin, mousy-haired woman in her late fifties, answered the doorbell. She moved like a nervous chipmunk, speaking in a quick, clipped Irish accent. But she had a warm smile as she said, "Ah, hello, Diane, it's good to meet ye and yer right on time as well." She motioned me inside while staring at my khaki hiking pants and boots. "Come this way and I'll make us a cuppa tea first."

She ushered me through a door that led into the kitchen. I was surprised because, while it's very common for the hostess to offer tea in the sitting area upon arrival, it's very out of the ordinary for a "lodger" to be invited into the usually off-limits kitchen. *This is weird. Does she do this for everyone?* But I followed obediently and sat down at a round table covered with a blue gingham tablecloth as she scurried about pouring tea and opening tins of biscuits. The kitchen was larger than I had expected and appeared to be stuck in the '70s with its orange flowered wallpaper and its avocado-green stove and refrigerator. The kitchen smelled of baked bread and I noticed two loaves of Irish brown bread cooling on the counter.

She joined me at the table, remarking as she sank into her chair, "Ah, yes, then, it's good to get off my feet and rest for a bit. I've been runnin' about all mornin'."

I didn't doubt that.

"These chocolate biscuits are delicious. I don't eat them very often as they go directly to my middle. Here," she said, passing the tin to me. "Take a bite. Aren't they brilliant?"

"Absolutely," I agreed, thinking that she didn't need to be so concerned about her thin middle.

"Here, have another then."

We sat there for a while drinking tea and chatting about things in general. She was kind and certainly attentive, but all the while I was thinking, *What's this about? Why can't I just go to my room and relax?* After all, it had been a long day of driving through the mountains of County Mayo and hiking in Connemara National Park. I was exhausted and ready for a nap.

It was about then that our conversation took a bizarre twist.

"So dear, where are you from?"

"Indiana."

"Really? Isn't that someplace in the middle?"

"Yes, it's between Ohio and Illinois."

"So how did you end up here doing this?"

"Well, I became obsessed with Ireland several years ago. I've wanted to travel here for so long. Finally, I was able to save up enough money to make the trip. This is really a dream come true for me. I still can't believe I'm actually here."

"Ah, I see," she said, though she didn't look like she did. "So, does this suit ye?" she asked.

"Oh yes, the west of Ireland is so beautiful—much more beautiful than I ever thought it would be. And I've loved exploring it on my own, not being tied to a definite schedule, you know. That part is great."

Another confused look crossed her face.

"Well, I guess this would be one way to explore it though I wouldn't think ye would have much time for sightseeing what with yer job and all. Perhaps on yer days off then?"

Now it was my turn to look confused.

"So, what about your family? Any children?" she asked.

"I have two daughters, ages twenty-four and nineteen."

"How do they feel about your being over here?"

"Oh, they're fine with it, although they worry about me traveling alone. Everyone back home does, but I tell them that it's much safer than in the States."

"And your husband?"

"I've been divorced several years now."

"Oh, I'm so sorry," she said as she sympathetically passed the biscuit tin my way. "Well, do ye like yer work then?"

"Oh yes, I love being a children's librarian. I've been doing it for so many years now, you know. Although it will be nice when I can retire."

Yet another confused look crossed her face.

Suddenly, she pointed to my bag and asked, "Well, don't you think you should get on with it?"

"Uh, get on with what?"

Just then, the doorbell rang. As she excused herself to answer it, I let out a sigh of relief, gulped down the rest of my tea, and wheeled my bag behind her, hoping that she would point the way to my room.

She opened the door to a smartly dressed young woman toting a vacuum cleaner.

"Mrs. O'Malley?"

"Yes."

"My name is Diane Finley," she said in a brisk Irish brogue. "I'm sorry for being a bit late. There was a mishap on the road from Roundstone and the traffic was backed up horrendously. I do hope it's not too late for my demonstration."

With a look of both surprise and absolute horror on her face, Mrs. O'Malley slowly turned to look at me and my bag, then turned back to stare at the woman and her vacuum cleaner with her bag of attachments.

"Mrs. O'Malley?" the woman asked uncertainly. "Are you all right?"

"Ohhhhh, noooo," she moaned repeatedly, still looking back and forth with her hands glued to her face. Then, regaining her composure, she added quickly, "I mean, yes, yes, I'm fine. Do come in." Mrs. O'Malley closed the door with a tense and embarrassed movement that told me she was anything but fine.

"Oh, grand. Shall I set it up in there, then?" she asked, pointing to the living room.

"Oh, yes, please do that."

As I was taking all of this in, I realized that despite the fact that I was dressed in my hiking attire, poor Mrs. O'Malley mistook me for the vacuum cleaner saleswoman who just happened to share my first name. No doubt she imagined that my large duffel bag on wheels contained a vacuum cleaner. I have to admit I was a little disappointed to realize that I had been given the royal treatment in the kitchen only because she thought she was entertaining an American woman peddling an Irish vacuum cleaner.

Mrs. O'Malley remained absolutely mortified and continued to apologize profusely. Being so exhausted, I was feeling a bit punchy and found myself responding by laughing uncontrollably. Between guffaws, I assured her that she needn't feel embarrassed, that with both of us having the same first name it was bound to be confusing.

"Oh, I'm sure you think me totally daft," she kept repeating.

"No, no, it's all right. I'll just go to my room now and leave you and the other Diane to yourselves," I said as I made a beeline down the hallway trying, albeit not very successfully, to control my laughter.

Later that evening when I returned from dinner, she stopped me at the door and continued to apologize and fret over "the things I must have said to ye." I reassured her once again but added that since I had explored Clifden much faster than I had planned, I wouldn't need to stay a second night and that I would be leaving after breakfast the next morning.

"Ahh, I knew it!" she exclaimed as if she had just made a huge, earth-shaking discovery. "Yer leaving early because of my stupidity. I can't say that I blame ye a bit, girl. Why, if someone had treated me the way I treated you, I'd . . ."

"No, no, Mrs. O'Malley," I protested. "Really, Clifden is a charming place and you have been so kind." I thought it best not to mention how much comic relief she had provided to a lone traveler. "I've enjoyed my stay. It's just that I'm anxious to drive on to Clonbur and explore Joyce Country. I'm acquainted with an Irish musician who lives there"—that was true—"and he's playing in the local pub." That, I wasn't sure about.

"Oh, and who would that musician be?" she inquired accusingly, as if I was making the whole story up.

"Pearse Dougherty. He used to play with The Saw Doctors."

"Ahh, yes, The Saw Doctors," she said, beaming. "I know them. Had a big hit called 'I Useta Lover,' right?"

"Yes, that's the song," I said, nodding, surprised that she was familiar with such a rambunctious Irish rock band. Classical music had been wafting from her radio the entire time I was in the kitchen being confused with the other Diane.

"Ahh, well then," she resigned. "I'll fix ye up a good breakfast in the mornin' and ye can be on yer way then."

And she did. A real Irish breakfast (prepared more often for tourists than for the Irish, I suspect) with eggs, sausage, and rashers (Irish bacon). I ate what I could, all the while moving the bloody sausage and rashers around on my plate with a fork trying to bury them under the eggs. I didn't want to spin her into another apologetic tizzy. She never knew that I'm vegetarian.

I said goodbye to the forlorn donkey, trying, without success, to cheer him up by making funny donkey-like noises. He just stared at me like I was crazy. "I give up, you sad thing. I don't blame you though. I'd be more than sad if I were stuck in this poor excuse of a pasture," I said as I stroked his bristly gray neck over and over. He gazed at me again with those sad brown eyes. "I'll bet you're related to Eeyore, huh?"

"Haw," he quietly replied, his curled lips revealing his yellow teeth.

CHAPTER TWENTY-TWO

Red Cortina in Clonbur, Black Dog in Cong

WHEN I thought about where I was going next, the movie *The Quiet Man* with John Wayne and Maureen O'Hara came to mind. It was filmed in that hilly region with valleys and lonely roads known as Joyce Country. It takes its name not from the famous Irish writer James Joyce but from his Welsh ancestors who settled there in the 13th century. This lovely area bordering Mayo and Galway is filled with lakes, woods, and walking trails, and is well-known to both anglers and hikers.

I had arranged to spend the night at Ballykine House on the edge of Clonbur, a village that sits between Lough Corrib and Lough Mask. As I drove down the hill into the village, I felt as though I were entering a fairy tale. Even the name, Clonbur, sounded like it was right out of a fairy tale. The little shops were painted in bright colors, window boxes were filled with flowers, and the streets were bustling with a few tourists but mostly with locals. I found a parking spot and entered a small grocery store to look for some snacks and my ever-hard-to-find iced tea.

"I just got into town. So . . . am I in a fairy tale?" I asked the cheerful cashier as I dropped my armful of snacks and two bottles of iced tea next to the register.

"I'm afraid not, ma'am," she laughed. "Just a small town like any other. Maybe a bit prettier, that's all."

"You could've fooled me," I said. "I expected to see the Seven Dwarfs come marching across the street at the crosswalk."

"No dwarfs, but ye might come upon some fairies in the woods," she half whispered as she took my euros and handed over my paper bag. "Watch yer step now!" she cautioned, and she wasn't talking about the step leading out the shop door.

I put the bag in my car and went window-shopping around the village. I saw the usual gift shops, hardware stores, restaurants and pubs advertising dinner specials. I came to a pub window and read a small white sign in the corner: PEARSE DOHERTY, SUNDAY 8:00, BENEFIT FOR SUSAN FOLEY'S CHARITY TRIP TO INDIA, 10 EURO MIN. DONATION.

Hot dog! He is going to play in a pub tonight. And on a Sunday night, the one night I'm going to be in town! How lucky is that?

I ended my window-shopping and followed my dashboard directions to Ballykine House, a two-hundred-year-old limestone structure with a modern annex and glass garden room on beautifully landscaped acreage. There I was met by Orla O'Connor, the friendly owner who showed me to my small but comfortable room in the older part of the home and offered me tea and biscuits in the garden room.

"I hate to leave ye so soon," she said after telling me all about the walking paths on the grounds and giving me directions to nearby Mount Gable in case I wanted to take the "easy" walk up, "but our son has a football match in Corofin this afternoon. We'll be back in a few hours. Ye have yer key, so just make yerself at home and come and go as ye please."

I decided to forgo the "easy" walk up Mount Gable for the time being. I'd had enough mountain climbing, but I was restless, so I took a long walk into the woods. The path was lined with forest undergrowth of moss and ferns and the sun dappled through the tree branches. I heard the soothing sound of a stream with a waterfall in the distance. The forest was enchanted, I felt sure of it. I slowed my pace and inspected the undergrowth more closely. I wasn't sure what I was looking for. I don't believe in fairies, and yet I have enough respect for all of the folklore and firsthand accounts I've heard about them not to disbelieve in them either. I don't have any respect for the Irish tourist trade that holds "Fairy Night Encounters" for gullible tourists, but I do respect the Irish citizens who demanded that a proposed major roadway be rerouted around a fairy hill. (It was.) Whatever I believed or didn't believe about fairies, I knew not to mess with them. They were known for being mischievous and easily pissed off. I quickened my pace and quit looking. After about an hour of walking and seeing signposts for paths leading to Clonbur, Cong, and Lough Mask, I lost my bearings and decided it would be best to turn around and retrace my steps back to the house. Damn those fairies!

I relaxed in the garden room drinking tea and eating more than my share of biscuits until the O'Connors returned with the happy news that their son's team had won the football match.

"So did ye hike up Mount Gable, Diane?" asked Orla, taking a seat in the chair across from me while her husband and son wandered off to another part of the house.

"No, but I did take a long walk in the woods," I answered. I didn't mention the part about the fairies messing with my sense of direction.

"The woods are so lovely. Was it a good walk?"

"Yes, it was. I also walked around Clonbur before I came here, and I noticed that Pearse Doherty is playing in one of the pubs tonight. Do you know him?"

"Pearse? Oh yes! Lovely man!" She smiled broadly. "He married a Clonbur girl, and they're raising their family here. Both of them are very involved in community affairs, they are. Lovely people. So, are ye a friend of Pearse's?"

"No," I said, laughing, taking another sip of my tea. "I'm a fan of The Saw Doctors. I've seen them a few times in the States, and I was sorry when Pearse decided to leave the group earlier this year."

"Yes, that was a tough decision for him, let me tell ye," she said. "He loves the group, but he was travelin' so much, ye know? And he has his family to think about now. He decided it would be better to return to university and finish his degree."

"Yes, it must have been a difficult decision for him to make," I said. "But the music business is so erratic and, honestly, I don't know how they can stand all that traveling. If he can use his degree toward supporting his family, it's probably for the best. He'll always have the music."

"Yer so right, Diane," agreed Orla. "Well, if I weren't so busy tonight I would tag along with ye, but I have several more guests checking in, so I'd best get busy. Burke's Bar is a good place to eat, and it's just across from the pub."

"Thanks, Orla. I'll give it a try."

"Yer most welcome, Diane. Have a good night. I'll see ye at breakfast."

I sat inside the entrance to Burke's Bar and waited to be seated. And waited and waited while a young waitress with badly bleached blond hair, wearing a smug smile, seated couple after couple who had arrived after me. The young man behind the counter motioned to her a couple of times to point out that I was waiting, but to no avail. Finally, I'd had enough. I walked right over to her and said, "One for dinner!"

"Oh, yer here for dinner?" she asked in fake surprise.

"What did you think I was here for?" I demanded.

"Follow me, please," she said with fake sweetness. She nonchalantly sashayed her ample rump as she escorted me to my seat. I glanced over toward the young man working behind the counter in time to see him shaking his head in embarrassment.

I continued my assertive, not mean, but assertive, manner toward her during dinner, and Her Fakeness let up a little. Still, I don't know why I didn't think to ask for the manager. I'm one who doesn't like conflict, and I seek to avoid it, but this piece-of-work-for-a-waitress was something else—especially in Ireland where service workers go out of their way to be gracious. I'm accustomed to getting strange looks when dining alone, but I've never been treated rudely because of it. That might have been part of my problem; I think I was in shock at being treated so badly. Also, I'm pretty easygoing except when someone is trying to take advantage of me. That will raise my hackles faster than anything—no doubt an extreme reaction left over from the similar incidents during my marriage. Therefore, when I paid at the counter, I made a point of giving a generous tip to the young man in full view of Her Fakeness, lowering my voice to say, "And make sure she doesn't get a penny of it because she doesn't deserve it!"

"Yes, ma'am," he said as he pocketed the money.

I walked across the street to the pub and seated myself at the far end of the bar. Pearse would be playing in an hour, and I wanted to sit where I would have a clear view of him. I really wanted a drink after the debacle at Burke's Bar, but I knew I couldn't risk it, since I would be driving the curvy road back to the B&B, not to mention driving it in the dark. So I ordered a Diet Coke and sat back to wait for Pearse's arrival. A couple of young men sat at a corner table singing Tom Petty songs until the owner booted them out, telling them that a session would be starting soon. He was wrong. We waited and waited. I tried to make small talk with those around me. They were polite enough, but not eager to include me in their tight-knit group. The small pub was filled with locals, and here I was, this middle-aged woman from Indiana. A stranger all by herself. I couldn't say that I blamed them, but I sure wished that Orla could have come with me. What a difference it would have made to be in the company of a well-respected local.

Pearse arrived in typical Irish fashion—ninety minutes late. He sat at the other end of the bar and played several songs, some traditional, some not, but none of them were Saw Doctors songs. In between songs, Pearse downed several pints as he and the crowd got happier and happier. Cigarette smoke was wafting through the air along with frequent use of the f-word, which I came to realize was far more common in Ireland than it was in the States. Pearse introduced the girl who was doing charity work in Calcutta, and we passed our donations down the bar. I was sipping on my third Diet Coke when I heard the opening chords to The Saw Doctors song

"Red Cortina." The crowd cheered as he sang the first verse, and we joined in on the chorus.

I had never expected that such a simple song about a schoolboy's first love for a girl whose father drops her off at school in a red Cortina would provide such a magical moment in a small pub in an Irish village with a fairy-tale name, but it did. For a few minutes the room quieted, and we all joined together in song, the locals and this stranger. Whatever was happening in our lives, whatever hardships or problems were eating away at us, was forgotten for that harmonious, magical moment.

The moment passed and Pearse pulled out his penny whistle and played some traditional tunes. His playing became more erratic the more he drank. It was getting late, and I was nervous about the drive back. I finished my Diet Coke, made a stop in the ladies' room, and paused to talk to Pearse as I headed toward the door.

"Hi, Pearse," I said. He turned in his chair to look at me.

"Do I know ye?" he slurred.

"No," I laughed. "You don't know me. I saw you with The Saw Doctors in Indianapolis and Chicago. I'm from Indiana, here on holiday."

"Yer from India?" he stammered.

"I-n-d-i-a-n-a," I said slowly.

"Oh, and are you enjoying your holiday?" he asked slowly.

"Absolutely, and it's even better now that I got to see you. Best wishes to you, Pearse."

"Ahh, brilliant. And to you as well." He rose from his barstool to give me a hug and one of his mates grabbed him to prevent him from falling on me.

"Whoa! So sorry, luv. I seem to have drunk a wee too much," he said as he steadied himself.

"Yer feckin' drunk awright," his friend laughed.

I gave Pearse the same sad smile I would give anyone who was drunk, waved goodbye, and walked out the door. The streets were deserted, and I didn't see any signs of dwarfs or fairies as I left this village with the fairy-tale name and nervously drove the dark road back to the comfort of Ballykine House.

Orla had a full house at breakfast. I watched her small figure glide from table to table, impressed with how she engaged everyone in conversation while keeping up with the breakfast orders. I enjoyed visiting with the anglers and the women who had attended a ceili dance (similar to an American square dance) the night before, but I was anxious to make a quick stop at nearby Cong before driving on to Lisdoonvarna for tonight's Luka Bloom concert.

I caught sight of Orla as I was dragging my suitcase to the door and filled her in on the previous night's adventures.

"Let me tell ye, Diane," she said, her hands planted on her hips. "That girl at Burke's won't last long. The nerve! Indeed, ye should have complained! Why, I've half a notion to complain myself!"

"It's okay, Orla," I said. "What goes around comes around."

"Right so," Orla agreed. "And Pearse, what can I say? I suppose he's having a rough time of it."

"Yeah, that huge life change has got to be stressful for him. Unfortunately, getting drunk is how some people deal with it."

"Indeed, and we will pray that it's a one-night-off for him," she said, carrying my backpack to the door with one hand and patting me on the back with the other. "So where are ye off to next, Diane?"

"I'm going to take a look around Cong, and then drive to Lisdoonvarna to join some friends for a concert tonight." It felt so good to say that I would be joining friends.

"Lovely. And who will ye be seeing?"

"Luka Bloom. Do you know him?"

"Luka Bloom. Yes, yes, from the Moore family! Another talented singer and songwriter just like his brother Christy. Oh, lucky you!"

"Yes, I'm friends with his sister, Anne. That's who I'm meeting, so it's very exciting."

"My, girl! You do get around, I must say!" Orla laughed. "Well, ye enjoy yerself and have a wonderful time. I'm so glad we met."

"Me too, Orla. Thank you for everything," I said, taking my backpack and giving her a hug. "It's been wonderful."

The village of Cong boasts two claims to fame: it's the picturesque village where much of *The Quiet Man* was filmed, and The Edge, the lead guitarist for the Irish band U2, owned a home there. I love U2 and The Edge is near the top of my list of the best guitar players ever, but I wasn't interested in stalking a rock star. I wasn't particularly interested in The Quiet Man either. I found John Wayne's portrayal of an American boxer who "tames" a wild Irish woman (Maureen O'Hara) to be stereotypical of the Irish and chauvinistic toward women. But I loved the scenery, and I wanted to see for myself if it was as idyllic as it is portrayed in the film.

I started out by making a quick run through the touristy *Quiet Man* Museum in the center of Cong. As expected, it holds many artifacts from the movie—the famous marriage bed, the kitchen table and chairs in the cottage, etc. The tour guide was quite kind and very knowledgeable, and fans of the movie (and there are legions of them) would love it. But truthfully, the entire village is a *Quiet Man* museum. Little has changed in the looks of the village since the movie was filmed there in 1952. The Cong River still flows through the center of it, past 12th-century Cong Abbey, and drains into Lough Corrib. The most recent addition to Cong seems to be a statue in the village center with John Wayne lifting Maureen O'Hara up into his arms. Everything is about *The Quiet Man*. It's Cong's bread and butter.

I wanted to be outside that morning enjoying the warm sunshine, so I decided to take a walk along the river and explore the Cong Abbey grounds. I entered the path toward the river and was approached by a black Labrador retriever coming across the bridge, his tongue hanging and his tail wagging, looking nothing like the Black Dog in my dreams.

"Well, hi there, buddy," I said, bending down to pet him, realizing how much I missed my two greyhounds. I looked around expecting to see his owner, but no one was about. "So, did you get loose and decide to go on a little adventure?" I asked, noting that he wasn't wearing a collar. He walked a short distance ahead of me, stopped, and glanced back as if to say "C'mon, what are you waiting for? I'm going to show you around." I moved forward and so did he, his tail wagging slightly and paws moving with purpose. We started across the bridge, walked halfway, and then paused. *Let's stop here for a moment and take in the view of the rushing water and the anglers just upriver by the woods. Isn't it beautiful?* he seemed to say. I was mesmerized by the clear rushing water, the sound of it so clear and pure with the sunlight bouncing off it. He walked ahead and looked back at me again. I knew what to do.

Our next stop was the Monk's Fishing House on the abbey grounds. A narrow bridge led us out to a limestone hut with a hole in its floor. There, centuries ago, the monks would rig a net and attach it to a rope that was attached to a bell in the kitchen. When fish were trapped, the bell would ring, alerting the monks that there was fish to gather for dinner.

My four-legged tour guide and I watched the rushing river under the hole for a while before he headed back across the bridge with me following close behind. We walked all over the Cong Abbey grounds this way. I kept expecting his owner to call for him, but I didn't see or hear anything other than birdsong, rushing water, a gorgeous landscape, and the mysterious black dog leading the way.

I sat on a bench among the abbey ruins. The black dog sat on the ground beside me looking off into the distance. I thought about the symbolism of the Black Dog and how it's been used throughout the ages to symbolize darkness, depression, and evil. "It's not fair," I said to the black dog sitting next to me. "You're a great dog, and my black greyhound, Eddy, well, I call him my 'black angel' because he came into my life during my divorce when I needed him most. He loves me without any strings attached, and when I'm feeling down, rubbing his warm suede belly comforts me." The black dog looked at me with wise, understanding eyes that spoke volumes. I didn't feel spooked by it. Like all of the other "mystical" situations I had experienced on this journey, it felt normal and it didn't last very long. Here, then gone.

I rose to leave, and the black dog walked me to the gate and back over the bridge to where our tour had started. We paused for a moment and I said, "The tour is over, isn't it? You're going to leave now." He started to turn toward the bridge and looked back at me. "Thank you," I said. "For the tour and for helping me understand that black can be both dark and light."

The black dog turned, looking satisfied. I watched him prance back across the bridge and out of sight.

The black dog was right, but it's far more complicated than that. And it's not a straight road forward either. I knew that I was on a journey to bring my darkness and my light together. Or, in Jungian terms, to integrate my shadow self with my authentic self. And I knew that it was still a work in progress. But there was progress.

I walked back to my car repeating my mantra:

And all shall be well, and all shall be well, in darkness and in light, all manner of thing shall be well.

CHAPTER TWENTY-THREE

With Luka in Lisdoonvarna

MY VISIT With the black dog in Cong coupled with the anticipation of seeing Luka Bloom made me restless, and my talking stomach reminded me that I hadn't eaten in several hours. I stopped in Ballyvaughan for a late lunch of the usual boring, but cheap, soup and brown bread. The soup, being a pureed mix of God-knows-what vegetables, was getting old. I longed for my own homemade vegetable soup back home. As I sat alone at a small table covered with a red-and-white gingham cloth, I could imagine the aroma of green beans, corn, cabbage, and herbed tomato juice simmering in a large pot on the back burner of my stove. I felt a pang of homesickness but quickly shook it off, reminding myself that I was about to have the time of my life tonight.

Driving on, I maneuvered the car up, down, and around Corkscrew Hill, congratulating myself on my newly acquired driving prowess, and entered the town of Lisdoonvarna, passing the Lisdoonvarna Spa, with its healing mineral waters for which the town is famous, on my right. I really wanted to check out the spa, but from a brochure I had seen, I knew that its prices were well beyond my budget. Just beyond the spa is the town center with its colorful pubs and shops. The town of about eight hundred is famous for its music and matchmaking festivals too. Its most famous music festival, The Lisdoonvarna Folk Festival, is a thing of the past. The last one was held in 1983 with performances by such big names as Jackson Browne, Emmylou Harris, Van Morrison, and Christy Moore. Sadly, the festival was marred by riots, caused in large part by the unfortunate decision to hire bikers to assist with extra security, and by the accidental drownings of eight festivalgoers (three of them brothers) at a beach near Doolin. The locals had had enough, and future large music festivals were banned. An effort was made to bring back the festival in June 2003, but it was voted down. I was relieved since I would be visiting at that time, and though I loved the music, I had no desire to be competing with thousands of festivalgoers vying for the same accommodations, not to mention the crowded roads and pubs. Still, I found myself singing the chorus of Christy Moore's famous song named about the festival: "Lisdoonvarna. Lisdoon, Lisdoon, Lisdoon, Lisdoonvarna."

The most famous and continual happening in Lisdoonvarna is its matchmaking festival held every year for the entire month of September. During that month at least 60,000 lovelorns of all ages swarm into the little town in hopes of finding that special someone. I smiled as I drove past the yellow facade of the Matchmaker Bar, where matchmaker extraordinaire, Wally Daly, offers his services from his small office. Every pub and social venue in town also assists with the matchmaking search by hosting dances and other socials. The locals tend not to complain about this festival because it brings in lots of money to the tourist town without attracting the biker gangs and rowdy, inebriated music fans.

I wasn't coming to town for matchmaking, but I must admit that I did have a schoolgirl crush on Luka Bloom, and I was far from alone. This handsome singer-songwriter of extraordinary talent is worthy of a crush. Songs like "Monsoon" and "Exploring the Blue" cause no-nonsense women such as myself to swoon. And swoonier-causing still is his popular remake of the LL Cool J classic, "I Need Love." Think of a sexy-voiced Irish rapper with a trad backup band and you'll get my drift.

Barry Moore reinvented himself as Luka Bloom in the late 1980s. Seeking to escape the shadow of his older brother, the folk icon Christy Moore, and prove himself as a stellar musician in his own right, he moved to the US to play in clubs and venues along the East Coast. It didn't take long for word to get out about the young Irish lad wowing audiences night after night with just his voice and guitar. Warner Brothers signed him to a record deal, and he was off and running, enjoying success across the country with moderate, consistent airplay on radio and video stations in addition to a poignant performance on NBC's *The Today Show* singing "Sunny Sailor Boy." He did a cross-country tour with the Irish rock band Hothouse Flowers, sang backup on the Indigo Girls hit "Closer to Fine," and hobnobbed with the popular musicians of the time: Suzanne Vega, Lou Reed, Rosanne Cash, and David Byrne, among others. Though his albums with Warner Brothers met with critical acclaim, they didn't meet the sales standards set by a major record company. Consequently, he was dropped from Warner Brothers. He recorded one album with Sony Records in the Abbey Road studios, but he felt that the album, *Salty Heaven,* was overproduced and parted ways with Sony. In the meantime, he was devastated when his mother died suddenly, and being terribly homesick for Ireland, he moved back to his homeland, started his own record label and has been recording and performing ever since with name-recognition success in Europe and Australia. He has a devoted following in the US, but he hasn't maintained his earlier success, largely because he doesn't tour there very often.

I discovered his music when his name kept cropping up in practically everything I read about contemporary Irish music. (Synchronicity at work again.) Finally, I heard several of his songs being played on satellite radio, and I was hooked. Not only was his voice and musicianship superior, but his thoughtful lyrics perfectly reflected my own feelings about love, living, and Ireland. Attending his Chicago concerts had been a treat, but the opportunity to see him play on his own turf made the experience extra special, never mind the fact that I was on the guest list with his sister! Anne confirmed that she would be there and that we should meet up in the lobby of the Royal Spa Hotel, where the concert was taking place. It's a small venue and Anne mentioned that Luka was performing there as a thank-you to the owner for his support. Following the Irish custom of late-starting performances, the concert wouldn't start until ten in the evening, giving me several hours to kill. I had made a reservation at a B&B in town, hopeful that I would have a room similar to the one at Mountain View in Drumcliff, where I could relax and take my time getting ready for the special evening.

Alas, it was not to be. Booking a room at O'Donovan's Town B&B proved to be a mistake. Though the listing in the

Town B&B booklet looked and sounded good, the accommodations were a few steps below the B&B in Tuam. Last decorated in the '70s, the house was clean but stuffy. Oranges and avocado-greens appeared on heavy, striped window coverings, floral sofas, and shag carpet. Fortunately, Mrs. O'Donovan wasn't wearing plaid pants topped with an orange shirt. Tall and slender, she wore black slacks with a pink pullover sweater. Her long, just-past-middle-age face was framed by a well-coifed bob of silver-gray.

"Diane, I think you will find your room most comfortable," she said, glancing back at me as she led me up the stairs. We turned left and walked to the end of a long hallway, past unoccupied rooms that I thought looked nice enough. Then we came to my room. "Let me know if you need anything, dear," she stated as she turned and walked back down the hall. Almost as an afterthought she paused and said, "Breakfast is from seven o'clock to nine o'clock."

"Thank you," I said as she faded down the stairs.

I entered the small room. Holy crap! It was actually two rooms in one. The bedroom on one side and the bathroom on the other. The dividing feature was the hideous red-tiled wall and floor of the "bathroom." Even the telephone booth–sized shower was outfitted in red tile. Then I rolled my suitcase onto the dark-blue shag carpet of the "bedroom" and gazed at the light-blue floral bedspread. My eyes floated upward to the headboard and I was astounded to see a piece of bare plywood fastened to the wall. I stared at it in disbelief. *I'm supposed to sleep against that? Well, shit. This special evening is off to a great start . . .*

Actually, it wasn't evening yet. There were a few hours left in the afternoon and several hours left until the 10 p.m. concert, giving me plenty of time to stew about the accommodations, about how tired I was of being alone, about how tired I was in general. It never occurred to me to go to Mrs. O'Donovan and demand a better room. I simply didn't possess the confidence yet. Despite the episode with the waitress in Clonbur, I didn't like confrontation, and I avoided it at all costs. The cost in this case was that I was going to see red for several hours and spend my sleeping hours keeping my head from coming into contact with a bare piece of plywood.

I took a shower. I lay on the bed (away from the headboard) in my robe listening to the kids in the backyard next door scream and squeal. I pondered what to wear and, since there wasn't much to choose from in my casual travel wardrobe, I settled on a pair of black slacks and a light-blue sleeveless sweater topped with a matching cardigan. Not exactly a sexy little black dress, but it would have to do.

Next, I stood in front of the "bathroom" mirror working with what little makeup I'd brought along. I spent more time applying the travel-size generic-colored foundation, blush, eye shadow, and lipstick than I did with my plethora of makeup at home. I wanted to look pretty. I knew I would never be drop-dead gorgeous, but I wanted to be attractive enough to be noticed and maybe even remembered in case I did get to meet Luka again. At least I could say I tried, but not too much. Obsessing over my looks, spending hours primping in front of a mirror has never appealed to me. I would much rather be doing something else, anything else, besides looking at myself in the mirror.

I plugged in the curling iron, quickly restyled my hair, and sprayed it down. I looked at my watch and saw that I still had several hours to kill. I paced around the room some more going over in my head what I was going to say to Anne and to Luka in the event that I had the opportunity to talk with him. How many family members were going to be there anyway?

The Moore family is big. Luka is the youngest of six—three boys and three girls. Plus, countless cousins, nieces, and nephews. His family alone could have occupied most of the room. I wondered if his son, Robbie, would be there. Like me, Luka married young and became a parent too soon. The marriage was short-lived, but both parents remain devoted to their son.

I was too wound up to feel hungry, but I knew I needed to eat some dinner. The weather was sunny and warm, so it was ridiculous to remain holed up in this red-tiled, plywood nightmare. I checked my small purse to be sure I had my room key, lipstick, compact, tissue, and billfold. Fortunately, the town center was a short, safe walk, so it wasn't necessary to drive. I headed out and prayed that I could settle my stomach, say the right words, relax, and enjoy myself.

Unfortunately, with it being Monday, the Matchmaker Bar was closed. I wandered on, circling the small town several times. I didn't mind walking though. The movement helped to ease my nervousness and reckon with my chattering mind. *What am I doing here? How did a librarian from Indiana end up getting on the guest list for a Luka Bloom concert? Where is all of this leading? Will I strike up a friendship with Luka or will it end as it always does: rejected or ignored? Oh, just shut up and enjoy yourself for a change! You're so damn serious!*

All those questions were legitimate, and I knew I needed to think them through. I glanced at my watch. Thirty minutes left until I needed to meet up with Anne. I glanced down a side street and noticed a lone bench just right for resting and reflection in a secluded, grassy spot. I walked over to it and made myself at home. It felt good to rest my feet. It was a lovely evening. I was glad it was not raining. I closed my eyes and my mind and wandered back to the dilemma of my romantic feelings toward men.

I have a long history of falling for unattainable men. They're usually, but not always, musicians. Maybe that's because I relate to music so much and, therefore, to those who make it. This started at a young age with Ricky Nelson, then the Beatles (well, maybe not Ringo), and then on to the Association, Jimmy Webb, James Taylor, Dan Fogelberg, Todd Rundgren, and, of course, Luka Bloom. I'm convinced that this infatuation with men who, let's face it, wouldn't give a librarian from Indiana a first glance, let alone a second, is a result of my father's death when I was ten years old. The unattainability of my father's love due to his long battle with depression, which, ultimately, resulted in his suicide, taught me that loving a man would result in rejection and abandonment. That's it in a nutshell, but it took me over thirty years of introspection and therapy to come to this conclusion. Make no mistake, my father loved me as best he could. I have some precious memories of him looking at me with loving eyes. But mainly, he just wasn't there. Even if he was in the house, he was shuttered in his bedroom, and we children instinctively knew not to disturb him. After his death, he was rarely spoken of, and we didn't visit his grave. There were no family portraits on display to trigger memories of him because there weren't any family portraits to display. My mother even gave away his Hank Williams records, one of the few things that seemed to bring him moments of joy. We were given unspoken instructions to act as though he never existed, but, of course, he had existed. The undertow of his illness and suicide rippled throughout my and my siblings' lives, affecting the choices we made and the turns we took at the various forks in the road on our life journeys. His death, coupled with my unhappy marriage, definitely affected my attitude toward men: Don't get too close. If you do, you're going to get hurt. It's better to love from afar. Better to be infatuated with someone famous than to be in love with a real man.

I was realizing that this understandable but warped philosophy didn't really apply to Luka because I wasn't so sure that my feelings were merely infatuation nor that he was unattainable. The few times I had talked with him I'd felt a connection, but it was more like a déjà vu feeling than an I-want-to-go-to-bed-with-you feeling. Yes, I was attracted to him, but I was more interested in being friends first, then seeing what developed. I was naively out of step with the real world of sex and rock 'n' roll. But Luka had shown himself to be down-to-earth, attentive, and kind. We were the same age, had lost our fathers at an early age, and seemed to have issues with finding a happy, long-term relationship. So maybe there was hope?

But who was I kidding? Luka had traveled the world from an early age. He had a cosmopolitan attitude, while I rarely left Indiana. Still, I couldn't help but be excited about this evening's concert and the possibility of a new friendship, an anam cara.

It was time to head to the Royal Spa Hotel. I stood up, brushed my pants with my hand and walked the two blocks to the entrance in the warm, calm evening. A small crowd was gathered outside laughing and chatting away. I walked to the entrance and gave a young man holding a clipboard my name. *I'll bet it's not on there,* I thought as he scanned the list. "Ah, yes, Diane, here ye are," he said, placing a big check mark beside my name. "C'mon in, luv, and enjoy the show."

"Thank you. I will."

I entered the carpeted lobby festooned with low-lit sconces and spotted Anne standing near the doorway to the ballroom. She was talking with a woman who resembled her in age and dress, someone who struck me as being an old friend. Anne turned and saw me at the same time.

"Diane, ye made it!" She rushed toward me and engulfed me in her strong, bare arms.

I laughed and said, "It's so great to be here with you. I still can't believe it!"

"Luka is so excited," Anne said. I couldn't tell if she meant he was excited about seeing me or excited about the concert or both, and I was afraid to ask.

"Diane, meet my friend Alice. We're old chums from way back, eh, Alice?"

"Right so," said Alice extending her hand. "I'm happy to meet ye."

I found it both amusing and empowering that both women were dressed in knit pants with floral rayon sleeveless blouses covering their ample midriffs but leaving their aging upper arms exposed. Neither woman seemed to be concerned about her appearance. In fact, each seemed very comfortable with her own body, which, to me, made them all the more beautiful.

"Let's make our way to our table, shall we?" said Anne, steering us into the ballroom. "Diane, dear, you look so lovely tonight."

"Thank you, Anne. I was just going to say the same about you and Alice."

Anne and Alice tittered with delight. "You are such a sweetheart, dear," laughed Anne.

"Hey, it's true!" I countered.

"Oh yes," added Alice, "we're the twin Roses of Tralee."

"Nah," Anne responded. "We're the Thorns in Der Sides."

We fell into fits of laughter as Anne guided us to our seats at a large round table that was reserved for us in the back of the room. I recognized a few family members. Anne introduced me to her husband, Davoc, who took my hand and told me how happy he was to meet me, and I waved across the table to Niall, who was engaged in conversation with a man I didn't recognize. I saw Donnacha sitting off to the side in his wheelchair. A younger man whom I presumed to be Michael, his caregiver, was assisting him with something to drink. I walked over to greet them.

"Hi, Donnacha. It's good to see you again. Are you excited about the concert?"

"Yes," he said slowly, "but not as excited as ye, I'll bet." His smile was lopsided, but I could detect the mischievousness in it.

"You're right about that," I laughed. "And you must be Michael, the man who has to put up with this bloke." We shook hands and laughed as Donnacha said, "Help! These two are torturing me!"

"He's always up to something," Michael said. "But, seriously, he's quite the man. It's an honor to be with him."

"No—yer the man," Donnacha said in fits and starts.

"No doubt you're both quite special," I said, looking at Donnacha, "but we all know who the real man is tonight. Your Uncle Luka."

"He steals the spotlight from me," Donnacha stopped to catch his breath, "every time."

I noticed Anne beckoning to me. I gave Donnacha a hug, shook Michael's hand, and went back to my seat. A waitress came over to ask what I wanted to drink. Although I really wanted a cocktail, I wanted to keep my mind clear.

"Water," I said.

"Sparkling or still?"

I had never heard of plain water being referred to as "still," so it took me a moment to realize what she was asking.

"Still, please."

She returned shortly with a glass of ice and a cold bottle of still water. I reached for my purse.

"No, it's on the house, Diane," said Anne.

I surmised that this was another perk to being on the guest list. Maybe I should have ordered a cocktail after all.

"How was your trip to Donegal?" I asked Anne.

"It was lovely. We stayed in a charming cottage near Bunbeg on the coast. We took long walks. Walked until our feet were so tired we couldn't walk anymore. The landscape up there is so wild and beautiful."

"'Tis," Alice chimed in. "The only downside was it's the season for those nasty little biting bugs that no one can see."

"Nasty little buggers they are," added Anne. "Look, I have some bites on my arm here, see?" She thrust her right arm over to show me.

"Do ye have those where ye live, Diane?" asked Alice.

"Yes, I'm afraid we do," I said.

"What do you call them?" asked Anne.

"No See-ums."

Anne and Alice thought that was hilarious. They were still laughing when the lights dimmed and the packed room grew quiet.

A smiling Luka ambled onto the stage, guitar in one hand, waving to the crowd with the other. His under-six-foot, compact frame was dressed in his usual jeans, knit shirt, and sneakers. He had what he called his "summer haircut," cut shorter than usual. The crowd continued to roar as he approached the microphone stand and fine-tuned his guitar. He smiled sheepishly, holding up one hand signaling for them to stop, but they kept it up with their cheering and catcalling until finally he had had enough. He stepped up to the microphone and shouted, "Aw right, aw right, enough with ye now! This isn't Riverdance, ye know!"

The audience laughed and quieted down as he played the opening chords to his beautiful ballad "Exploring the Blue."

I settled back into my seat and traveled on a two-hour-plus magical journey of songs about the joy and pain of love, the holy ground of the Burren, dreams in America, mermaids singing in their salty heaven, and so much more. The concert was like living inside the best dream of your life. Its contents remain a blur, but a few special moments stood out.

When Luka unexpectedly began to sing the folk classic "The Water is Wide," Anne took my hand and squeezed it. She remembered that I had told her at the bakery that I had been practicing that song in case I was asked to sing in a pub. Another moment of synchronicity to add to the list. And when Luka sang "Sunny Sailor Boy," Anne and I harmonized on the chorus, a symbol of our own harmony that night.

Luka also performed his anti-war song, "I am Not at War with Anyone." It was directed at then–President George W. Bush and the American military aircraft stopping to refuel at the nearby Shannon Airport on their way to Iraq. I couldn't be certain, but I think I was the only American in the audience and, not approving of the war myself, I felt awkward because I couldn't justify my country's actions to the Irish.

Fortunately, the mood switched gears, and Luka was joined onstage by two young women fiddlers. In addition to performing some classic trad tunes, they closed the show with Luka's trad-inspired "You Couldn't Have Come at a Better Time."

Before I knew it, he was taking bows and doing a rockin' rendition of his early hit "Delirious" before exiting the stage for the last time. The lights came up, and I felt a shock to my system like someone waking up from general anesthesia when her name is being called over and over.

"Diane, what did ye think?" Anne was staring at me. "Diane?"

I came back to myself, brought my hands to my face, and answered, "Oh, it was fantastic! Simply fantastic!"

"Wasn't it though?" said Alice.

"He was in fine form, fine form," agreed Anne.

She stepped over to talk to Davoc about their arrangement for him to catch a ride with Alice's husband while I chatted with Niall. The crowd was beginning to thin out, many of them heading for the hotel bar. As I was giving Niall a goodbye hug, I heard Anne say, "Well, I'm goin' up to see him." I swung around to see her heading for the stairs. In an instant I realized that she was going up to Luka's dressing room.

"Can I come with you?" I asked, walking quickly behind her. Anne either didn't hear me or was ignoring me.

I knew it was now or never.

"Well, I'm coming anyway," I mumbled as I ran to follow her up the steps. She didn't seem to mind, so I kept following.

We strode down the hotel hallway, and it dawned on me that we weren't going to his dressing room—we were going to his hotel room.

Oh, wow! This is going to be interesting.

Anne muttered something about how she hoped he wasn't stuck in the shower. She stopped at one of the doors and pounded on it with her fist.

"Barry! Barry!"

"Wha?"

"Open up!"

"Give me a minute! I'm getting dressed!"

Ooh!

The door flung open and there stood Luka, freshly showered, wearing only jeans.

He and Anne embraced each other and what followed was a mini family reunion full of hugs, laughter, and talk about how long it had been since they had seen one another, what other family members had been up to, and on and on.

"I didn't know if ye would make it," said Luka, giving Anne another hug.

"I wouldn't have missed it for the world," answered Anne.

I was standing in the doorway, slightly behind Anne, taking in the wonderous sight of a shirtless Luka when he looked at me with a quizzical smile and said, "Hello." Anne, realizing that she hadn't introduced us, said, "Barry, this is my friend, Diane. She's visiting from Indiana. You two have met before, I hear."

"Yes," I said as Luka took my hand. "We talked after the Chicago show a month ago."

"Yes, of course, I remember. Ye asked me about Anne, and we chatted about the cliffs and Brigid's Well," he said, pulling his knit shirt over his head. "It's so good to see ye again, Diane." He stepped toward me to give me a hug, stopped to look at Anne, and said, "So she did finally make it over the pond to visit ye, Anne."

"And as it turns out, to visit ye as well," added Anne.

"Well done, Diane. Well done." Then he leaned in for the longed-for hug. God it felt great.

Luka stepped back and motioned around the room with his hand. "I'm sorry about the mess." His room was nothing fancy. A double bed with the usual plain hotel furniture and generic "art" on the wall. I noticed an open suitcase on the bed and a few items of clothing strewn about. It didn't look messy to me, but I was touched that he thought he needed to apologize for it.

"Well, in all fairness, it's not like you were expecting company, right?"

"True," he laughed, "but I can always count on my sister to surprise me."

"That's me! I'm full of surprises," laughed Anne.

Luka seemed genuinely happy to see me again. There was no hype to him, and he was a true gentleman. Even though I realized the surrealness of the situation, I felt very comfortable talking with him. He repeated my name a lot in his lovely Irish accent as we, along with Anne, of course, talked about the concert, his drive from Dublin, and his love of Chicago. I loved his genuine, kind, quick-witted nature.

"The crowd seemed a bit flat," he told us. "I couldn't get a rise outa them."

Anne and I agreed, although, to be honest, I was so caught up in La La Luka Land that I hadn't noticed.

"Well, I don't give a shite," he said. "Just wanted to do Paddy a favor. I think I brought him a good-sized crowd, don't ye?"

"That you did, Barry. That you did," said Anne.

"Definitely," I added.

At that, he ushered us out the door and down the hallway. On the stairway we were met by a waiter carrying a large cheese pizza. "Ahh, pizza!" said Luka as he ripped off a piece. "I am so hungry. Would you like some, Diane? Anne?"

"None for me," answered Anne.

"No thanks, Luka," I said.

When we reached the ballroom Luka was swept into the crowd meeting fans and signing autographs. A girl young enough to be his daughter was flirting with him. He flirted back. I was afraid that my visit with him was over, but a few minutes later he was by my side with his arm around me cajoling Anne to take our picture. Anne wasn't the best photographer, so the final image was of me with my mouth wide open and Luka swallowing a swig of his sparkling water. But he was pulling me close with his arm around me. That was all that mattered to me.

He was off again. Anne introduced me to several people, none of whom I remember except the aforementioned Paddy. We found Alice. She was watching the mostly young crowd in the bar.

"Look at them, Anne," she said. "Remember when we could throw back the drinks like that."

"Ah, yes, could we ever," laughed Anne. "We were wild, eh, Alice?"

"Aye, as wild as they came," sighed Alice.

I didn't doubt that for a minute.

Luka found us as we were preparing to leave. "Oh good, yer still here," he said to me. "I was afraid I had missed ye, and I wanted to tell ye how much I enjoyed seeing ye tonight."

"I enjoyed seeing you too, Luka," I smiled. "You made a lot of people, including me, very happy tonight. Thank you."

"Ahh, thank you, Diane," he said, giving me a big hug. "Safe travels home, and I hope to see ye again soon."

"Goodbye, Luka."

"Goodbye now."

Apparently, Anne and Luka had already parted ways. She and Alice were waiting outside. I knew it was time to say so long to her too.

"Diane, I'm so sorry," Anne said. "I should have made plans for ye to spend the night at my house. I don't know what I was thinking. I guess I wasn't thinking at all."

"It's all right, Anne," I reassured her. "You've done enough already. You've made this the most memorable night of my trip."

I turned to Alice. "It was so wonderful to meet you, Alice," I said. "I hope we can go pub-hopping the next time I'm here."

"Oh, not to worry, Diane. You let me know when yer comin', and I'll make all the arrangements." Alice laughed as she hugged me.

Anne and I looked at each other with tears in our eyes before one last long hug.

"Now, you type me when you get home," said Anne. "Promise?"

"I promise."

I started to walk away, but then turned to blow her a kiss.

"Are ye sure ye'll be all right? Do you want me to drive you to the B&B?"

"I'll be fine, Anne. It's just a few blocks away. Goodnight."

"Goodnight, luv."

It was two in the morning when I got back to the red-tiled, plywood headboard room. I was exhausted, but too wired to sleep. I wrote about the day in my journal, something I had made myself do at the end of every day of my trip no matter how tired I felt. I took a warm shower and put on my cozy pajamas, but still felt wired. *Oh, what the hell.* I rummaged through my pill boxes and found one of the sleeping pills I kept for these special occasions. Then, placing my pillow diagonally on the bed so that my head wouldn't come anywhere near the plywood headboard, I fell into a restful sleep filled with dreams of singing mermaids, sunny sailor boys, and Luka giving me warm hugs while my smiling father looked on.

CHAPTER TWENTY-FOUR

Lady Gregory, Yeats, and Journey's End

DESPITE THE plywood headboard incident, Mrs. O'Donovan proved to be a kind, chatty host at breakfast. I filled her in on the concert, leaving out the after-concert scenario, and she filled me in on the history of the Lisdoonvarna Festival. According to her, the village of Doolin was responsible for voting against it this year. We talked about that and everything else it seemed, except my room.

The sun was shining after I checked out. I drove past the Royal Spa Hotel, hoping I would see Luka in the parking lot loading his car. I didn't see any sign of him, but I whispered goodbye to him anyway. That bittersweet moment left me in tears. My emotions felt exposed, like a live wire with the insulation stripped off. No doubt part of it was due to lack of sleep, but another part was due to the fact that I would be flying home tomorrow. I was both looking forward to it and dreading it. I was excited about telling my friends and family about my adventures and about relishing a decent glass of iced tea or cup of coffee. But I was dreading the return to "my reality" of living on my own with no prospects for a romantic relationship. My relationship with my daughters was dependent upon their current mood status and whether or not they were believing their father's relentless lies about me. The efforts from his lawyer and me admonishing him to stop bad-mouthing me to the children went unheeded.

Get a grip, Diane. You're still in Ireland. You have one full day left to explore Coole Park and, hopefully, spend one more night in a much nicer B&B. Don't forget, you're the one who brought yourself here. Make the best of it.

I navigated the narrow roads of the Burren as they wound around the limestone-layered Mt. Mullaghmore and the clear waters of Lough Bunny, where I paused to take more photos, understanding how lucky I was to be experiencing such unique beauty. I instinctively knew I was meant to be here in this place, in this beauty. I just didn't know why. Was I supposed to live here full-time or part-time? If so, how on earth could I afford it? Was I supposed to meet someone? And how important was the "why" anyway? How about if I just relaxed and lived in the moment during these last few hours here? Wouldn't that be enough?

I needed a break from the narrow roads as well as from my thoughts. I stopped for tea in Gort and purchased two turquoise candle holders and a small blue-and-purple ombre bowl at the Michael Kennedy pottery shop. Although the pieces were far from expensive, the lovely woman working in the shop treated them as though they were and carefully wrapped them in layers of tissue paper. She placed them in a large box stuffed with paper and Bubble Wrap to be shipped across the ocean and then by land to my little house in Indiana. She told me to expect the box in about three weeks.

I drove a few miles south on the main road from Gort to Coole Park, the 1,000 acre former home of Lady Augusta Gregory, folklorist, dramatist, and leader of the Irish Literary Revival in the early 20th century. Lady Gregory was a force of nature, decades ahead of her time, whose influence on Irish artists, writers, and actors is felt to this day. She was a close friend and mentor to William Butler Yeats and together they founded Dublin's Abbey Theatre. She entertained her friends often, and many, especially Yeats, found solace in the woods and ponds during extended stays at her home in Coole Park. Yeats wrote at least two poems about it and several famous visitors carved their initials into the copper beach tree that still stands on the grounds.

The land was left to the National Parks and Wildlife Service shortly before Lady Gregory's death in 1932. Unfortunately, her magnificent home was not maintained and, to a great outcry, was demolished in 1941. Today the park, with its wooded trails, ponds, gardens, and, of course, new teahouse, is an oasis for tourists and locals alike.

Just as Yeats did, I found solace in walking the wooded trails and sitting by Coole Pond to watch the swans meander on the calm water. And just as I had at Yeats's grave, I felt his presence. His poetry played in my head like a movie, and for the first time in days I felt calm.

By midafternoon the wind had shifted and it began to lightly rain. I walked one last trail wearing my raincoat but sheltered from the rain by the tall trees, and I encountered only one lone jogger the entire time. It was so peaceful, and I didn't want to leave, but I had other sites to see. Reluctantly, I walked to my car and studied my tattered road map to decide what sites I had the time and energy left to visit. Nearby, "just up the rood aways," was Yeats's summer home, Thoor Ballylee. I decided it might be worth a look and aimed my car in that direction.

I nearly ended up in the ditch again while trying to navigate the sharp turn from the highway onto the narrow side road, but with what felt again like divine intervention from the auto angels, I managed to straighten the wheels just in time. The road led back to a 15th-century Norman tower standing beside a flowing river. I read in the brochure I had picked up at Coole Park that the grandiose Yeats thought this nearly windowless tower would make a great summer home for his family. In 1919 he converted all four floors, eventually adding a small, thatched-roof kitchen extension. There was one window and one room on each of the four floors connected by a spiral stone stairway built into the seven-foot-thick outer wall. One floor was the living room, another floor was Yeats's study, another a bedroom, and so on. Each window overlooked the Streamstown River and the entire area was uniquely scenic. The Yeats family lived there until 1928. Yeats's romantic vision of a summerhouse by a river failed to consider that rivers tend to flood, and the Streamstown River was no exception. As a result, floodwaters overtook Thoor Ballylee many times and Yeats's wife finally put her foot down. I wondered how his wife managed to put up with all of the flooding and restoration for as long as she did. Flooding has continued to be a problem over the years and the tower has endured several restorations. There are plans in the near future to erect a floodwall and other measures to keep the floodwaters at bay.

The narrow river flowed gently now as the sun peeked from behind the clouds, casting a golden glow on the water. It reminded me of the stream in Drumcliff. I sat on a bench gazing at the water for several minutes, lost in thoughts of Yeats, the friends I had made, and of all the adventures packed into these two short weeks. "You're at peace here," the river seemed to say as it meandered around the rocks in its path. Or maybe it was Yeats speaking to me again. I was too tired to tell.

"Yeah," I whispered. "Finally. Right here, right now, I'm at peace. Now, if I could just pack that feeling into my heavy black suitcase and take it home with me."

I went inside the small cottage, now converted into a visitor center/gift shop crowded with tourists. It cost five euros to tour the tower, and I decided that it wasn't worth spending my last few euros stuck on a cramped spiral staircase with tourists. I could use those extra coins for a snack before boarding the plane tomorrow.

I walked to my car and planned my route to my next, last, farmhouse bed and breakfast, taped the directions to my dashboard, and drove to the conveniently close-to-the-airport village of Quin.

The B&B was more than I could have dreamed for on my last night. I arrived late in the afternoon to a charming, red, two-story modern farmhouse. My room was upstairs with a bay window overlooking the pasture. The room's cheery yellow walls, dark antique furniture, and white eyelet bedspread were a welcome respite from last night's plywood palace. I opened one of the windows and heard the sounds from the barnyard compete with the annoying "song" of the rooks perched along the utility lines, but I kept my window open to listen to it anyway. I didn't want to miss anything. I wanted to remember everything about this place, this journey, and take it home with me. I turned on my tape recorder and reflected upon my trip. The magic of it, but also the stress of traveling solo, the driving—always the driving. But I felt proud of my increased confidence with my driving, with my interactions with strangers, and with making friends that I hoped would last a lifetime.

I was anxious to get home. I missed my friends, my daughters, and my greyhounds. But at the same time, I didn't want to leave. There was still so much to see and learn. I instinctively knew that I wasn't finished with Ireland yet.

I packed as much as I could so that I wouldn't need to rush around in the morning. I watched the cows in the pasture and smiled as I remembered singing to the Sullivans' cows. *So many stories to tell when I get back home,* I thought as I drifted off to sleep while repeating my mantra . . .

And all shall be well, and all shall be well, and all manner of thing shall be well.

CHAPTER TWENTY-FIVE

Back Home

BUT ALL was not well when I returned home. My friends had left a bouquet of flowers for me on the kitchen table along with a handmade WELCOME HOME sign. Beside it, however, I found a letter they had written explaining that my youngest daughter and her friend had managed to get into the house while I was gone. Something they knew they were not supposed to do. They had made themselves quite at home by the time my friends got wind of it and paid them an unexpected visit to unceremoniously vacate them from the house. I felt disappointment and anger with my daughter and embarrassment that my friends had to deal with it, but grateful that I had good friends who were looking out for me and who didn't want to disturb my trip.

I straightened the house, unpacked my bags, and picked up the dogs from the Greyhound Resort. I was tired and depressed—feelings I expected to have after returning to my "real" life after experiencing such a fantastic adventure. I thought about my Ireland friends a lot and stayed in touch via email. Anne told me how much Luka had enjoyed meeting me and that she hoped I would be "crossing the pond" again soon. I was so happy to hear that. Jessie wanted me to consider staying with her during my next visit. I was delighted and grateful for her generosity. I returned Pat Monaghan's cell phone and filled her in on my adventures. "We must go over together next time, Diane." I agreed. Perhaps the biggest surprise came from my cousin, the bestselling author, who admonished me about my visit to the hermit nun. "That woman is crazy!" she screamed over the phone.

"What do you mean?"

"I emailed her after you left for Ireland. I just wanted to connect with her and tell her how excited I was about your trip and your upcoming visit with her. And she sent a really bizarre response. She is a nutcase and you're lucky you weren't hurt."

"Hurt? What did she say?"

"Oh, things like 'What makes you think I'm Catholic?' 'Who told you I'm a nun?' and even worse, 'Your cousin isn't going to visit me because *no* one visits me unless I will it and lead them here.' That last one scared me the most. I feared for your life."

"Oh, Charlene, don't be so dramatic," I laughed. "That's just the fiction writer in you coming out. I was not afraid of her and, yes, she is eccentric, but we had a good visit."

"Well, you must have caught her in one of her more lucid moments, that's all I can say because the woman is more than eccentric. She's crazy!"

"Oh, Char."

"Don't 'Oh, Char' me! You were out in the middle of nowhere with someone you met on the internet and didn't really know at all. She could have poisoned you! She could have had a gun and shot you! For all you knew, she could have been a man dressed like a nun who raped and killed you! And who would have known? None of us would have had a clue until you didn't return from your trip."

I assured her that the "nun," though eccentric, was harmless and that I had never felt my personal safety was in jeopardy. Still, I knew that I would need to be more careful in the future about visiting people I've "met" on the internet—even nuns—and that I wouldn't do so without having others verify their authenticity.

I didn't contact Sister Hilda nor did she contact me, but I checked her website every now and then fearing that I'd see a picture of myself posing with her cats accompanied by a bizarre story about how she saved this wayfaring woman's soul. Her website has changed a little. She's removed the pictures of herself and her cottage—as though she's growing more paranoid, wanting to be more anonymous. As winter approached I thought of her being by herself in that cold damp cottage, and I wondered how her health was holding up. I continued to pray for her.

Did I provide some solace to her? I'll never know, but unbeknownst to her, she gave something to me. The following summer I entered one of the photos I had taken of her in a prestigious juried photo competition and it won top honors. The image of her sitting outside her cottage laughing with her cats on her lap has brought a smile to countless others who have seen it. I smiled as I gazed at her sitting in her white plastic chair in front of her cottage, and I think about how we never really know where the road we choose to follow is taking us.

After my return home, I didn't really know where the road was taking me either. I was back into the old routine. The rest of the summer passed quickly, and my journey to Ireland seemed like a dream. Soon enough I was caught up in teacher meetings, library orientation classes, library administrative duties, and wondering if this was how I was supposed to spend the rest of my life. Retirement was years away, I had to support myself and assist my daughters financially and often emotionally. I wasn't in any position to give up my career. I refused to abandon my children as their father had done, and I needed the reassurance of a steady income. So relocating to Ireland was out of the question for now. Still, even though I knew that my children were my priority and I valued being present for them, I had my eyes and my heart set on moving to Ireland someday. In the meantime, I wondered what it would be like to visit Ireland in the winter. As fall turned to winter, I found myself contacting Jessie and Anne to ask if they would be up for a visit right after Christmas.

PART THREE

Dark Night of the Soul

Knowing your own darkness
is the best method for dealing with
the darknesses of others.

Carl Jung

CHAPTER TWENTY-SIX

Best-Laid Plans

"THE WEATHER has been promised to be wet and windy this evening," said the announcer on Clare FM. I was maneuvering my rental car around the curves and stone walls on the road to Doolin while sheets of rain splashed against my windshield. Thank God it was the offseason so the traffic was light.

"No kidding," I answered, talking back to the radio. "I hope this isn't a preview of the whole week. If so, I'm screwed."

I had missed Ireland so much that I had decided it would be a great idea to return for a week right after Christmas. I could experience what Ireland was like in the winter, spend New Year's Eve at the Black Box Theatre in Galway, and stay with Jessie while in Clare. Anne would be available for a meetup too and, of course, I was hoping that Luka might make an appearance.

Instead, the day before my flight, Jessie had emailed to say that she was sick and that I would need to find another place to stay. I contacted Anne. Her son Niall was staying with her and he was sick as well. Practically everything was closed this time of year including the farmhouse bed and breakfasts where I liked to stay, but I had high hopes that Maeve Sullivan would open up a room for me. Either way, I knew that I would be staying in or near Doolin, since I was so familiar with that area.

The rain was relentless. I made it through the village of Ennistymon and inched toward Doolin with my wipers on the highest speed. I began to question whether this trip was such a good idea and that thought gave the inner critic the perfect opportunity to express its unwanted advice.

Well, you wanted to experience Ireland in the winter, so here you are, driving in a downpour on dangerous roads in a foreign country by yourself with no place to stay. You paid top dollar with money you don't have to experience winter in Ireland and to spend New Year's Eve in a strange city by yourself just to see a has-been Irish rock band. Enjoy your stay, dear.

"Oh, shut up!" I said to that pesky voice. It wasn't the most eloquent answer, but it was heartfelt. Maybe coming here *was* a mistake, but I vowed to make the best of it. At least I wasn't sick, and I had brought along a supply of antibiotics just in case.

I wound my way along the coast road and on to the downhill drive into Doolin. I squeezed into a parking space next to a phone booth and used a calling card, regretting that Pat Monaghan's cousin in Mayo was using her cell phone. Once inside the booth I performed the arduous task of punching in the Sullivans' number along with all of the other numbers on the calling card. I had to start over twice. Finally the call went through and I heard the familiar voice of Maeve Sullivan.

"Ahh, Diane, it's so good to hear yer voice. Did you have a lovely Christmas?"

"Yes, it was a good Christmas. How was yours, Maeve?"

"Brilliant! We had a splendid time with our family." After a pause she asked, "So what can I do for ye?"

"Funny you should ask," I said as I struggled to put my calling card back in my purse and hold on to the receiver at the same time. "I'm in Doolin and I'm needing a place to stay for a few nights. I know you're not open." I rushed on without giving her a chance to answer. "But I was wondering if it would be possible for you to open a room for me." I took another breath and went on. "You wouldn't need to cook breakfast or do anything extra. My lodging plans fell through at the last minute, and I'm desperate for a place to stay."

"My, I'm glad yer here, and I wish I could help, but, as ye said, we are closed for the winter, and the painters are set to come tomorrow to paint the entire upstairs. I'm afraid I can't help."

"Are you sure you can't open just one room?" I persisted.

She must have heard the desperation in my voice, but she didn't budge.

"I'm so sorry, Diane. Truly I am, but I'm afraid I can't help ye," she repeated. "Have ye tried looking in Doolin? They should have some lodging, I would think."

"No, I haven't tried that yet," I answered, trying not to sound too dejected. After all, she had every right not to open her place to me.

"Well, I suggest that you give Erin House a try. It's located directly across from McDermott's pub."

"Thanks, Maeve. I'll do that," I said, knowing that my voice reeked with disappointment.

"So how long will ye be staying?" she asked.

"Not more than a week. I'll be staying here for a few nights and then spending New Year's Eve in Galway before heading back here and flying home."

"Well, ye must come by for a visit," she insisted.

"I would love to, Maeve. I have some gifts for the kids. I'll call you later and we can set a time."

"Brilliant. I'll talk with ye soon."

I left the phone booth and ran back to my car in the pouring rain. The weather reflected my mood—dark and rainy.

I drove a few blocks up the road to McDermott's and glanced across the street. Yes, there was the Erin House and there was a vacancy sign in the window. The place wouldn't win any B&B beauty awards. A one-story brown building, looking halfway between a B&B and a motel. It didn't matter. I needed a place to stay and I couldn't be picky. I parked in front and ran to the door, landing in a puddle on the way and splashing muddy water onto my hiking pants.

I stepped inside and was greeted by a middle-aged woman with short brown curly hair. Her thick black glasses rested on the tip of her nose.

"May I help ye," she asked, pushing her glasses into place with her index finger.

"Yes, I just arrived here from the States and I'm looking for a room."

"Just yerself?" She glanced at the door to see if anyone was following me.

"Yes." I tried not to sigh. "Just myself."

"How many nights?"

"Three."

"Yes, I have a room that should suit ye. Follow me."

I followed her to the end of the hallway while she opened a door on the left.

"Here ye are." She pushed the door all the way open and I stepped inside. There was brown indoor/outdoor carpet, beige walls, and twin beds covered with matching blue-and-brown bedspreads that sort of matched the carpet. To the right of the only window there was a small bathroom with a telephone booth–sized shower. But it was clean and that was all I needed.

"How many euros per night?" I asked, hoping that it wouldn't be too much. I hadn't brought vouchers this time, thinking that I wouldn't need them.

"We're on winter rates now, so forty-five euros it 'tis."

"That's fine," I answered with a smile, relieved to find a room with a reasonable rate.

She filled me in on the breakfast time and pointed to the phone across from the desk where I could use my calling card.

"Thanks so much," I said.

"Yer most welcome, dear."

One advantage of staying on the main drag in Doolin was that I could walk to and from the pubs. No need to drive at night. Plus I could drink more than one Irish coffee. *Hot dog!* I told myself. This will be a new experience!

After spending the rest of the afternoon trying, without much success, to rest my jetlag away, I walked down the street to McGann's. The usual older men in their tweed caps were sitting just inside, some with their panting, contented dogs on the floor beside them. There was a crowd starting to form though it was still early in the evening. I ordered a sandwich at the bar along with my Irish coffee and searched for a place to sit. I spotted a table close to the musicians. A young couple was sitting there. I waved to them and they motioned me over. Their smiles looked friendly enough, so I plopped down on the bench next to them so that I could face the musicians and introduced myself.

"I'm Tristan and this is my wife, Cindy," the young man said as he made more room for me. I recognized his Australian accent.

"It's nice to meet you," I said while taking a sip of my Irish coffee. "So are you visiting from Australia?"

"Yeah, and we're having a crackin' ole time," answered Cindy, brushing her blond bangs away from her eyes. She was the epitome of how I wanted to look—tall, thin, long blond hair, lovely blue eyes full of life. I didn't care about the blond part, but I wanted the rest.

"What about the weather here? You know, with it being summer back home," I asked between bites of my fish sandwich. "The weather here this time of year can be depressing."

Tristan took a sip of his beer and said, "Yeah, that's a thing, but there's always a pub to duck into, and the pubs are great, don't you think?"

I nodded.

"And we'll be on our way home to summertime next week." Tristan looked like the rugged outdoor type. His longish light-brown hair highlighted his tanned face. His dark-green fleece shirt brought out the hazel in his eyes. "Meanwhile, we're going to enjoy every minute of our time here. Right, Cindy?"

"You're so right, luv."

"That's the spirit," I said, raising my glass. "Slainte!"

"Slainte!" We clicked our glasses together, and this lonely traveler said a prayer of thanks for finding such kind people along the road.

I knew that Luka wasn't touring, and I was secretly hoping that he would drop in with his guitar for the session, as he often did. Instead, who did I see but Jessie's neighbor pounding away on his bodhran at the table next to ours. I was sure he wouldn't recognize me, especially since he appeared to be drunk already. We exchanged glances and his locked onto mine as if he was trying to place where he had seen me before. I was afraid he might strip down to his boxer shorts and pose for me. I quickly turned away and continued my conversation with Tristan and Cindy.

The pub was filling up with revelers of all ages, and the noise level was off the charts. I thought about leaving, but the musicians were great and I wanted to hear them. There were five of them, young and old, seated at the table farther down from us, playing fiddle, penny whistle, guitar, and, of course, Jessie's neighbor on the bodhran. My foot was tapping along with the tune, and the beer was flowing freely. I walked to the bar and came back with my second Irish coffee. While I was away the people on my left had moved to another table, leaving me with the only option of sitting next to Jessie's neighbor. I sat as far away from him as I could, but the space between us was getting smaller and smaller as he kept scooting toward me. If I scooted farther away I would be on Tristan's lap. He glanced at me again as he poured a small amount of beer onto his bodhran and rubbed it in like he was greasing a skillet. I thought it was disgusting.

"Why are you doing that?" I blurted out. *Damn, I wasn't going to talk to him!*

"Well, me lovely, this is goatskin and wetting it improves the sound."

"Oh."

"Have we met before?" he asked before downing the rest of his beer.

"No," I answered. Not "I don't think so" or "I'm sure you're mistaken" but a firm "*No.*" I fiddled with my drink. "You must have me confused with someone else."

"But ye look so familiar like," he insisted. "Are ye sure?"

I shot him a surely-you-don't-think-I'm-going-to-fall-for-that-lame-line-do-you? look.

"Absolutely sure."

"Awright then," he conceded. "Can't trust me memory nowadays."

Especially when you're drunk all the time.

He went back to playing his bodhran along to the tune of "Banish Misfortune." When the song ended the musicians took a break, but instead of getting up and moving around, as I hoped he would do, he looked straight ahead and scooted closer to me, pressing his thigh against mine. I scooted. He scooted and pressed my thigh harder. I couldn't believe it. The guy who had posed for me in his stupid boxer shorts and wellies was lewdly hitting on me.

Okay, enough of this! I lifted my leg and kicked a hard punch into his calf.

"Ow!" he yelled. "That hurt!"

"It's going to hurt even more if you do that again," I said, giving him a look that could burn right through him.

"Awright then, have it yer way." He scooted away but not far enough for me.

The fiddle player sitting across from him said, "Are ye causing trouble again? Man, ye'd best behave yerself and act more like a gentleman toward this pretty lass." Then he winked at me. I didn't wink back.

Tristan and Cindy witnessed the incident. "I'll put an end to this," said Tristan, taking my place while I moved to the end next to Cindy.

"I don't know if this will take care of it," I said to Cindy. "He's so drunk he's likely to take a swing at Tristan."

Cindy guffawed so hard she almost spilled her beer. "Now that would be somethin' to see, eh luv?" she laughed, giving Tristan a flirty look.

"Ah, let's not even go there," said Tristan, putting his arm around Cindy. "Just like Ringo says," he said, making the peace sign. "Peace and love, peace and love."

The musicians played another set and the drunk bodhran player left me alone. I tapped along with my right foot, my left foot being a little sore. I was hot, thirsty, and a little light-headed. I'd finished my drink almost an hour ago, and I dared not order another one or I would be stumbling instead of walking back to my room. I glanced at my watch. 11:05. I decided to call it a night. My first late night in a pub. I thanked Tristan and Cindy for their company and wished them well. I made a point of ignoring Jessie's neighbor.

I know he has an alcohol problem, I told myself as I walked (not stumbled) back to my room. I hoped that someone would convince him to give up the drink. I wondered if he knew Luka. Luka had battled the drink several years before and won. Maybe he could help him.

I was too wound up to sleep. I wrote in my journal until three in the morning. As I turned out the light I thought about my visit with Anne tomorrow. How wonderful it would be to see her again. Then I drifted off to sleep repeating Julian's words, my mantra:

And all shall be well, and all shall be well, and all manner of thing shall be well.

CHAPTER TWENTY-SEVEN

A Cup of Tea and a Walk on the Beach

I OVERSLEPT THE next morning and barely made it to breakfast. I was invited to the Sullivans' at eleven for "tea and a chat" and then on to Spanish Point to meet Anne for a walk.

I smiled as I pulled into the Sullivans' driveway. There was Finn running out the front door to meet me with Murphy fast at his heels.

"Finn!" I shouted, running to meet him. "You've grown, little man."

"I'm big now," he said. He looked so cute in his jeans and denim jacket.

"May I give you a hug?" I asked.

"Just one," he said, looking a little shy.

"Thank you," I said, giving him a bear hug that made him laugh. I gave Murphy a hug too. He rolled over inviting me to rub his tummy, which I did. Finn laughed some more.

"Now, let's go back to my car. I have some things to bring in."

Maeve met me at the door. I was glad to see her, and I hoped I would see Brendan too.

"Welcome Diane." Maeve smiled as she hugged me. "'Tis wonderful to see ye again. I'm so happy that ye could schedule some time for us." She paused and looked at Finn as he stood next to her pulling at her skirt. "I hope Finn hasn't been a bother."

"No, not at all. I can't believe how much he's grown!"

"They're all growing too fast," laughed Maeve. "Come in for some tea. Brendan will be joining us soon."

"Oh, good!"

I followed her into their living room. I'd never been in here before. The room was a large square with cream walls and dark-beige carpet. A large front window framed one wall, and a brick fireplace faced the opposite wall, its mantel covered with family photos. It looked the way a growing family's living room should look—light, cozy, and comfortable. I sat down in a blue wingback chair and Maeve sat on the adjoining sofa. Finn ran out back to get his two older brothers, Rory and Ronan. Maeve and I were catching up on the latest news in our lives when the boys poked their heads in the doorway.

"Hi guys!" I said. They shyly walked into the room. They had grown too. Rory, tall and thin, was beginning to look like a young man. Ronan, dressed in his County Clare blue-and-yellow football jersey, looked like a typical nine-year-old who would rather be outside.

"Boys, sit down and chat with Ms. Hartman while I gather the tea," Maeve said as she headed toward the kitchen. The boys started to sit down when I said, "Come here, guys. I brought some books for you." I opened my tote bag and pulled out a paperback book for each of them.

"Rory, have you read any books by Gary Paulsen?"

"No, ma'am."

"Well, I think you'll like this story. It's called *Hatchett* and it's about a boy named Brian who tries to survive in the wilderness after a plane crash. Ronan, I brought you one of Gary Paulsen's western stories called *Mr. Tucket*. It's about a boy named Frances Tucket who escapes from the Native American tribe that kidnapped him and becomes a cowboy. Here, Finn, I brought you a Gary Paulsen book called *Dogteam*. It's about riding on a dog sled in Alaska."

Each boy gently took his book from my hand and remembered to thank me without being prompted. So different from their American counterparts. Rory and Ronan sat on the floor and opened their books. Finn brought his book to me.

"Read please," he said.

"Okay, do you want to sit on my lap so that you can see the pictures?"

He climbed onto my lap and opened the book.

"Here," he said, pointing to the first page.

Just as I was finishing the story I heard the back door open and close and in walked Brendan, dressed in his farming outfit of jeans and wool sweater, followed by Maeve carrying a large silver tray of tea, cookies, and cake. Brendan greeted me while Maeve placed the tray on the coffee table.

"Maeve, that looks delicious, but you didn't need to go to all that trouble for me."

"'Tis no trouble at tall," she insisted as she poured the tea into china teacups.

It was then that I realized that I had made a major faux pas. The Irish consider it rude to make a fuss when offered tea. It's especially rude to refuse a cup of tea, even if you don't want one. I was still feeling full from breakfast, but I thanked her when offered the cup of tea and a small plate covered with cookies and a slice of white cake. I wondered how I could possibly eat all of that, but Finn came to my rescue by offering to eat the cake and a few of the cookies. Meanwhile, Rory and Ronan had quietly helped themselves to cookies before going back to their books.

"Thank ye for the books," said Brendan. "That was very kind of ye, and it looks as though ye picked the right ones."

"You're welcome," I said as I took my last sip of tea. "Oh, I almost forgot. I brought some of the photos I took last summer." I pulled an envelope from my tote and stood by Maeve and Brendan as they oohed and aahed over them.

"These are brilliant, Diane," said Brendan.

"Yes," agreed Maeve, "and you brought these for us?"

"Of course," I said. "I love the photo of Rory and Ronan waiting for the school bus. And the one of Murphy walking on top of the stone wall."

"And there's Finn mucking about in the mud." Maeve laughed.

"Look at this photo of the ocean, Maeve," Brendan said. "It's gorgeous."

"I took that one from the trail behind your house," I said. "The light was just right. And, Maeve, I think there's a photo of your clothesline in there somewhere."

"Oh, you tease," Maeve laughed. "Are you certain these are ours?"

"I'm certain."

"Oh, thank ye, Diane," said Maeve.

"Yes, thank ye," said Brendan. "Yer so kind. We don't get around to taking as many pictures as we should and ours wouldn't be as good as yers anyway. Now we are blessed with pictures of our children and our property to remind us of last summer's beauty."

Maeve nodded in agreement.

"That's so sweet of you," I said, my eyes welling with tears. "I enjoy taking photos of your beautiful family." The conversation paused while I fished a tissue from my purse and dried my tears.

"Now, Brendan and Maeve," I said, "tell me the latest about the goings on in Doolin and the Burren."

"Right so." Brendan smiled. "There's much going on, some good, some not so good."

"We will begin with the good," said Maeve.

They described the latest happenings, and each was not shy about stating their opinions. I got an earful about the developers whose proposed building plans would destroy the Burren and the Cliffs of Moher, their outrage at the hypocrisy of the local church, and Brendan's plan to continue improvements to the trail to the Cliffs of Moher.

My visit passed too quickly, and I needed to head for Spanish Point. The boys thanked me again for their books, and the entire family walked me to my car. Each one of them gave me a hug, even shy, awkward Rory. I looked in my rearview mirror as I drove away and saw them smiling and waving from their doorstep.

God, I love that family.

I beeped my horn and turned onto the road toward Spanish Point.

I stopped at Brigid's Well on my way to meet Anne and had the place to myself. I lit a candle and said some prayers. When I pray I don't often ask for anything specific. Since God knows the person I'm praying for much better than I do, including myself, I visualize the person and ask that God's will be done. Most of the time I sit in silence and listen. Even when we pray, we tend to spend too much time talking instead of listening. It was easy to listen in this quiet, holy space, but I needed to move on. I cupped my hands into the well and drank the cool water. I took a few more photos and drove on down the coast road.

I wasn't nearly as nervous driving through Lahinch and Miltown Malbay. There were few cars on the coast road, making it much easier for me to maneuver the twists and turns. Still, I was relieved to see the Armada Hotel at Spanish Point. In the usual Irish fashion, Anne was late, but I didn't mind. It was a slightly chilly, but sunny, beautiful day. Perfect for walking on the beach wearing a light coat, no hat or gloves needed. I sat on the wall in the parking lot and watched the dogs running along the beach.

Pretty soon I heard the gear-shifting, clutch-bearing sound of Anne's car. I got down off the wall and walked toward her car as she parked it. We hugged and hugged. Anne suggested that we take a walk on a beach south of Quilty, so I piled into her car with my camera and off we went.

Anne was chatty and in good spirits, but tired from the holidays.

"Not only that, Diane," she said as she steered her car around a sharp curve, "but I'm tired from taking care of everyone. Niall is still sick with his chest infection. My daughter, Ainne, is staying with us too. Thank the powers that be that she's not sick. Well here we are at last." Anne sighed. "Ready to walk the most beautiful beach in all of Ireland?"

We were parked along the side of a dirt road, and try as I might, I didn't see any sign of a beach. "Where's the beach?"

"It's just behind those two buildings," answered Anne. "C'mon, I know a shortcut."

Sure enough, just beyond the buildings was the most beautiful sandy beach I had ever seen. "Anne, it's beautiful!"

"'Tis. Come and we'll walk a little closer to the water."

There weren't many people on the beach. I didn't spot anyone who looked like a tourist—no families, no shorts. Just a few adults, some with their dogs happily splashing along the shore.

The wind had picked up, but it wasn't bad. Anne's short salt-and-pepper hair was standing up in the breeze and mine was blowing to one side.

"We're going to come out a bit windblown, eh?" Anne asked, squinting behind her black glasses from the bright sun.

"For sure."

Anne was moving fast. Her legs were a lot longer than mine, so I was having a hard time keeping up without breaking into a sprint. Finally, we settled into the same stride and began our long "walk and talk."

We started by talking about books. Anne is a voracious reader, and we've enjoyed sharing our favorite books and authors.

"Have you read Paul Auster's latest?" Anne asked.

"I'm not familiar with him," I confessed, stopping to pick up a small shell that caught my eye.

"Oh, girl, ye must get familiar with him. He's fab. Read *The Book of Illusions*. Ye'll love it. It's about this professor from Vermont who loses his wife and son and eventually becomes obsessed with writing a book about a silent film comedian who vanished in 1929."

"Wow! Sounds interesting," I said. "What about Niall Williams's latest, *The Fall of Light*? I just finished it and loved it. He's such a romantic."

"Indeed he is. I've read *Four Letters of Love* and I adored it, but I haven't read his latest yet. Is it as good as his others?"

"Definitely," I answered. Anne stopped to say hello to a couple she knew. "Have you met Niall Williams?" I continued. "He lives south of here in Kiltumper."

"No, I haven't had the pleasure, but I'm sure I'll run into him and have a chat someday," Anne said.

"I'm surprised you haven't met him," I said. "You seem to know everyone in the county."

Anne laughed. "No, I still have a few left to meet and he's one of 'em."

We continued to walk. Anne asked a lot of questions about my home, my children, and how I was doing.

"How is your work?" she continued.

"It's stressful," I answered. "With all of the new technology, more and more responsibilities are thrown at me. I love the teaching aspect and all of the reading guidance I do with my students. It's dealing with all of the administrative stuff, you know, and a few parents who want to ban books."

"Which books?" asked Anne.

"Oh, Harry Potter and books with witches and the supernatural."

"Oh, begobs!" said Anne. "Some people. I'll bet they're hypocrites and read sexy fantasy novels on the sly."

I laughed. "I wouldn't be surprised. Maybe I've just been doing this job too long." I continued, "But these last few years it's been hard for me to be excited about my career. I'm fully engaged when I'm there. But my career is not my entire life. I would rather be writing and pursuing other interests and be free from all of the restrictions that are being thrust upon us. I can tell that the Irish respect their teachers, but there's little respect for them in the States."

"The whole lot of it is sad," said Anne. "Do ye think ye might fancy leaving soon or is that not possible financially?"

"I wish I could, but it's not possible. I would have to work, and any other job I can think of couldn't compete with the pay and health insurance benefits."

"Oh, that's right. You Americans have to scramble and make sacrifices just to get health insurance." Anne shook her head. "What a pity."

"Yes, it is. But I can't see us ever having national health insurance in the States. Too many, especially the insurance companies and lobbyists, think it reeks of socialism. Social Security is socialism too, but they conveniently overlook that. Anyway, I'm in for another twelve or so years and then I can retire and start another life."

"Another life," Anne repeated. "Yes, I like that. You can be wild and free!"

"Yeah, right," I laughed. "Although I do think the artistic side of me will flourish. I'll probably get a tattoo and retire my librarian wardrobe for a more flamboyant one."

"Oh, I can't wait to see that!" chortled Anne.

"Me either," I laughed.

The wind had calmed down, and the light from the late-afternoon sun reminded me of a Nordic sky, with streaks of white shooting through blues and grays. It seemed magical, and I was so happy to be here with Anne. We had walked a good mile by then when Anne suggested that we turn around.

"Anne, you'll get a kick out of this," I said. "I visited a psychic a while ago because I wanted to see what she thought of this Ireland obsession of mine, you know, like what in the hell is this Irish thing all about? Instead, she tells me that my father is with her and proceeds to tell me all of these things she couldn't possibly know about him."

"Such as?" asked Anne.

"Such as, he was sorry that he took his own life, that he didn't realize how much it would hurt everyone. She knew that he worked with trains, and she said that he wanted me to know that he was very proud of me and that I should keep writing."

"Oh, my!" Anne said. "What do you make of it?"

"Well, I don't think it really matters whether or not it's real. It's more about how these things make us feel upon hearing them. And about how this information might help to heal and comfort us."

"It is a comfort to hear such things," agreed Anne. "You know my father died when I was about the same age as ye were when yer father died. Ten was it?"

"Yes."

"He died in surgery, but it was a simple procedure, nothing life-threatening, so it shouldn't have happened. It was such a tragedy. Luka was only eighteen months old, so he doesn't remember him but, still, it's left its mark on him. On all of us."

"Yes, and he's used his music to help heal that wound," I said. "It's what inspired him to write 'The Man is Alive.' Such a beautiful tribute to his father."

"Right so," said Anne.

"A father's death has such an overwhelming effect on daughters, especially when he dies young," I said. "We feel like we've been abandoned, don't we?"

"Indeed, we do," Anne agreed. "And then we try to fill that void by marrying someone who reminds us of him."

"Exactly!" I was so relieved that she came to this insight. "That's exactly what we do! You were young when you married Davoc, but that's worked out very well for you. Not so much for me. You found the best version of your father while I found the worst version of mine."

"Ah, but Diane," Anne insisted. "Ye came out of it with two beautiful daughters and all the wiser from what I can tell."

"You're right, Anne. My daughters can be a thorn in my side, but they will always be the light of my life. I wouldn't change the past. I would like to think that if I were ever in another relationship, I wouldn't make the same mistakes."

"And you will have a good relationship by and by. I feel it in me bones, gal," she said, putting her arm around my shoulder.

"Thanks, Anne." I rested my head on her shoulder as we paused to watch a young man playing frisbee with his golden retriever.

"Brilliant catch!" yelled Anne. The man waved and the dog wagged her tail as if she knew she was being complimented.

"So, what is Luka up to?" I asked.

"Ah, Barry. Let's call him by his real name, shall we?"

"Sure." I said.

"He spent a quiet Christmas with our sister, Terry, who is on her own and suffering from shingles in her eyes."

"Oh my God, how awful!"

"Yes. Terrible. But Barry said that he wanted her to have some Christmas, so he stayed with her. He said he hasn't watched that many movies in years!" She laughed.

"I'm not surprised that he spent Christmas with her," I said. "It seems to me that he is very devoted to his family. That's another thing I love about him."

"Yes, there's much to love, I tell ye. One couldn't ask for a better baby brother, but he can be stubborn too. And like me, he can be impulsive and not think things through."

"We all have our weaknesses," I said. "Our blind spots."

"Right so," agreed Anne. "Barry's taking a much-needed rest after working so hard. He's seeing a physical therapist at least weekly about his tendonitis and his carpal tunnel."

"I'm surprised that he has played so many gigs around Ireland while undergoing such intense treatment."

"I agree," said Anne, shaking her head. "But I have a secret to tell ye. Barry's been recording an acoustic album at his home and it will be released soon. The announcement should be on the website in the next few weeks."

"That's wonderful!" I said. "Tell him that I'm so glad he's getting back to the basics."

"Ahh, I can't tell him!" Anne gasped. "If he knew that I had told you about it he would kill me! It's supposed to be top secret."

"The secret's safe with me," I assured her, feeling honored that she trusted me.

Before long we had arrived back to her car. She drove back to the Armada parking lot, and we sat in the car for a while talking more about Barry, her family, her brother Christy, her son Donnacha's deteriorating health, and more books.

Our visit ended all too soon with hugs and "Are you coming back next summer?"

"I don't know," I said. "I want to but we'll have to see."

"I hope you do," Anne said. "We can arrange more time to spend together."

"I would love that, Anne."

"As would I," she answered. There was a pause before she asked, "Are you sure you want to spend New Year's Eve in Galway with The Saw Doctors? Will you be safe?"

"I'll be fine," I said. "I'm staying in a hostel a short walk from the venue. It should be fun."

"The Saw Doctors are always a good time," said Anne. "But if ye change yer mind, we're having some friends over to play cards and yer welcome to join us."

"Thanks, Anne. I'll call you when I get back to Clare. Jessie has assured me that she will be well enough for me to stay with her before I fly home."

"Yes, do call." She took my face in her hands and kissed my cheek. "I so enjoyed our walk together. Keep writing me."

"I enjoyed it too, Anne. Thanks for spending time with me."

I gave her one last hug before gathering my things and getting out of the car. I waved as she beeped her horn and left the parking lot. *What a surreal afternoon. I'm so lucky to have her for a friend. Who would've thought that asking a few questions on her brother's fan site would lead to such a close friendship? Synchronicity again.*

I thought of everything we had talked about on the drive back to Doolin. Things I said, things I forgot to say, things I wished I'd said. I felt sad that our visit was over, but I was excited about spending tomorrow night, New Year's Eve, with The Saw Doctors.

CHAPTER TWENTY-EIGHT

My Night in Hell

I AWOKE THE next morning to the sound of rain thrashing against my window. It continued to pour, coming down in lashes as the Irish say, as I loaded my car and left for Doolin, and it never let up all the way to Galway. I was hoping this wasn't an omen for my New Year's Eve adventure. Fortunately, I had remembered to tape my trusty note with directions to the hostel on my dashboard. Despite the downpour, I managed to take the correct roundabouts into the city center and found my way to the hostel. The young woman at the desk told me that I could park my car in the lot across the street.

"It is surrounded by a high brick wall, so it will be locked for the night. That way yer car will be safe tonight. Call this number in the morning when yer ready to leave and the owners will come and unlock the gate for ye."

"Great," I said. "Is there anything else I need to know?"

"Yer not allowed to have any visitors in yer room. This is strictly enforced. Check out is at 11:00 a.m. There's a cold breakfast of cereal and such in the kitchen until 10:00 a.m."

Staying in a hostel was new to me, so I didn't know what to expect. I only knew that it was a cheap way to spend the night close to the Black Box Theatre. I knew that I would be sharing a room, but I didn't expect it to be with five girls young enough to be my daughters. Though it was only midafternoon, they were already primping and prepping themselves for a big night out as they chatted away. They barely looked at me when I entered the room. The walls were lined with bunkbeds. I chose a lower bunk as far away as I could get from the girls. I settled in and lay down on the bed, but I couldn't rest with the sound of the blow dryers and the girls' incessant chatter. I needed to find something to eat anyway, so I donned my raincoat, grabbed my umbrella and purse, and went in search of a restaurant. I decided to walk toward the Black Box to scout out the area.

The rain had turned to a mist, just enough to require an umbrella. I crossed the street and walked the two blocks to the theater. As I approached, I spotted Davy Carton, The Saw Doctors' lead singer, unloading his guitars from a dark-blue compact car parked in front of the theater.

"Hi, Davy," I shouted.

He looked up. I crossed the street and walked toward him. The expression on his face told me that he didn't want to talk to me, but I braved on.

"I don't want to bother you," I assured him. "I just wanted to see where the theater is located." His face relaxed a little. "I came all the way from Indiana to see you guys tonight," I went on. He smiled. "Well ye sure picked a good day fer it." He laughed, pointing up at the rain. "That's brilliant that ye came all that way fer tonight," he said, closing the trunk. "Enjoy the show," he said, looking at me and smiling for the first time.

"Oh, I will." I smiled back. "Fair play to you, Davy."

"And fair play to ye as well."

He carried his guitar cases into the theater, and I hurried back toward the hostel hoping to find a place to eat along the way.

There's a fine line between being a fan and being an obsessive fan. I didn't want to cross that line by trying to engage him in a longer conversation. It was clear that he was in a hurry to get inside, and it was foolish of me to be standing outside in the rain anyway. I was a mature middle-aged woman, not a teenybopper hoping to get an autograph. I felt a gnawing in my stomach and saw a fish and chips shop across the street. But the gnawing wasn't from hunger. I had this sinking feeling that coming to Galway was a big mistake. First, there was the miserable weather, then I was sharing a room with a bunch of girls, finally I was going to a concert alone on New Year's Eve.

The girls were still primping and priming when I returned to the hostel. I nodded to them, hung up my wet things, headed straight for my bunk, and tried to read. The chatter went on.

"So, how does this look? Is it too much eyeliner, do ye think?"

"Ah, no luv. It looks grand."

"Is me skirt too short?"

"Well, what's wrong with that? You want the guys in the pub to notice ye, don't ye?"

"Fer sure, but I don't want 'em looking up me arse."

And so it went for a few more hours until they exited for their big night out. I wondered which area of Ireland they were from. Going out was a big deal for them. I hoped they wouldn't be disappointed, but I said a prayer that they would be safe too. I wanted to tell them that they needn't have wasted so much time on their appearance. If a young man was truly attracted to them for all the right reasons, it wouldn't matter if their eyeliner was on straight. But what did I know? No doubt they thought I was a strange old lady anyway, being alone in a hostel on New Year's Eve. I was beginning to think they were right.

Finally, having the bathroom to myself, I hurriedly changed my clothes, fixed my hair, and applied a little makeup. If I wanted to stand close to the stage, I needed to get there early.

The Black Box Theatre was exactly as described, a huge black box on the outside and the same inside. Nothing fancy about it, just a bare concrete floor with standing room only and a big bar in the back. I walked to the front and looked for someone to talk with. I approached a small group of thirty-something New Yorkers I had overheard talking to one another.

"Hi," I said in my friendliest voice. "I'm from the States too."

They barely looked at me.

"Are you big Saw Doctors fans?" I blabbered on, but I couldn't get a response. They let it be known that they weren't interested in talking to me. "Well, enjoy the show you New York snobs," I muttered the last part under my breath as I moved to the other side of the stage.

Before long, an older couple stood beside me and smiled. I took a chance and introduced myself.

"I'm Liam," he said, "and this is me wife, Nora." Nora smiled and shook my hand. "Ye say ye are from Indiana. What brings ye here tonight?"

"I'm visiting friends in Clare, and I'm a Saw Doctor fan, so I decided to come to the concert."

"All by yerself?" asked Nora.

"Yes, just for tonight."

"Where are ye staying tonight?" asked Liam.

"At a hostel close by."

"Ahh, that's a shame," said Liam. His West Ireland accent was thick. I could barely understand him. "When ye travel to Galway next, ye must stay with us."

"Indeed," said Nora, nodding in agreement. "We have lots of room. There's no need to stay in a bloody hostel, I tell ye."

"Right so," said Liam. "We live not far, near Spiddal."

"Oh, yes," I said, remembering my "bog man" bus trip with Ms. Snooty. "It's a lovely area."

"'Tis," said Nora.

"So what brings you here tonight?" I asked.

"Our daughter is in the opening band—RiRa. She sings and plays fiddle."

"That's wonderful," I said. "I can't wait to see her. You must be so proud of her."

"Indeed, we are," answered Nora.

We talked some more and, due to their heavy western Ireland accents, I was embarrassed to have to ask them to repeat themselves. The area where they live, northwest of Galway, is a Gallach area where many still speak Irish. That explained their accent, but accent or not, I was so happy that they had chosen to stand next to me and strike up a conversation. And what a friendly, generous couple they were. Inviting a strange woman to stay with them! But that's the Irish, at least it is in the west. They seemed to have a sixth sense about them when it came to discerning who might need some extra generosity.

I looked away, and I was surprised to see that the floor was filling up quickly with young revelers, many holding more than one pint of beer.

"Uh-oh," I said. "I was hoping otherwise, but it looks like there will be lots of heavy drinking tonight."

"That's right," said Liam. "I hope they don't get too rowdy and try to rush the stage."

"Right so," agreed Nora. "But they likely will."

Just then the lights were lowered, and I could tell from the cheering crowd that it was going to be a rowdy night.

The curtain opened and there was RiRa, a group of five young male and female musicians in their early twenties all dressed in black and white. I motioned for Nora to point out their daughter and she pointed to a lovely brunette picking up a fiddle.

"She's beautiful!" I said to both of them. They smiled and nodded in agreement.

They began to play a set of traditional tunes and then sang a beautiful rendition of Leonard Cohen's haunting ballad "Hallelujah." I could see this band going places. Their set ended too soon. The curtain closed and the lights came on.

"They come back later to play with The Saw Doctors," said Liam.

"Oh, great!" I said. "They have a bright future ahead of them."

"They do," replied Nora, "but it takes a lot of hard work and just plain luck."

"They're lucky that The Saw Doctors took them under their wing," added Liam. "It's opened some doors for them."

The lights lowered again and the crowd roared as The Saw Doctors took the stage and broke into their hit "N17."

I took out my Sony Mavica camera and began shooting. Before long, what looked like a teenage boy dressed up in a white button-down shirt, black slacks, and shiny black shoes appeared beside me.

"At the request of The Saw Doctors you are not permitted to take video of this concert."

"This isn't a video camera," I replied. "It's a digital camera."

"At the request of The Saw Doctors you are not permitted to take video of this concert."

"You've memorized that line very well," I shouted above the crowd, "but this is not a video camera!" I turned my back to him and continued to shoot.

"If you do not cease, I will have no alternative than to call in more security, and we will confiscate your video camera."

"It's not a . . ." I was so exasperated by his lack of knowledge. "Oh, you're security are you? Well maybe you could do your real job and keep the drunks behind me from pushing me into the freaking stage!"

He stood in silence, staring at me. I think I saw his lower lip quiver. Clearly I had rattled him.

"And by the way," I continued, "I know The Saw Doctors, and I have taken hundreds of photos of them. They've put some of them on their website, and I know for a fact that they don't mind if I take some pictures of them with my *digital* camera!"

"Ma'am, I'm sorry, but if you refuse to put your camera away, I will have no choice but to confiscate it."

"Oh, whatever!" I shouted, stuffing my camera into my bag. I was tired of this, and it was impossible to take good shots when I was being shoved from behind anyway. "Why don't you quit harassing me now and go take care of these drunks behind me?"

He walked away without answering, and it was clear to me that "security" was more interested in harassing me than dealing with the rowdy drunks.

"Well done, well done," said Liam, patting me on the back. "Mighty spunky of you."

"Maybe," I said, "but I just don't have any patience with stupid people bossing me around." Then I realized what a stupid statement that was, given that I work in education, where stupid people boss me around on a regular basis.

We went back to watching The Saw Doctors. When they finished "Same Oul' Town," Davy Carton invited RiRa onto the stage to join them in a romping rendition of "Joyce Country Ceili Band." The proud parents beamed. But when RiRa left the stage and The Saw Doctors moved into their more rambunctious songs, the crowd got that way too, and the pushing from behind became shoving. I was knocked against Liam time and again. "I'm sorry," I said again and again. I was knocked into Nora too. "I'm sorry." I was knocked against a stranger in front of me. "I'm sorry."

As it neared midnight and they began their most rambunctious song, "Hay Wrap," I'd had enough. I waved goodbye to Liam and Nora, moved away from the stage, and managed to find the door to the lobby. The door slammed shut behind me, and I was standing in the quiet lobby with Ollie Jennings, The Saw Doctors' manager.

"Are you all right?" he asked. "You look quite upset."

"I am upset. I was being slammed into others by the drunks behind me and nothing was done about it. Instead, this young security guy threatened to confiscate my digital camera because he thought it was a video camera even though I told him several times that it wasn't." I was welling up with tears by now. "I came all this way to celebrate New Year's Eve with The Saw Doctors, not to be harassed and shoved into the stage. I'm really disappointed, Ollie. Coming here was a big mistake."

"I'm sorry," said Ollie. "New Year's Eve brings out the drinkers, and it's hard to control them."

"I understand that it's hard to control them, but you and the venue should have a plan in place for dealing with them. They're harassing and possibly hurting those of us who came to hear the music. And security did absolutely nothing. Instead, they were threatening to throw me out if I didn't put my video camera away. And I kept telling them that it's not a video camera, it's a digital camera . . ." My voice trailed off and I realized, much to my frustration, that it was because I was choking up. *Damn! I don't want to be sniffling and sobbing in front of The Saw Doctors' manager!*

"Well, ye have brought up some valid points," said Ollie, moving closer. "We've met before, haven't we?"

"Yes, I'm Diane. We met at the Vic in Chicago. You let me in for the sound check."

"Oh, now I remember. You asked for me at the ticket office."

I nodded.

"I'm sorry that this wasn't a better experience for you. Where are you off to?"

"The hostel, a few blocks away."

"Will you be all right?"

"Yes, I'll be fine, just disappointed. But it's my own fault. I should have known better than to come."

"Be that as it may, I'm sorry ye had such a bad experience. Shall I call ye a taxi?"

"No, thank you. That's not necessary. It's just a few blocks."

"Well, I hope we meet again under better circumstances."

"We will, especially if you and the boys come back to Indianapolis."

"No doubt we will one of these days. Take care, Diane. I will be talking this situation over with the boys."

"Thanks, Ollie. You take care too."

I walked out the door into the cold, misty night. I felt a little afraid. Who knew what might happen on the way back to the hostel? But my purposeful stride didn't reveal my fear. If anything, it was a warning to anyone who saw me to stay away.

I entered the hostel, greeted the older guy staffing the desk, and went straight to my room. Fortunately, it was empty. The girls were still out partying.

I continued to chastise myself as I got ready for bed. *What a way to start the new year for an almost fifty-year-old woman, huh?* The tears were welling up again. *You have only yourself to blame for getting into this mess. What were you thinking anyway? It's not like you're a young beauty looking for someone to screw, for God's sake. Get yourself together and get out of here as fast as you can.*

Instead, I took a sleeping pill and overslept. I remember hearing the man at the desk shouting at a girl who was trying to sneak a young man into her room at what must have been around three in the morning, and the sound of retching coming from the bathroom. But it was almost ten now. The girls were dead to the world. I was hungry and wanted to take advantage of the free breakfast. I had laid out my clothes the night before, preparing to make a quick getaway. I glanced in the bathroom mirror and saw a haggard-looking woman with swollen eyes. I splashed cold water on my face, hoping it would help. I packed my bag and headed downstairs. When I found the kitchen, the man at the desk was talking to a woman who looked to be close to my age, a full backpack by her side. *So*

I wasn't the only woman who traveled alone after all! The only food left was tea and toast, which was enough to clear my foggy head and settle my stomach.

"How was yer concert?" the man asked. I had told him about my plans yesterday.

"It started out fine, but it became full of drunks pushing me into the stage. I left before it was over."

"I'm sorry to hear that," he said.

"I should have expected it," I replied.

"Ah, don't be so hard on yourself," the woman chimed in with her English accent. "It's too bad so many feel they have to get bloody plastered to have a good time."

"It sounded like you had your hands full last night too," I said, looking at the man.

"Indeed, there's always some who drink too much and try to break the rules."

"That's too bad. What a bother," I said. "I plan to catch up on my sleep tonight. I'm driving to Liscannor today to stay with a friend."

"Good for ye," he said. "Be careful and have a good stay."

"Thanks, and best of luck to you," I said, addressing both of them. I left them deep in conversation. The young woman at the desk called the parking lot owner for me. She told me he would meet me at eleven. That gave me about forty minutes. I needed cash, so I stashed my bag behind the desk and headed out the door toward Eyre Square to find an ATM machine. The morning was bright and sunny. *Thank God I don't have to drive in the rain.*

The streets were empty save for a few young people wearing backpacks. There was a strange, uneasy quiet following a night of noisy revelry. I heard a male Irish voice saying, "Wake up, man. Wake up! Are ye all right? Wake up, mate."

I looked toward the sound at the parking garage on the corner. I saw a young, bearded man bending over a young man slumped over in the recessed wall beside the parking garage. I ran over. The bearded man was patting the young man's face. "C'mon, mate, wake up now." My heart dropped. The young man was clearly unconscious. His thin, baby-smooth face looked strangely at peace. His short, dark hair was neatly cut and groomed, and he was wearing black designer glasses. He had on beige dress pants with a white polo shirt and shiny brown loafers. He looked out of place.

"Do you know him?" I asked the bearded man.

"No, I just found him here," he answered, practically slapping the young man's face. "C'mon mate, can ye hear me? Wake up!"

"I don't think he's going to come out of it," I said. "Do you want me to call an ambulance?"

"Aye, I imagine we'd better."

"Okay. I'll go back to the hostel and have them call."

"Right, then. Thank you, luv."

"I hope he turns out to be okay."

I ran back to the hostel and told the woman at the desk what had happened and that she needed to call an ambulance at once. She seemed reluctant at first.

"Are ye sure he needs one? Is he just a little passed out from drinking too much?"

"No, he's out stone-cold and he won't wake up."

"All right then," she sighed as she reached for the phone.

"Thank you," I said, grabbing my bag from behind the desk and heading out the door.

"An ambulance is on the way," I shouted to the bearded man. He waved an "okay" and kept pleading with the young man, "Wake up, man."

I forgot all about the ATM. I walked to the parking lot and waited outside the gate for the owner. Shortly before he arrived, I heard the siren heading toward the parking garage. I looked up the street and watched as the EMTs loaded the young man onto a stretcher and placed it into the back of the ambulance. The bearded man shook the EMTs' hands and walked away. I stood, my feet glued to the sidewalk, and watched as the ambulance pulled away in the opposite direction, its siren fading in the distance.

"Will all be well?" I asked Julian of Norwich.

She didn't answer.

I loaded up my car, taped the directions to Jessie's on my dashboard, and waved to the man holding the parking lot gate open for me. I let out a big sigh of relief when I exited the last roundabout in Galway and eased onto the N18 toward Clare. Jessie would be waiting for me. We would talk over a late lunch. I would play with her dogs and visit Clint, the donkey, out in his field. Maybe I would end up laughing at myself when telling her about my New Year's Eve in Galway. Someday I might, but not yet. I had a lot to process and some hard questions to ask myself first. But I would feel better after some rest, and Jessie's kind voice and warm hospitality would be a balm to my wounded soul.

CHAPTER TWENTY-NINE

Refuge and Rest

THE DRIVE south through the Burren and Corkscrew Hill seemed second nature now, allowing me to slow down and take in the scenery. Frost covered the green vegetation and the rocks resembled white moonstones on the hills. All of this unique beauty belied the fact that I felt like crap. True, my head wasn't foggy, but it felt heavy, and my stomach hadn't gotten over the stress from the night before. I was hoping I wouldn't need to stop in Lisdoonvarna to look for a tearoom with a toilet. I was anxious to get to Liscannor to see Jessie.

As I drove I thought about why I had decided to come to Ireland now. True, I wanted to experience Ireland in the winter without all the tourists, and taking advantage of the opportunity to see The Saw Doctors on New Year's Eve had seemed like a great idea at the time. What had happened? Well, for the most part, the weather was gloomy and darkness descended by five o'clock, making the memory of last summer's warm evenings and long sunsets all the more precious. And then there was the New Year's Eve debacle at The Saw Doctors' concert. I had been so naive and foolish for thinking that I would be having a good time with fellow fans. No wonder I was disappointed. My expectations had been idealistic, and they had shattered like a favorite teacup crashing to the floor once I realized my mistake. So, now what? Being more pragmatic this time, I told myself that I would make the best of my last day and night with Jessie. I had the long plane trip home tomorrow evening to ponder this journey.

I turned south onto the familiar coast road and headed toward the Cliffs of Moher. I glanced in awe at the rushing waves caressing the shore. The vastness of the Atlantic reminded me of how insignificant my problems were in the grand scheme of things. I regretted that it was too misty to stop and take photos. I snapped out of my reverie as I approached the cliffs. I needed to look for Jessie's road. With no one behind me, I slowed down and eased onto it without landing in the ditch.

Jessie and her dogs greeted me when I pulled into her drive. It was quite a welcoming party with the dogs barking and Jessie yelling, "Hello, Diane! Hello!" I felt so happy to see them, especially after being alone for the past few days.

"Are you feeling better?" I asked Jessie before giving her a big hug.

"Oh yes, much better." She hugged me hard. "That flu is nasty stuff, dammit! So how are you?"

"I'm fine," I lied. I followed her into the house with the dogs close behind. "Just tired because I didn't sleep much last night."

"How was the concert?" asked Jessie as she motioned for me to sit at the kitchen table while she made tea.

"Why don't we talk about that later?" I shifted in my chair and changed the subject. "How was your Christmas?"

"Fine. Fine," answered Jessie, placing a cup of steaming hot tea in front of me. "Just Tim, Siobhan, and me. We had a lovely Christmas Eve dinner and a quiet Christmas morning. How about you?"

"It was good," I said, before taking a sip of my tea. "Just me and the girls. I went along with what they wanted to do. It's easier that way, you know? We fixed our traditional quiche on Christmas Eve and opened presents Christmas morning."

"Not like the Christmases when the kids were little, but good in its own way," Jessie said, looking wistfully at her Christmas tree. I nodded in agreement. Big Jack stood beside me and rested his head on my lap. I caressed him behind his ears.

"Your house looks great. Is that table new?" I asked, pointing to a lamp table by the window.

"No, it was here last summer, but it was covered with books and papers probably." Jessie laughed. "Speaking of papers, I was wondering if you would mind helping me sort through some stacks of papers in my office tomorrow?"

"Sure," I said. "My flight doesn't leave until four o'clock."

"Lovely," said Jessie. "That will give us more time to visit. Tim will be fixing dinner tonight. They're house-sitting for some friends down the road. They should be here in a few hours. Come on and I'll show you your room."

At the top of the stairs was a small bedroom with a bright-yellow comforter and matching curtains. "Oh wow!" I said. "This looks so bright and cheerful."

"Yes," agreed Jessie. "Every little bit of brightness helps on winter days like these. The bathroom is down the hall next to my bedroom."

"Thanks, Jessie. This bed looks so comfortable. Would you mind if I take a little nap?"

"Of course not. I'll go downstairs and watch TV, but I'll probably doze off too."

Two hours later I staggered down the stairs. Jessie and the dogs were watching TV.

"I'm sorry. I didn't mean to sleep so long. I don't know what happened." I sat down in a chair across from the sofa. The dogs were dozing but, once again, Big Jack joined me.

"Hey, it's okay." Jessie smiled. "You must have needed the rest. Quite a party last night, huh?"

"No, quite the opposite," I answered. I told her all about my unfortunate New Year's Eve. She listened attentively, her blue eyes softening as the story unfolded.

"My God, Diane. What an ordeal! I'm glad you're safe. Anyone could have followed you back to the hostel."

"Yeah, I know, but I was aware of my surroundings. Besides, I think everyone out that night was more interested in getting plastered than in paying any attention to me."

"Well, maybe so, but you know what's weird?" Jessie paused. "A past concert of The Saw Doctors was on RTÉ last night."

"You're kidding!"

"Nope," she replied. "You could have been here nestled on the sofa with an Irish coffee watching it with me."

"Damn! I would've much preferred that to being shoved against the stage by a bunch of drunks."

"I'll bet," she agreed. "But at least you got a good story out of it. Just don't do that again."

"Not to worry," I laughed.

Just then the dogs began a ruckus and ran to the door. In came Tim and Siobhan each carrying a bag of groceries.

"Happy New Year!" I said, standing up to receive their hugs.

"Well look what the new year brought us!" Tim laughed, putting down the grocery bag to give me a hug. Siobhan did the same.

"It's so good to see you both," I said. "I hear you're cooking dinner tonight, Tim."

"Indeed, a delicious pasta dish with fresh sausage is on the menu. You do like sausage, don't you?"

"Oh dear, I'm afraid Diane is vegetarian," Jessie piped in.

"It's okay," I said. "I can eat the sausage. Don't go to any trouble for me." *Damn, I hope I can stomach it, but I don't want them to make a big deal about my food preferences.*

"Are you sure, Diane?" Tim asked.

"Yes, I'm sure."

"Brilliant! Let's catch up a little before I head to the kitchen."

"Have you enjoyed your visit so far?" asked Siobhan.

"Well, yes and no," I said. I told her about my visits with Anne and the Sullivans before I repeated the story of the New Year's Eve debacle.

"Oh, my dear girl, what possessed you to go to the Black Box on New Year's Eve?" asked Siobhan.

"Right so," Tim chimed in. "That could have been dangerous, especially for a woman by herself."

I told them about my talk with Ollie Jennings and assured them I was fine.

"What about the young man passed out in the street," asked Tim. "Did you ever find out what happened to him?"

"No, I don't have any idea. I would like to think that he is okay now. I prayed for him all the way to Doolin."

Tim filled me in on his teaching job in Ballyvaughan, and Siobhan told me how busy she was with Salmon Poetry.

"It sounds like things are better for Salmon," I said.

"Much better," said Jessie. "We received a grant from the Arts Council and that got us above water."

"Then we were able to publish a slew of wonderful poets," added Siobhan.

"I'm so glad things are better. I was worried last summer."

"So were we!" they both said.

With that, Tim and Siobhan excused themselves to the kitchen. Jessie and I decided to brave the chilly mist and pay a visit to Clint and Hilly. Clint saw us approaching and galloped to the fence. Hilly stood back, her feet planted in place.

"Hee-haw! Hee-haw!" Clint roared. I took his head in my arms and nuzzled him.

"Clint, my friend, how are you? I missed you, old buddy." Clint nuzzled even more, making whining sounds as if to say "I missed you too."

I took several shots of Clint. He seemed more than happy to pose. Hilly, not so much. When we walked back to the house we were serenaded by Clint's pathetic cries.

"Poor Clint," I said.

"Oh don't worry about him," said Jessie. "He's fine. He can be such a spoiled baby sometimes."

We laughed and walked to the house, where a delicious dinner awaited us. As tasty as it was, I struggled with the sausage, even hiding a few pieces under the pasta and hoping no one noticed.

The next morning I sat on the floor in Jessie's office sorting stacks of papers into piles. One for the trash, one for things she should look at, and one for things I wasn't sure about. Jessie was busy at her computer, but we carried on a conversation.

"Did you apply for the fellowship again this year?" asked Jessie, peering up from her computer screen.

"Yes, I applied," I sighed. "Let's see, this is the fifth year now. I'll know around St. Patrick's Day."

"Is your proposal about Ireland, still?"

"Oh, yes. As always. Something about immersing myself in the folklore and culture of Ireland."

"Well, I hope you get it."

"Thanks, Jessie. I do too, but I'm not holding my breath."

"Will you be coming back anyway?"

"Yes, I've said from the time I first applied that not receiving the fellowship wouldn't determine whether or not I travel to Ireland—even if I go broke in the process."

"You won't," Jessie said. "You were meant to be here and you'll return."

I said goodbye to Jessie and her animals later that afternoon and drove to Shannon Airport to catch my flight home. Although I remained ambivalent about whether or not I should have made this trip, I had no doubt that I would return next summer. I would want to see Jessie and Anne again and explore new places. Ireland had become so much a part of me. But, as it turned out, life had a way of intruding on my plans. I took on more and more responsibility at my school. My daughters needed help with their expenses. Since their dad wasn't around and wasn't willing to help, that left me to pick up the slack. The extra expense ate into my travel budget. On top of that, my mom's health continued to deteriorate, necessitating many trips to her home in Texas. My beloved greyhounds, Eddy and Rosie, died within three years of each other from bone cancer. And, no, I didn't receive what I came to refer to as "that damn fellowship."

Although Julian of Norwich continued to assure me that "all would be well," it would be six more summers before I would return to Ireland.

PART FOUR

Bloomin' in the Burren and the Beara

All our hurts we wade through,
still we find,
blackberry time.

Luka Bloom

Introduction

FINALLY, AFTER ten attempts, my proposal won over the anonymous committee of educators, and I was awarded the Lilly Teacher Creativity Fellowship. I was both surprised and elated when I opened my mailbox and saw the big white envelope on top. I was expecting to see the regular-sized envelope containing the rejection letter. I immediately contacted my friends and family with the good news. They were elated too. I had $8,000 (before taxes) to spend toward my goals of mastering the techniques of digital photography, honing my writing skills, and immersing myself in the land and culture of western and southwestern Ireland. I had three months to prepare for a three-week stay—half in the Burren studying with a renowned landscape photographer, and the other half working with writer and editor Sue Booth-Forbes at Anam Cara Writers Retreat in Eyeries, Beara Peninsula, County Cork.

As I finished up my twenty-ninth year of teaching, I was consumed with making contacts for the photography and writing workshops and securing airline reservations, vouchers for B&Bs, an Irish cell phone, car rental, and photo lenses and filters.

Jessie and Anne were pumped that, after six years, I was finally coming back.

"Can't wait to see you," said Jessie. "We can go exploring!"

"With the dogs?" I asked.

"Of course! They're anxious to see you too."

Anne talked about all the fun we would have.

"We'll take a long walk on the beach and visit some pubs. You can sing a tune or two."

"Only if you sing with me," I laughed. "By the way, do you know what Luka's schedule will be? Does he have any gigs planned for June or July?"

"I don't know yet, luv," she answered, "but either way, I know he would like to see you. He enjoyed visiting with you after his last gig in Chicago a few years ago. That photo of the two of you was so cute."

"Tell me about it," I laughed. "My parents saw the photo and already had us married! I had to explain to them that we're just acquaintances, but they weren't buying it."

"Ha! Ye gotta love parents who want their daughter to be happy," Anne said. "Speaking of Luka, do ye have tickets for his Chicago gig this May?"

"Yes, and I'm bringing my daughter and son-in-law with me."

"Brilliant! I'll tell him that yer coming."

"Thanks, Anne," I said. "I'll check in later to see if he wants to have dinner with us before the show."

"Excellent. I'm so glad yer coming back," said Anne.

"Me too."

A lot had changed in the last six years. My oldest daughter married and moved to Chicago. My youngest became engaged, and she and her fiancée offered to house-sit during my trip. I was so relieved that my daughters had found good, responsible partners. So much of the previous parental responsibility was off my shoulders now. I was dogless and free to travel without having the expense of a boarding kennel.

My school had a new, young principal, and I could sense a shift in the school system's priorities, with the school library program quickly plummeting down the list. My school leadership role was diminishing and a new, much younger, female teaching staff was taking over. All of them looked alike to me, tall and slender with long light-brown or blond hair and a superior attitude. I had trouble matching their names with their faces. I was still dedicated to the importance of instilling a love of reading in students while the new teachers were dedicated to measuring and evaluating data. I felt more and more undervalued. My years of experience meant nothing to them. Ageism, very prevalent in the teaching profession, was rearing its ugly head. Despite the number of years my fellowship proposals had been rejected, this felt like the right time to receive it. Winning the fellowship boosted my self-confidence and highlighted my talent to the rest of the school community. Still, I knew that my position was in jeopardy.

Things had changed in Ireland too. It was reeling from the economic recession that had enveloped much of the world. The Celtic Tiger, Ireland's economic boom, was dead. The Irish, whose bread and butter was tourism, were begging tourists to return, and they were willing to lower their prices to lure the tourists back. The young Irish were once again leaving the country to find employment.

In many ways, at least externally, life was much the same as it had been. Being in a romantic relationship was as elusive as ever, but the years had made me more accepting of that fact. There was no more dreaming about unattainable men or of being in a romantic, supportive relationship with anyone.

I had grown quite accustomed to doing things by myself and being alone was second nature to me. Fortunately, I was blessed with deep, lasting friendships that nourished me and kept me grounded, along with the promise of being a grandmother someday. My internal life, though, was in transition. My spiritual journey continued to grow. I practiced contemplative prayer nearly every day, resulting in a more positive and patient attitude. I devoured books by spiritual writers from all faiths, and I became more at home in my own spiritual beliefs. I began meeting monthly with a spiritual director, a nun, whose kind and compassionate counsel encouraged me along my path. She "got" me, and I felt so grateful for her friendship.

June finally arrived, and I packed my suitcase with everything I thought I would need. It weighed fifty-four pounds, largely due to the extra photography equipment and computer gear, leaving just a little room to bring home extra treasures. I felt excited, nervous, and apprehensive, but happy for the opportunity to return to the friends and the country I had missed so much. I was ready for a new adventure to begin.

CHAPTER THIRTY

Cliff Crawling

I WAS CRAWLING on my hands and knees along the trail behind the Sullivans' house to the Cliffs of Moher. Only I wasn't sure I was still on the trail. It wasn't marked well. Maybe I had veered onto a secondary trail meant for those who loved the thrill of looking over the edge. Being afraid of heights, I wasn't one of them. I was alone and petrified that the strong wind would hurl me over the edge into the air and onto the rocks below. I couldn't see the edge, but I knew it was close. The curving edge of tall, blowing grass made it impossible to determine where it ended and certain death from falling began. I had touted my camera gear a couple of miles already, passing fields of horses and cows. Feeling brave, I had ignored the BEWARE OF THE BULL sign and trudged on, crawling under barbed wire fences and getting shocked by the electrified ones meant for keeping the livestock away from the cliffs. I wasn't feeling so brave now.

"Oh, shit," I sobbed. "This can't be happening!"

The saying about one's life flashing before one's eyes in times like these is true. Mine did—in flashes of Technicolor detail capturing me in kindergarten, at a high school dance, my wedding day, rocking my infant daughters, and working in my library. It was too much. There was so much more I wanted to experience—more love, more travel, more everything.

"Dammit, God," I shouted, raising my fist to the heavens. "You didn't bring me all the way over here to fall off a cliff, did you?" I tried again to crawl uphill, but the wind picked up, blocking my attempt to move in that direction. It was always windy along the cliffs, but the relentless gusts were stronger than usual. Not only was I frustrated, but now I was furious too. "Is this your idea of a joke, God?" I screamed. "And what about you, Julian of Norwich?" I shouted mockingly. "Are all things well now?" I knew better than that, but my anger had fueled my adrenaline, and I used that adrenaline to fling my body toward the hill away from the edge. It worked. Eventually, I was able to cling to my camera equipment and stand upright. My beige hiking pants were splattered with mud, and my hiking boots reeked of cow manure. I didn't care. Relieved, but still frustrated, I made the decision to hike up to the coast road instead of risking another mile on the trail to the Cliffs of Moher Visitor Centre.

As I walked, tired and hungry, I thought about what had just happened, realizing how close I'd come to dying. Or at least I thought I'd come close. I didn't really know how close to the edge I had actually been, but it was close enough to scare the bejesus out of me. An average of eight people per year fall to their deaths from the Cliffs of Moher. The vast majority of those falls being accidental, just as mine would have been. My knees were still shaking, my mouth was dry, and that mile-long walk seemed to take forever.

Brendan Sullivan was to blame for my brush with death. Or so I told myself. Shortly after my return to his Doolin Farmhouse, he had waxed eloquently about the benefits of hiking the trail to the cliffs as opposed to driving to the new visitor center and paying eight euros to park across the road. "The trail's rough," he had said. (A vast understatement, it turned out.) "But walk to the cliffs, then, and take a moment to look at the faces of those who came on one of the tour buses. Ye will know that ye've had such a richer experience for it." He had neglected to mention the risk of being blown over the edge. I wanted to tell him off, but I realized that, seasoned hiker that he was, he had simply underestimated my navigational skills. I had only myself to blame for wandering off the trail and getting too close to the edge.

The Celtic Tiger had pounced onto the visitor center before the recession hit and turned it into what to me was an unwanted extravaganza. Now billed as the Cliffs of Moher Experience, the previous, humble cottage-like visitor center had been replaced with a modern, expansive limestone-brick-and-glass edifice built into the side of a hill. The ample new parking lot had been moved across the coast road and was filled with tourist buses and hundreds of cars. I couldn't help but look at it and recall how, during my first visit, the attendant had waved me through the gate late one evening in the original lot, telling me there was no need to pay. That wouldn't happen now. Everything was touristy, from the expansive snack bar to the enormous interactive multimedia "experience" with nothing lacking except an adequate number of toilets. As for photographing the cliffs, I didn't bother because new, tourist-filled fenced trails had been created so that any full-view photo would be peopled with tourists. I knew that I could erase them in the final image but having to put forth the effort to do so ticked me off. Instead, I ate a sandwich in the snack bar and decided to take a chance and call Jessie.

Jessie hadn't responded to my last few emails, so I was nervous about whether or not she was sick again as well as if and when we might meet. Thankfully, she was home. I told her where I was and how I'd gotten there.

"Ahh, Diane. That is too bad. That trail can be treacherous. Are you all right?"

"Yeah, I'm okay," I said. "But I sure could use a rest. There's no way I can hike back to the Sullivans' right now. Would it be okay for me to come over?"

"Well," Jessie hesitated, "I don't know. I'm really not feeling up to speed right now."

Jessie was pulling the "I don't feel good" excuse on me again, and I didn't have the patience for it after what I had just been through.

"Jessie, I won't be any bother, I promise," I pleaded. "I'm really in a mess here."

"Well, I don't know . . . maybe tomorrow? I might feel better then."

"Jessie, we haven't seen each other in six years! Maybe you would feel better if you had a little company."

"I do want to see you." Jessie paused, and my heart raced. "Well, yes, it's okay for you to come over."

"Thanks, Jessie," I said, feeling such a sense of relief. "I have to trudge up your hill, so it might take me a bit. My legs feel like aching jelly. You'll know I'm there when the dogs start barking."

Jessie laughed. "Yes, that's true. Be careful and I'll see you soon."

I crossed the coast road and headed up the narrow, curving lane to her house, all the while wishing that I had worked out more before coming over here. I came to her neighbor's cottage, the bodhran player who had hit on me in the pub. Thankfully, he wasn't home, so I was spared the sight of seeing him in his boxer shorts and wellies. A little farther at the top of the hill overlooking Liscannor Bay was Jessie's house. The dogs began barking as soon as they sensed my presence. Jessie met me at the door.

"Oh, Diane, there you are!" Jessie wrapped her arms around me and gave me a big hug as the excited dogs jumped in a circle around us.

"Thanks for seeing me on such short notice, Jessie," I said while trying to brush some of the mud off my pants. "As you can see, I'm a mess."

"Oh my God, you are!" Jessie said, looking me up and down. "Are you sure you're all right?"

"I'm just tired and a little weak-kneed, but I'm so glad to be here." I took off my muddy hiking boots and left them on the step. The dogs and I followed her into the house.

"Wow, Jessie, you've done some remodeling!"

"Yes," said Jessie. "And wait till you see this." I followed her to a door on the other side of the office. "Ta da!" She opened the door with a flourish to reveal a lovely furnished living room with a wood burner. "It's an addition for Tim, Siobhan, and Eve. There are two bedrooms on the other side. We did this so they could live with me yet have their privacy too."

"It's beautiful, Jessie! And so thoughtful of you too. It must be a comfort to have them so close. And to be able to spend time with your granddaughter whenever you want. By the way, congratulations on becoming a grandmother! She is such a beautiful child."

"Truly, she is. She's an angel. But I have more to show you," she said. "Come, follow me out back." I followed her through the kitchen and out the back door with the five dogs trying to nose their way in front of me.

"Big Jack, Zeke, Freck, Shannon, Zena," Jessie scolded. "Have you no manners?"

I laughed. "They just want to lead the tour too."

"Take a look at this," Jessie said, pointing to a darling tiny house, complete with a door, two windows, and a red roof. A full-size one-room doll house without the dolls. Inside, the room was large enough for a desk, office chair, and a comfy reading nook.

"Wow! Your own private retreat?" I asked.

"It's my writing shed," Jessie answered, her eyes brightening. "I'm going to write my memoir here."

"What a great idea!"

"Yes. People have been after me for years to write it, and I've been wanting to do it. No more excuses now. I have the ideal space to write."

"And what a story you have to tell," I added. "It's perfect for you. Now, when are you going to write it?"

"Oh, I don't know." Jessie hemmed and hawed. "Eventually." We laughed and went back inside. "I'll make some tea, and we can catch up," she said, heading for the kitchen.

We talked all afternoon, drinking cups of tea around her kitchen table and highlighting our happenings over the past six years. Jessie was thrilled that I had received the fellowship, and I was both happy and relieved that her business was doing so well. And clearly, our talk over tea brightened her mood.

"Are you hungry?" Jessie asked.

"Yes, I am," I said. "I haven't eaten since breakfast."

"Let's go to Stonecutters," said Jessie.

"Great idea!" I said as we both got up from the table and rounded up the dogs. "It'll be just like old times. We can eat banoffee pie."

"Ahh, yes," said Jessie in a dreamy voice. "We'll be in heaven."

The dogs followed us to the car and we piled in. Big Jack leaned forward from the backseat and parked his head between me and Jessie. Down the hill we went toward Stonecutters with the windows down and the dogs happily panting all the way.

Everything at Stonecutters was the same as six years before. We were led to a table by the window so that we could keep an eye on the dogs. We had a delicious dinner topped off with the banoffee pie.

"Oh my God, this is so good," I said between bites.

"Mmm," Jessie replied. "I could eat this stuff all night."

Jessie wanted to take the dogs for a walk in the nearby village of Ennistymon, so we piled back into the car and drove to the Falls Hotel, where there was a stream perfect for walking along. It was a gorgeous summer evening—warm and sunny with a light breeze. The air felt enchanted to me, and as we left the car and walked toward the water, I wouldn't have been surprised to see fairies skittering along the stream's edge. But there weren't any fairies that I could see, just the dogs galloping straight into the water. Zeke was the first dog in. He quickly found a large stone to carry around in his mouth (one of his favorite things) and splashed downstream with the others following. None of the dogs were leashed and I worried that they might run off, but with a slight high whistle, Jessie had them under her control. They ran and played ahead of us while Jessie and I strolled along the stream enjoying the beautiful evening and each other's company. After my perilous adventure earlier in the day, this peaceful evening with a friend was exactly what I needed to come back into myself and, for the first time since my arrival, feel content.

It was after eight thirty when we gathered the dogs and drove back to Jessie's. It was a monumental ride, with all five wet dogs jockeying for a place closest to Jessie and me, their soaked snouts and hot breath brushing against our necks. I recalled my previous eccentric car rides with them years before and decided that this ride topped all the others.

"Shoot, Jessie," I said as we left the car and walked toward the lawn chairs with a view of Liscannor Bay, "I haven't been in touch with the Sullivans since I left for my hike this morning. I'd better call them. They're probably worried that I've had an accident on the trail." Chuckling at the irony of what I'd just said, I pulled out my cell phone and punched in their number. Sixteen-year-old Rory answered and seemed amused by my apology for not being in touch. "Ma and Da were wondering what happened to ye," he said. "But Ma told Da that ye could take care of yerself."

"Well, that's right—sort of," I said. "Just tell them that I'm at a friend's house up the road aways and that she'll be bringing me back soon."

"Brilliant," he said. "I'll let 'em know."

"Rory is such a young man now," I told Jessie. "When I checked in yesterday I was amazed at how the boys had grown. Ronan is a preteenager now who lives for soccer, and Finn isn't a toddler anymore but still has a mind of his own."

"How are their parents getting on?" asked Jessie.

"They seem to be doing fine. They have a hectic life with the three active boys, along with running the B&B and the farm, but they seem happy. They're such a great family."

"They're well-liked and active in the community, that's for sure," said Jessie. "Did you notice the white dog running around at Stonecutters?" She didn't wait for me to answer.

"It seems that the Sullivans' dog had a liaison with the Stonecutters' owner's dog which resulted in . . ."

"You mean Murphy fathered that white dog?" Jessie nodded. "Why that sly old dog!" I laughed. "I would've thought he was too old for that."

"Apparently not," laughed Jessie. "They're trying to find a home for her."

"So, you gonna take her?" I asked. "You already have five. What's one more?"

"I think one more might just put even me over the edge." Jessie laughed.

"How is your neighbor doing?" I asked. "It didn't look like he was home when I passed his cottage. Is he still posing in his boxer shorts and wellies?"

"Actually, he has turned himself around. He's not drinking like he was, if at all, and he's living part of the year in Greece. That's where he is now."

"That's fantastic, Jessie," I said. "I'm so glad to hear that. I'll miss seeing him in his boxer shorts and wellies, but I guess that's the price I'll have to pay for him getting sober. It's worth it."

"It certainly is," agreed Jessie. "He was always a good man with heart, but now even more so."

Jessie dropped me off at the Sullivans' around ten o'clock just as the sun was setting over the Atlantic behind their house. She invited me to a poetry reading she was hosting at the town hall in Ennistymon the following Friday. I told her I would try my best to be there.

I checked out of the Sullivans' the following morning so that I could move to a B&B closer to where my photography workshop was being held. Brendan was already out in the fields, but Maeve gave me a hug as Rory carried my suitcase down the stairs and loaded it into my car.

"You and Brendan have done a great job raising the boys," I told her.

"Thank ye, Diane. We're very proud of them."

"As you should be," I said. We stood in the driveway looking at each other, each feeling the awkward pause. Maeve broke the silence.

"I'm so glad ye came back, Diane," she said with a smile. "We're going to miss ye." She took my hand. "Please stay with us again when ye come back."

I nodded and gave her a hug, but I didn't tell her what I was thinking. I was thinking that while I loved the Sullivans, I felt that my time with them had run its course. The boys were much older now. Rory would be going to college in a couple of years. My room had seemed too small this time. There was too much noise from the other lodgers. Maybe I would stay with them again and maybe I wouldn't. I waved to Maeve and blew her a kiss as I drove away.

CHAPTER THIRTY-ONE

Foxglove Farm and the Terrible Tutor

I HAD SOME time to kill before I could check into the B&B, so I decided to revisit Inisheer. Maeve told me the boat service was offering discounts to tourists in order to beef up business. I parked by the Doolin pier, bought my ticket for the next trip, and waited and waited. The weather had been a mixture of sun, then clouds and rain and then sun again. I knew that the boat's departure time was dependent upon the weather, so I found a place to sit out of the wind and rain and waited some more.

The rain finally let up and we were able to board the boat for Inisheer. On the way I glanced at the cliffs and shivered. The sheer drop straight down onto the rocks and the swirling water below scared the bejesus out of me. *God, I came so close.*

Inisheer didn't have the romance it had once held for me. Maybe it was the weather—slightly chilly and rainy—or maybe, being here for the third time, I noticed how touristy it had become over the years. There were old men in shabby horse-drawn wagons offering rides up the hill to O'Brien's Castle, and some makeshift booths had been set up near the pier by locals selling their wares. When I ate my lunch, the restaurant was filled with chatty people, but they looked right through me as if I was invisible. It's not that this hadn't happened before, but this time I was left feeling lonely and tired. I took some photos of the stonewalled landscape and captured a candid moment of several local fishermen sitting at the bar in their waterproof overalls and boots. Staying busy helped to quell the loneliness and pass the time. As the time to board the boat approached, I was good and ready to get back to Doolin and check into my next bed and breakfast.

I drove northeast of Doolin down one-lane roads until I came to the driveway for Foxglove Farm. The two-story white farmhouse with green shutters looked welcoming and the grounds were immaculately landscaped with lilies, foxgloves, fuchsia, and all kinds of greenery. I parked in the wide driveway close to the house and walked to the front door. A young woman with long dark curly hair greeted me. She was tall and big-boned with clear, glowing skin.

"You must be Diane," she said. "Welcome!" I was surprised by her American accent. "Let me find Ella, and she will decide where to put you." She walked toward the back of the house and called out, "Ella, Diane is here."

"That's good," I heard an older voice with an Irish accent say. "I'll be right there."

I stood in the foyer admiring the fireplace and high-quality but comfortable-looking furniture in the adjoining rooms. The inside was as immaculate as the outside.

Ella joined us. "Hello, Diane. How many nights are ye staying with us?"

"Three," I answered.

Ella was tall and thin with short coifed red hair. She appeared to be at least in her mid-sixties. She spoke in a thick western Irish accent and moved about in a brisk businesslike manner.

"Ye have such a large suitcase, dear. I wouldn't want ye to have to carry it up these stairs. Besides, wouldn't ye want to have a bit more privacy anyway?" She paused and looked at Melissa. "Let's put her in the studio apartment," she said.

"Great idea," said Melissa.

Ella looked at me and smiled. "That way, ye can have some extra room to spread out. It's attached to the house, but ye will have yer own entrance. Melissa will take ye there and give ye the key."

"Thank you," I said before following Melissa out the door. "I'm really grateful to you."

"Ah, don't mention it, darlin. Enjoy yer stay."

Melissa opened the door to the annex, and we stepped inside.

"Wow!" I said. "This is incredible." The sitting room was bright and airy with hardwood floors and a sofa with colorful throw pillows. Beyond the sitting room was a large bedroom with an ensuite bathroom. "I can't believe this," I said to Melissa. "This is the perfect place for relaxing and editing my photos."

"I'm so glad this works for you," Melissa said as she walked toward the door. "Enjoy yourself and let me know if you need anything."

"Uh, Melissa, I couldn't help but notice your American accent. What brings you to Ireland?" I asked as I sat down on the comfortable sofa.

"I arranged to come here for six months through an organization called WOLF, that is Willing Workers for Organic Farming. I help with the farming and assist Ella with serving breakfast. I'm doing this so that I can decide whether or not I want to buy and run a farm back in the States."

"And have you made a decision yet?"

"Well," she said, twirling a strand of her hair with her finger, "I'm realizing that I probably wouldn't be able to do it without a partner."

"Who knows, you might meet someone with the same interest in running a farm," I said.

"Maybe," she laughed as she opened the door, "but that hasn't happened yet."

As I settled in and began to unpack, I suddenly realized how exhausted I felt. It was as if jet lag or my treacherous morning on the cliffs had snuck up behind me to surprise me with brain fog and the urge to stretch out on the sofa. The thought of having to go out for dinner just added to my exhaustion. I needed to get up early in the morning to begin my photography instruction with Sean in Ballyvaughan. I needed to rest. I decided to take a chance and ask Melissa for something to eat. I explained to her how tired I was and how I didn't have the energy to go out. She took pity on me and made the most delicious cheese sandwich I've ever had—several slices of cheddar cheese, crisp lettuce, a slice of tomato, and mayonnaise sandwiched between two slices of homemade Irish brown bread. She included potato chips and a tall glass of ice water too. I couldn't thank her enough.

Early the next morning I had a delicious breakfast with the other guests before making the thirty-minute drive to Ballyvaughan. Sean wanted to meet in a café on the main drag, which meant I had to parallel park. After maneuvering the car backward and forward several times and steering from the opposite angle I was accustomed to, I finally managed to tuck the car between two others without incident. I breathed a sigh of relief, grabbed my camera gear, and entered the café. The tables were covered with red-and-white checked vinyl cloths and most of them were empty. I glanced at one of the tables by the window and saw Sean sitting with an older man close to my age. The older man's eyes smiled behind his black-rimmed glasses and his graying brown hair and plaid short-sleeved shirt made him blend right in with any other middle-aged man. I wondered what was going on. This was supposed to be a one-on-one workshop.

Sean introduced me to Gary from Dublin, indicating that he would be participating in the workshop too. Sean's communication skills left a lot to be desired. His responses to my emails about the best lens to buy for landscapes, the lightest tripod that wouldn't blow over, and the most efficient backpack had been met with vague answers or none at all. He never mentioned adding Gary to the group either. I had paid the one-on-one fee. I wondered what Gary had paid.

I joined them at the table and Sean gave a short review of exposure, shutter speed, and other basics. Gary seemed nice enough, and he followed Sean's instructions intently. As the lesson wound down, I asked for an agenda for the rest of the workshop.

"Uh, I don't have a formal agenda, like," Sean answered. "Much of it depends on the weather and since it's sunny today, I thought I could drive us into the Burren and perhaps we could photograph the wildflowers."

In the small amount of communication we had shared before my trip, Sean never mentioned how I might want to consider purchasing a close-up macro lens for taking flower photos. Instead, he said that I should buy a fixed wide-angle lens for landscapes, which I did and which turned out to be useless. I would have to rely on my zoom lens for the flowers. And I was surprised that he didn't have an agenda or lesson plan. This seemed strange for someone who had taught photography at the prestigious Burren College of Art.

On the way to Sean's car, Gary leaned toward me and whispered, "I thought he would be more organized."

"Me too," I whispered back. "And it doesn't look like he has any handouts either."

Sean drove us out of Ballyvaughan and onto the narrow one-lane roads of the Burren. The scenery was beautiful: flat fields topped with huge boulders and Mt. Mullaghmore in the distance. Sean drove very fast down the narrow roads—too fast. Gary and I hung on for dear life. He did stop briefly to show us the house that appeared in the Father Ted television series, but then he gunned it once more and we went flying down the road.

"Sean, what are you doing? Slow down!" I yelled as I was slammed against the car door. "You're driving too fast!"

"I'm not driving that fast," answered Sean, slightly amused. "There are many others who drive faster than this."

"Then those blokes are crazy!" shouted Gary from the back seat. "For the safety of everyone you must slow down now!"

Sean did as he was told, though he seemed disappointed at losing the opportunity to show off. Finally he pulled to the side of the road and stopped. "This is an excellent spot for wildflowers," he said. Gary and I piled out of the car as fast as we could, eager to stand still on solid ground. Sean walked ahead of us and we lagged behind. Gary whispered, "I'm a driving instructor in Dublin. He is crazy for driving like that. He could have gotten us killed."

"I'll bet he would have flunked your class," I said with a wink.

"You bet he would've. I hope he's better at tutoring than he is driving."

I decided that having Gary in the workshop wasn't a bad idea after all.

What followed were two days of taking photos in the Burren with little or no instruction from our tutor. He seemed more intent on taking his own photos. The more photos he took, the angrier I became. I began to call him over to assist me whenever he was in the middle of a shot. Gary caught on quickly and did the same. Sean didn't seem bothered one way or the other.

The third day Sean wanted us to drive to his house in Kilkenny so that he could teach us the finer points of editing. (I chuckled to myself when he used the word "teach.") Gary suggested that we could ride together and that he would drive. I was all for that, so we decided to meet at the church parking lot in Doolin. The drive took over an hour and that gave us plenty of time to chat. Gary said that he and his wife had amicably divorced three years ago and that they have four daughters.

"Four daughters!" I said. "Man, I nearly died raising two daughters! I can't imagine four!"

"Aye we had our trials, that's true. But they are good-hearted girls, and they've grown into successful young women. I'm very proud of them."

"And I'm sure they're proud to be your daughters," I added. We sat in companiable silence for a moment, each in our own thoughts, before I asked, "By the way, did you teach them to drive?"

"Oh no," Gary laughed, straightening his glasses. "Let's not talk about that."

We continued to talk about where we lived and worked as well as the cultural differences between Ireland and the United States all the while enjoying the sunny but windy day as we passed through serene villages along the beautiful Atlantic coast. I was reminded of my favorite Seamus Heaney poem, "The Peninsula," where he speaks of the big soft buffetings coming at the car sideways and blowing the heart open.

Sean was waiting for us when we pulled into his driveway. He invited us into his white modern cottage and escorted us to a small room in the back where he kept his big-screen Mac computer. Sean said that his wife was at work. "She's a nurse," he told us, "and loves her job." They had a toddler named Alec who was at day care. Except for breaking for lunch in his kitchen, we spent the rest of the day learning about Lightroom software as he demonstrated the editing process—using his photos of course. Gary and I agreed that this was the most useful part of the workshop, since he actually did some teaching. As we were leaving, he gave us autographed copies of his latest photography book. The photos were gorgeous and technically perfect, but the book was large and heavy. I wondered how I was going to get it home.

On the drive back to Doolin Gary said, "No doubt he's a brilliant photographer, but he's a terrible tutor."

"Yes," I said. "It just goes to show that no matter how well you know a subject, it doesn't mean you can teach it."

"Right so," Gary agreed. "I guess that explains why he doesn't teach at Burren College of Art anymore."

"Yeah, that should have been a red flag." I fumbled in my backpack for a mint and offered one to Gary. "You know," I said, setting my backpack on the floor, "considering how much we paid for this workshop, I wonder if we should ask for some of our money back?"

"In fairness, I doubt that it would do any good," Gary answered. "He didn't present us with any guarantee-type contract, like, so we really don't have any recourse."

"You're right," I sighed. "I don't like to burn bridges anyway. Who knows, I might need his recommendation someday. Besides, he has a wife and toddler to support, although I imagine his wife does most of it with her nursing job."

"Aye, fair play to her," said Gary.

"So, are you driving back to Dublin this evening?" I asked as we turned onto the road to Doolin.

"No, I want to take the boat to one of the Aran Islands this evening," he said. "I'll spend the night and drive home in the morning." He turned into the church parking lot and pulled up alongside my car. "It's been lovely being in this class with ye. I don't know how I could've gotten through it without ye."

"And I feel the same, Gary," I said as I tried getting out of the car as gracefully as possible while lugging my camera gear. "Safe travels. Thanks for driving and for being such a good classmate."

"And same to ye, Diane. Bye now."

I waved as he drove away thinking how nice it would have been if there had been a spark between us. But there wasn't.

Damn.

CHAPTER THIRTY-TWO

The Poetry Reading

ELLA WALKED me to the barn so that I could hang out with the cows. Ross, the border collie, followed close behind. He liked to hang out with the cows too, and apparently they liked to hang out with him.

"And here are the cows," said Ella, walking forward to pet one. "Go on, they love to be petted. Spoiled they are."

I leaned forward and ran my hand down the neck of a brown-and-white bull with soulful eyes. He leaned his head on my shoulder, his warm, moist breath against my ear.

"My uncle raised cows, but I wasn't around them much," I said. "I had no idea they were this cuddly."

"Aye, some are more friendly than others, but Liam Neeson here, well, he's a lover."

"Did you say Liam Neeson?" I asked, laughing as the bull moved even closer with a soft murmur as I scratched behind his ears.

"Indeed," she said. "All of my cows are named after movie stars. This one here is John Wayne." He looked at Ella when she said his name. She pointed to each stall and introduced the others. "Next is Clint Eastwood followed by Charlie Chaplin and Tom Hanks."

"And what is his name?" I asked, pointing to the next cow and hugging the lover boy tighter.

"That's Dracula," she answered. "I'm afraid his name doesn't quite suit him, like. I've thought about changing it to a romantic movie star like Daniel Day-Lewis or Cillian Murphy."

"Oh, I love Cillian Murphy," I gushed. "Those blue eyes . . ."

"Indeed. He's a dreamboat," Ella agreed.

"Oh, yeah, and he can act too," I added.

Ella laughed. "He's one of the great ones. Let's check on the chickens." I pulled away from Liam Neeson (he was not pleased and bellowed a *moo* to prove it.) We walked out of the barn with Ross in front of us and the cows mooing their disapproval behind us. The chicken coops were fenced a short distance behind the barn.

"I gather you've already heard the rooster," said Ella as she opened the gate and we stepped in. The rooster went berserk, flapping all over the chicken yard.

"Never mind him," said Ella with a dismissive wave of her hand. "He thinks he owns the place."

"What's his name?"

"Paddy."

"A good Irish name," I said.

"Right so," said Ella. She pointed at the hens. "And here are the girls—Katie, Frieda, Molly, and Lily."

"Hi girls," I called. Boy were they skittish! Squawking and moving fast, Frieda made a beeline to the henhouse followed by the others, except Paddy, who continued to let us know that we were invading his territory.

"Come," said Ella. "Let's walk back to the house and leave these nervous wrecks alone."

"Good idea," I said. "Ross, come here boy and walk with me." Ross came bounding across the barnyard and did just that.

I decided to extend my stay at Foxglove Farm to one week. I couldn't have asked for a better place, and I wanted to spend more time with Jessie and Anne. Jessie was hosting an evening of poetry reading at the Ennistymon Town Hall. Some of Ireland's best poets would be there, and, as an added bonus, a photographer would be exhibiting his underwater photos.

I dressed up as best I could for the poetry reading. Ella approved.

"Begobs, Diane," said Ella, coming out the front door carrying a basket full of laundry, "ye look so pretty this night."

"Thank you," I answered. "My friend, Jessie Lendennie, is hosting a poetry reading tonight in Ennistymon."

"Oh, lovely. I've heard good things about her, but I haven't had the pleasure of meeting her."

"Would you like to come with me?" I asked. "I promise my driving skills are pretty good on the road to Ennistymon."

"Oh, thank you, dear," she said. "But, as you can see, I'm afraid I have some things that need taking care of here." She walked toward what she referred to as the "laundry shed"—a separate building full of washers and dryers. Her own little laundromat. "Ye have a wonderful time, dear," she called over her shoulder.

I arrived in Ennistymon an hour early. The sun was beginning to set and the golden hour, that time of evening when the light is perfect for taking photos, would soon be here. I walked toward the Falls Hotel, the area where Jessie and I had walked her dogs, and wandered around taking photos. I reveled in the light becoming more and more golden. Being here, at this time of day, was more than I could have hoped for. I stopped on the bridge over the creek and looked toward town. The colorful shops were bathed in the golden light, and the creek's little waterfall made a perfect foreground. I took several shots before walking the few blocks to the town hall.

Jessie greeted me as I entered the large, square room filled with folding chairs and a lectern at the front. The walls were covered with underwater photos of dolphins and other sea life.

"Diane, you're here," said Jessie, giving me a hug. "I'm so glad you came."

"I wouldn't have missed it," I said, hugging her back.

"Come, let me introduce you to some of my friends who will be reading their poetry tonight," she said, taking my hand and guiding me across the room.

I felt shy about meeting these poets—similar to how I had felt the first time I met Jessie. All of them were published by Jessie's Salmon Poetry, and I had read enough of their poetry to know that they were first-rate poets. I, on the other hand, hadn't published anything.

First, Jessie introduced me to Nessa Mahoney. She was draped in a colorful scarf that highlighted her long, curly reddish hair.

"This is Diane, my friend from the States. She's here on holiday." *Please don't tell her I'm a writer,* I thought, *because she'll ask what I've published and then I'll have to explain how I haven't published anything yet!* Fortunately, she didn't mention it.

"It's so nice to meet ye, Diane," Nessa said, taking my hand. "Any friend of Jessie's is a friend of mine."

"Thank you," I said. "I've read some of your poetry, and I'm looking forward to hearing you read it."

"Well, I hope my reading does the poems justice." She laughed. She leaned closer and whispered, "I get downright nervous standing in front of a group of people, ye know. I hope I don't botch it up."

"Oh, I don't think you need to worry about that," I reassured her.

Hearing her talk about her nervousness made me feel less nervous, and as Jessie introduced me to the other poets, Kevin Higgins, Drucilla Wall, and Paul Perry, I felt more and more at ease. It was a fun gathering, not stuffy at all. It seemed like Jessie introduced me to everyone, and everyone seemed happy to meet me. Enjoying myself with a crowd of like-minded people was so different from my usual solo routine.

The photographer, a man of twentyish with short blond hair and bad breath, introduced himself to me and Drucilla. We both took a step back to distance ourselves from his breath.

"Taking these photos is my whole life," he said. "There's nothing I would rather be doing than taking underwater shots in County Clare."

"That must be wonderful to feel so passionate about something you love doing," I said. Drucilla took another step back and nodded in agreement.

"Oh, 'tis," he said, moving closer as we moved back. "I love it so much that I live in my truck, since housing here is beyond my means."

Drucilla and I didn't really know how to respond to that, so I quickly asked him some technical questions, and he was happy to go on and on about his camera gear. Drucilla and I stepped back again and exchanged glances.

"Well, I'm afraid it's almost time for the poetry reading, so I'd best get prepared," said Drucilla, pulling me along with her. "It was nice meeting ye."

"Oh, sweet Mary and Joseph," said Drucilla when we were out of his earshot. "I thought we would never get away!"

"I know," I said, taking a cup of punch from the refreshment table. "Do you think he really lives in his truck?"

"Who knows?" she answered. "I'm sure as hell not going to ask him! One thing's for sure though, he hasn't had the company of a toothbrush in quite some time."

"Yes," I said. "And you know what's sad? His photographs aren't that great. I mean, he has the technical skills, but the water has the same greenish, muddy-looking color to it, and the animals have that color too. It's like he's taking the same photo over and over."

"I'm afraid yer right," said Drucilla. "The poor lad."

Jessie motioned to Drucilla to come sit up front. I found a seat in the middle as Jessie introduced Nessa Mahoney, who, despite being nervous, did a wonderful fifteen-minute reading. Nessa was followed by the other poets. I loved all of it, and the evening flew by.

Afterward, Nessa took a photo of Jessie and me, our smiling faces cheek to cheek. I loved that she felt so much affection for me, this person she'd only seen twice. Again, I could feel the synchronicity at work. We were meant to meet at this point in our lives. I didn't know why. *Don't question it,* I told myself, *just go with the flow.*

And all shall be well, and all shall be well, and all manner of thing shall be well.

CHAPTER THIRTY-THREE

A Swim and a Session

"I DON'T BELIEVE in coincidences," said Anne.

We were walking on Sunset Beach on a warm, sunny, not-too-windy day. I was scheduled to return my rental car to the airport the next day and then board a bus to Cork city, where a driver would take me to Anam Cara Writers Retreat in the Beara Peninsula. I sensed that it would be a while before I would see Anne again. I wanted to make the best of our time together. I had driven to her home, a humble small white cottage just outside Miltown Malbay, for the day. We talked for a while before deciding to walk on the beach before lunch.

"Well, I don't believe in coincidences either," I answered. "I mean, just look at the synchronicity occurring in my relationship with Ireland," I said, stopping to pick up a shell. "I discover Luka's music by accident, feel so at home in County

Clare, meet you and Jessie and feel so close to both of you right away. All of it coming together at this time is no coincidence."

Anne looked at me and smiled. "Right so," she said, briefly touching my hand.

"I don't understand what the synchronicity is all about," I went on, "but I have no doubt that there's a higher purpose for this journey I'm on. I love being in Clare, but I have a sense that even better things are waiting for me in the Beara Peninsula."

"That's a very good possibility," said Anne. "Have you heard about the Buddhist retreat center there, Dzogchen Beara?"

"Yes, I've read a little about it. It's not too far from where I'm staying at Anam Cara, so I plan to visit and see what it's about."

"I can tell you that it's a wonderful, sacred, magical place," Anne said with a sly smile.

"You've been there?" I asked.

"Indeed I have. I attended a workshop there about a year ago on mindfulness and loving kindness." She stood still for a moment, a wave washing moss around her ankles. "It changed me life, I tell ye. I meditate every morning now, and I feel more at peace than I've ever felt. That's really something for me, ye know? I feel passionate about the world's injustices and at times the anger boils over in me. But not so much anymore. Meditation really helps, ye see. It helps me to focus on what's really important and to use my voice for change in a positive way."

"Wow, Anne, I'm so happy for you! What a wonderful experience. I can't wait to visit there myself."

"Ye will love it," said Anne. "Be sure to take some time to sit in the meditation room. It's full of windows that look out to sea. Very peaceful . . ." She paused. "Oh, I forgot to tell you, Luka is doing a benefit concert there."

"When?"

"July 10th."

I couldn't believe what I was hearing! "I'll be staying at the writers retreat then, so I can go!"

"Brilliant," said Anne.

"Jeez, talk about synchronicity!" I stopped and sat on one of the boulders scattered on the beach. Anne sat next to me. "I just saw him in Chicago, Anne. Please tell him that I'm not stalking him!"

"Oh, he'll get a laugh out of that one, he will," said Anne. We sat in silence for a moment, both of us looking out to sea. Anne stood up and said, "I'm going to take a wee swim. Would you like to join me?"

"No thanks. I don't have my suit," I said as Anne pulled off her shirt and pants to reveal a black swimsuit. I loved Anne's carefree spirit, how she was so unassuming and comfortable with her middle-aged body. "I'll walk on the beach some more while you swim," I said. "Take your time."

"All right, then. I shan't be long . . . just until the cold water takes over me bones." She bounded toward the water and squealed with glee as she dove into a wave.

I watched her taking freestyle strokes in the water as I walked along the beach shooting pictures of the bright-green foamy moss and the giant boulders standing like sentries guarding the shore. *You're so damn lucky to be here.* "I know," I said out loud.

Several minutes later, Anne came out of the water and stood behind a boulder, stripped off her suit, and quickly dressed. I met her at the boulder. "Let's go back to the house and have some lunch," she said. "I'm hungry!"

"Me too!"

Anne's husband, Davoc, was waiting for us and had set the round, wooden kitchen table for lunch. The two of them finished preparing the meal—soup and sandwiches on whole wheat buns—while I sat at the table and watched them move around the kitchen in sync with one another. *Only couples who have been happily married for a long time can do that,* I thought.

As we ate lunch, we talked about the local news, which inevitably led to the subject of trad Irish music. Davoc was a respected tin whistle musician who played regularly in the area pubs. He had recently begun to give Anne lessons.

"I'm not that good, ye know," said Anne.

"That's not true," said Davoc, looking at me. "She's making good progress, Diane."

"I would love to hear the two of you play," I said, then took the last bite of my sandwich.

"Right so," said Davoc as he stood up. "Let us clean up our lunch, and then we shall have a proper session."

"Let me help," I said, starting to get up.

"I won't hear of it," said Anne, taking my empty plate and bowl. "You sit and enjoy yerself."

Davoc went into the living room and came back with two tin whistles. He handed one to Anne and they sat back down at the table. Davoc's full head of gray hair and bespeckled smooth face belied the fact that he was several years older than his wife, and Anne looked ageless in her colorful bohemian blouse, a paisley scarf wrapped around her still-damp hair.

"Do you mind if I take some pictures?" I said, reaching for my camera bag.

"I knew ye were going to ask that," Anne mumbled dryly.

"Now what shall we play, dear?" asked Davoc.

"Ye choose and I'll join in," Anne answered.

"Let's begin with 'The Humours of Ennistymon.'"

"Right so, good choice," said Anne as she and Davoc put the tin whistles to their lips, and I prepared my camera for what I knew would be some classic photos.

They began to play, each in sync with the other, and I raised my camera. What followed was pure magic. Davoc was the master, but Anne clearly had been practicing and kept pace. I was transfixed and time seemed to stand still as they went on to play the "West Clare Jig" and "Rocky Road to Dublin." I took several photos, but I don't remember taking them. What will forever be seared into my memory is the image of this delightful, salt-of-the-earth couple sitting around their kitchen table making lovely music together, and what a privilege it was to witness it.

That evening Ella insisted on making an Irish coffee for me. We sat on the porch, and I recounted my day with Anne. Of course Ella knew her. Everyone seems to know her.

"Ah, yes, I got acquainted with Anne when I had a bed and breakfast in Miltown Malbay," said Ella. "She's doing well, I hope?"

"Yes," I said. "She's swimming in the ocean and learning to play the tin whistle among other things."

"That's Anne for ye. Always doing something to keep her on her toes." Ella laughed. "Well, fair play to her. I'm glad ye two are friends."

I took another sip of my Irish coffee. It was the best I'd ever tasted but was it ever strong! I was feeling a little dizzy.

"I really don't want to leave here," I blurted out.

"I know," Ella said. "Melissa and I have loved having you here. Ye've been such a delight, and ye are so brave to be doing all this travelin' on yer own."

"Thanks, Ella, but I don't think about being brave. I just knew that it was something I had to do for myself. Most of my adult life has been dedicated to being a wife, mother, and librarian. That's been my identity. I married young, so I never had the chance to know who I was by myself. Now I have that opportunity."

"So what are you learning about yourself, Diane?" asked Ella.

"How much time do you have?" I laughed. "Well," I went on, "for one thing, I've learned that I'm much stronger than I thought I was. I'm more comfortable in my own skin, and I'm making headway when it comes to sticking up for myself, but I'm still working on all of that. I'm not a risk-taker by nature, but I'm learning that it's okay to take risks that will serve me even if it makes me uncomfortable."

"Ye don't grow if ye aren't willing to take risks," Ella said. "When my husband died suddenly ten years ago I had to decide whether I should sell the bed and breakfast and the farm or run it myself. My son is a professional in Galway. He wasn't in any position to take over, so I opted to run it all, and I have no regrets. As ye know, the economy has not been good here for the past five years or so. Sometimes I wonder if I should have sold everything, but I'm still taking care of my eighty-nine-year-old mother—we would need to find another home, ye see, and I don't have it in me to give up the business anyway. I love it and the farm too much—even though the work is hard. This is my home. So go with your gut, Diane, and don't be afraid to take a chance on something you feel passionate about. Mark my words, there are naysayers who will try and talk you out of it. That was my experience too, but don't listen to them. Trust yourself."

I was moved to tears, and it had nothing to do with the amount of whiskey in the Irish coffee. *How did I come to meet these strangers who have been so kind to me? Who believe in me?* I knew that Ella wasn't the hugging kind, but I hugged her anyway and she didn't seem to mind.

"Thank you," I said through my tears. "Thank you for everything."

"Ye rest up now tonight, dear. Ye've got a big travelin' day tomorrow."

"I will. And you rest up too," I added. "I'll see you in the morning. Goodnight."

I paid one last visit to the farm animals and to dear old Ross and said a tearful goodbye to Ella and Melissa after breakfast.

"Promise ye'll send us some of your pictures of the Burren," said Ella. "I want to hang some in the house."

"And I would like to take some back to California with me," added Melissa.

"I promise."

With a heavy heart I left Foxglove Farm not knowing whether I would ever see Ella again. So often we want to stay where we're comfortable. Where we feel safe and loved. It's a struggle to motivate oneself to move on to new and unfamiliar adventures. But I knew I had to move on. I had to continue to grow into my own truth. I knew, in my gut, that there would be new, rewarding adventures for me in the Beara Peninsula.

CHAPTER THIRTY-FOUR

Excuse Me, Who Let the Dogs Out?

CORK IS a big city and I wasn't prepared for the noise and traffic after being in the quiet west. The bus station was hopping, but the woman working at the information desk was kind enough to draw a map to the hotel where the owner of Anam Cara had arranged for me to stay overnight. As I pulled my luggage up a steep hill I thought about my very first trip to Ireland when my confidence was as thin as an Irish lace veil. No more stomach churns at every little thing now. Though I was far from being free of anxiety, time and travel had strengthened my backbone, and I was more accepting of the necessity of learning to go with the flow. I knew that my resilience would be tested though when I found the hotel and noticed that the front was covered with scaffolding. Not a good sign. My room was small, but nice enough and clean. However, the room wasn't air-conditioned.

I opened the big window (without a screen, of course) overlooking the street and was greeted by a cacophony of street noise. Directly across the street was a noisy pub complete with late-afternoon revelers seated at sidewalk tables. So much for taking a nap. I was kicking myself already for deciding to spend the night in Cork before taking the three-hour minibus ride to Anam Cara tomorrow evening. Oh well, I had plenty of time to kill, so I might as well make the best of it and explore the city. I found my way to the lobby through a series of unmarked hallways and set out.

All of Cork's streets are narrow and busy with both car and pedestrian traffic. The pedestrian traffic reminded me of New York City's. No one made eye contact, and there was no clear path. I stayed to the right and had to walk around oncomers. Same for the left, and I quickly discovered that the phrase "excuse me" is not known to Cork pedestrians. People bumped into one another and kept moving. This perceived lack of manners frustrated my Midwestern sensibility, but I realized that Cork wasn't different from any other large multicultural city. The downtown area was full of shops, restaurants, and pubs on cobblestone side streets that resembled alleys. I discovered that the city was built on water and those side streets used to be canals. There were many bridges crossing from one quay to another. Thank God I had my map, although even the map was difficult to follow at times. Still, the hilly and winding streets with their multicolored buildings were charming, and I was happy to find a good vegetarian restaurant for dinner.

At ten o'clock that night I knew that even with earplugs and the window closed, I wouldn't get much sleep. The boisterous pubgoers would make sure of that. *Oh well,* I thought to myself, *I'll just sleep in tomorrow morning.*

At six o'clock the next morning I was jarred awake by a loud banging just outside my second-floor window. I flung the window open, stuck my head out, and saw two men on the scaffolding hammering away. I couldn't believe it! The men were very chatty and sprinkled their talk liberally with the f-word. They also fancied themselves singers. "Who let the dogs out? Woof, woof, woof, woof!" was followed by lots of laughter before they repeated the only song they seemed to know. I slammed the window shut and called the reception desk to complain, only to be told abruptly by a male voice, "I'm working on it." Except at six thirty the blokes were still singing away. Totally disgusted, I got in the shower. When I came out, the men were gone. Relieved, I got dressed and followed the maze of hallways to the lobby, where I saw a sign that stated there would be workers on the scaffolding at nine o'clock and that the hotel was sorry for any inconvenience. Apparently, those Irish blokes couldn't tell time either. The hotel clerk, a young woman now, told me that she had heard what happened and reiterated that the workers were not supposed to start until nine o'clock.

"Well, how do you plan to compensate your guests for being rudely awakened at six o'clock?" I asked. I knew that my crankiness was a result of being tired—tired from lack of sleep and tired of this time of transition between leaving County Clare and arriving at Anam Cara. Still, I wasn't going to apologize for it. I was tired of apologizing for every little thing. In my mind I had the right to feel irritated at having my sleep schedule so disrupted.

She looked confused at first, as if compensating the guests hadn't occurred to her. Finally she said, "I can offer you a free breakfast in our restaurant."

Since it was raining and the restaurant looked nice and expensive, I took her up on the offer. I enjoyed a huge breakfast of eggs, potatoes, fruit, and pastries along with several cups of delicious coffee. I returned to my room to relax and, sure enough, the one-song noisemakers started up again at nine o'clock sharp. "Who let the dogs out? Woof, woof, woof, woof!"

I checked out of the hotel, still frustrated with myself for spending the Anam Cara "discounted" cost of seventy euros on this place instead of taking the minibus to Anam Cara yesterday evening.

Oh, get over it, Diane. Travel doesn't always go as planned. You're supposed to be growing and learning to go with the flow, remember?

Determined to make the best of my full day in Cork, I stored my luggage at the bus station and spent the day walking around town taking photographs. I visited the Crawford and Fenton art galleries and ended up later that afternoon at the Cork City Library, where I could rest my tired feet and write. I was surprised that the library was rather small and drab with shabby furniture and no architectural interest whatsoever. For a city of Cork's size I had expected a large building with historical interest. But it was quiet and that was all that mattered. I spent the rest of the afternoon there before grabbing some dinner and going back to the bus station to take the minibus to Anam Cara.

It was July fourth and several pubs were hoping to attract American tourists with Fourth of July celebrations. I felt a tinge of homesickness when I saw the huge celebration banners and barbecue setups. I thought about my daughters and how they would be spending the day, one in downtown Chicago and the other at a lake in southern Indiana, and for the first time I realized how long I had been away from home and that I had two more weeks to go. I hoped that my stay at

Anam Cara would be worth it. I had such high hopes for my residency there to be a breakthrough in my writing journey. That I would feel like a real writer.

I found the minibus parked beside the bus station. It turned out to be a large van, and all but one seat was filled with men and women of all ages. I knew I wasn't late, so I guessed that they wanted to arrive early for the best seats. I was stuck in a seat with my huge suitcase at my feet facing another passenger directly across from me. The driver, a kind, soft-spoken older man with a thick Irish accent had driven this route to and from the Beara Peninsula to Cork six days a week for several years. It was the only mass transportation available in the sparsely populated Beara Peninsula. He told us that it would be about a three-hour drive and to settle in and relax. It was hard for me to relax with my suitcase at my feet. It would start to tip over toward the woman across from me every time we took a sharp turn, which was often, and each time I would say, "Excuse me." She would glare at me then, so I assumed that she was another Corker who had never heard that phrase.

And so it went for the first half of the trip until the man next to me suggested that I sit the suitcase on its side, which I did, and the woman stopped glaring at me. I wasn't paying much attention to her anyway. I was mesmerized by the scenery.

As we traveled farther southwest the landscape became more and more beautiful with green hills that could have passed for small mountains. There were wind turbines on top of some of the hills like the kind that dot the farm fields of northwest Indiana. The sun was low on the horizon, casting its golden light over the countryside. I was gobsmacked. I wished I could get out of the van long enough to take some shots, but then everyone would be glaring at me. Instead, I became enraptured with the view as the landscape took on more and more beauty. *How can this place be as beautiful as the west?* I continued to stare out the window, mesmerized, until the van came to a stop in the fishing village of Castletownbere. Several of the passengers exited, including Glaring Woman, and we continued farther west toward the village of Eyeries.

By now, the sun had set and dusk had settled in, filling the air like the comfort of a grandmother's lap. It was as if the air had shifted and a sense of peace had settled over me. It reminded me of the peace I had felt while sitting at Yeats's grave. I never expected to feel that again, yet here it was. The colors of the sea and hills took on such a rich vibrancy that, even though it was dusk, I almost had to shield my eyes.

I was the last passenger when the van pulled into the driveway of Anam Cara just outside the village of Eyeries. I saw a white stone house surrounded by flowers of every color. In front of the house was a tall, stone fountain. Greeting us in the driveway was a middle-aged woman with short blond hair and a welcoming smile. It was Sue Booth-Forbes, an American woman who had settled here and opened a renowned retreat center for writers and artists. I exited the van and walked toward her. She held out her arms and I received a warm hug. Although we had never met, I instantly felt as if I had known her all my life. I had been brought to this paradise for answers. Answers to questions about finding my voice as a writer, about self-acceptance and acceptance of others, and answers to questions that I wasn't totally aware of yet. And this wonderful woman was going to help me.

CHAPTER THIRTY-FIVE

Anam Cara and Annie Proulx

I AWOKE THE next morning in my comfortable upstairs room to a view of the sea. I stood at the window for several minutes transfixed by the beauty of sparkling water and puffy white clouds floating around like ballet dancers in the blue sky. The shapeshifting clouds merged long enough for a slight rain shower, and a fully arched rainbow appeared on the horizon. Oh my God. Could it get any better than this?

Shortly after I arrived the night before, Sue had taken me into the village to a pub where the other Anam Cara guests were waiting for me. I'd told Sue that I was tired, but she convinced me that it would be a good idea for me to go to the pub and meet the others, so I did. Much to my relief, I bonded right away with the other writers: Collette, Tara, Joanne, and Wendy. They came from all over—Belfast, London, Georgia, and Utah—for the same reason: to write and to gain constructive feedback by sharing our writing with each other. I could tell from their enthusiasm as we pulled our chairs closer around the table to one another that they were as grateful as I was to have this opportunity to share their work with other like-minded writers. Writing is a lonely pursuit, and non-writers do not understand the effort it takes to write a good sentence, let alone an entire book. It's a rare thing to spend several days living with other writers who understand. I had felt a deep sense of gratitude as we chatted away on the drive back to Anam Cara and settled into our separate rooms for the night.

I wandered around the house and the surrounding grounds before breakfast. Jack, Sue's black-and-white long-haired terrier, came with me. The modern, homey interior flowed from one room to the next with nooks and crannies filled with books and window seats. Our rooms were in separate wings both upstairs and downstairs. My favorite room was the large country kitchen complete with a new industrial range (Sue was quite the gourmet cook) and a large window above the kitchen sink overlooking the yard. Outside, there was a hot tub and a hammock on the patio. The yard was filled with huge, deep-purple hydrangeas, fuchsia, lilies, and palm trees. There was a rope swing anchored to a tree that overlooked the Slieve Misk Mountains just up the road. The lush grounds included several acres with seating areas tucked among the clearings. A wooded path led to a creek with rushing water noisily cascading down the rocks. I could have watched the falls all day, but it was time to join the others for breakfast.

Sue explained our schedule at breakfast. We would meet in the kitchen for breakfast at eight. Quiet hours in and around the house would begin at nine thirty and stay in effect until five thirty. We would fix our own lunch and meet as a group for dinner prepared by Sue. We could volunteer to read up to ten pages of our work aloud after dinner for feedback from the others, but we were under no obligation to do so. Afterward those who wanted could ride with her to the local pub. She stressed the importance of the quiet hours and that talking would not be tolerated. I loved the idea of having time to myself during the day to do whatever I wanted—write, walk around the grounds, visit the village, take a nap—and still have the company and comradery of other writers the remainder of the day.

After breakfast I sat with Sue at the round kitchen table tucked into a corner with a bay window overlooking the front yard. I was glad to have this time with her to myself.

"I felt when we met last night that we must have a lot in common," said Sue, getting up to pour another cup of tea.

"I'll bet we do," I answered. "How did you decide to come here from the States?"

"I was ready for a change. I was middle-aged, recently divorced, and sick of my job. I traveled to Connemara for a month-long literary retreat and fell in love with it. I had led some writing retreats myself, so I decided to relocate from Boston to Ireland. My daughter, along with my mother, helped me find this place in 1997, and I opened the retreat center in 1998."

"Why did you name it Anam Cara?" I asked.

"I was touched by John O'Donohue's book of the same name during my stay in Connemara. I became a big fan. The name is to honor both the idea of that type of love and to honor O'Donohue as well."

"Perfect," I said. "I'm a big fan too." I told her about meeting him at a book signing in Indianapolis.

"Wow! He really told you that you must come to Ireland without even knowing you?"

"Yes, he really did."

"Well, that doesn't surprise me really. He was prophetic in so many other ways, especially through his writing."

"Yeah, I have other friends who knew him well, and they say the same thing," I said. "I was shocked to hear of his sudden death last year. He was so young."

"Yes, I cried for days," Sue said, staring into her cup of tea. We sat in silence for a moment. "So, I take it you are divorced too, Diane," Sue said. It was more of a statement than a question.

"Yes."

"For how long?"

"Let's see, around thirteen years now. I was married for twenty-two."

"God, I was married for thirty." Sue sighed. "But I've been divorced the same amount of time as you."

"Did you want the divorce?" I asked. "I mean, no one wants a divorce, but did you think it was time for the marriage to end?"

"Definitely," Sue answered firmly. "He was cheating on me, for one thing, and he tried to make my life miserable during our divorce."

"Mine too," I said. "And you know what's funny? He thought his life would be so much happier without me, but now he seems more miserable than ever. He's remarried, but it doesn't seem to be a happy marriage. And, of course, he blames everything on me. He's still bad-mouthing me to my daughters even though we've told him over and over to stop doing it. At this rate he'll probably end up estranging himself from our daughters too."

"Yeah, mine has pretty much done that," said Sue, rolling her eyes. "So, is your life better now? Without him, I mean?"

"Oh God, yes! Let me count the ways." I laughed. "I'm not the same person I was then. I feel like I'm just now coming into my own. I'm so much happier."

"Funny how that works, isn't it? We go through hell, but then the outcome turns out to be so good for us," said Sue. "I'm glad you're here, Diane. I have a feeling this retreat will help you come into your own even more."

"Me too."

We talked about writing then and about her varied career as an editor. In addition to being the editor of *Exponent II*, an alternative magazine for Mormon women, she had worked for Cambridge University Press. But she made headlines for winning a lawsuit in Virginia against the discrimination of pregnant teachers when her teaching contract wasn't renewed due to her pregnancy in 1975. She had made headlines again recently when child actress Eliza Dushku accused a production assistant on the television show *True Lies* of an off-set sexual attack years after the fact. Sue, a friend of the family, was her legal guardian on-set and backed the actress's claim.

I was in awe of the path that had led Sue here to Anam Cara. Her bravery and tenacity were fierce, yet she presented herself as a compassionate, empathetic, down-to-earth teacher—a "literary midwife" she called herself.

Later that morning all of us traveled to Eyeries with jugs in hand to pump water from the village spring. The area water was being tested, and there was some question about drinking it. Sue took a photo of me and Collette in our raincoats wearing the wellies Sue had provided, laughing as we took turns pumping until our arms were sore.

After that, we fell into the routine of being on our own during the day and enjoying each other's company at dinner, sharing our writing, and then on to the pub with the locals in the evening. I loved walking the one mile to the village in the afternoons past lush fields dotted with horses and cattle, with the blue water of the bay in the background. The village itself was lined with brightly painted houses and shops. The village dog, a small gray terrier, always greeted me, as did the villagers. The locals held a deep respect and affection for Sue, and they felt the same way about the Anam Cara retreatants. I would be asked about my writing while visiting the post office or savoring a piece of delicious rhubarb custard pie at the local eatery. I felt as if I were living a writer's dream, and I guess I was. It was surreal to be there in that paradise, and I kept expecting to awaken from that luxurious dream.

There were ducks and chickens at Anam Cara, and I volunteered to look after them during my stay. My duties were to lead the ducks to the pond in the morning and back to their gated yard each evening. I fed the chickens and collected their eggs, but, fortunately, Sue assured me that I didn't need to clean the coop because a hired man would take care of that task. The chickens tolerated me, and being quite the escape artists, I would count them before exiting through the gate. One morning I told Sue that one was missing. She walked to the coop with me, looked over the chickens, and said that Nelly, one of the brown hens, was gone. "She probably got out when the gate was open for a moment," Sue said.

"That's strange," I said, "because I didn't see any chickens fly out the gate." I stood there feeling guilty as hell for neglecting my duties.

"Don't feel bad. Nelly is small and fast. This isn't the first time she's gotten out. I wouldn't be surprised if a fox has gotten to her by now," said Sue, leaving me feeling even more irresponsible. A few days later she was spotted roosting high up in a tree. Sue coaxed her down and carried her back to the coop. I felt so relieved.

The ducks weren't the mallard ducks I was accustomed to at home. They were large and came in a variety of colors, quacking up a storm as they swam in the pond. They had little tufts of feathers on top of their heads that looked like punk hairdos. One duck in particular sported a huge tuft of black, white, and green. Sue named her Madam Pompadour.

Sue had arranged for us to attend an evening with Annie Proulx (pronounced pru) at the West Cork Literary Festival in Bantry. I was excited to see the American author of *Brokeback Mountain* and *The Shipping News* in person and in Ireland no less. Though I wasn't that familiar with her work, I had seen the powerful movie version of *Brokeback Mountain* and knew of her reputation as a National Book Award winner. I was anxious to hear about her writing journey and her reasons for being in Ireland. Was she writing a book with an Irish setting?

We ate an early dinner and piled into Sue's car for the two-hour drive southeast to Bantry. There wasn't any road that resembled a highway in that remote part of County Cork, hence the two-hour drive on narrow, curvy roads. I couldn't believe the landscape along the way, lush with greenery, fuchsia, foxgloves, geraniums, and the occasional palm tree. We traveled through every picturesque village along the way—Adrigola, Glengarriff, Snave, Ballylickey, and, finally, Bantry. Sue pointed out highlights along the way, such as the area where Colin Farrell had filmed his latest movie. "He was very friendly, not at all standoffish or full of himself," said Sue. "I swear to God he's more handsome in person than he is on-screen." We passed a lush, gated yard with an adorable one-story cottage. "That's where Maureen O'Hara lives," said Sue. "She isn't in very good health now. I heard she has a full-time nurse living with her." *This is where I would choose to come to die,* I thought. *It would be as if I was already in heaven.*

Finally, we arrived at the hall where the festival was being held. Sue had the inside scoop on all of the behind-the-scenes activity. Annie Proulx was here to do research for a book on the old copper mines in this area and their relationship to the copper mines in Wyoming, where she lived. Apparently, some of the Irish miners emigrated to Wyoming, and she was interested in interviewing some of their descendants, but it turned out she wasn't exactly mingling with the locals. She had kept mostly to herself. Sue also pointed out some of the board members for the festival as we milled around in the lobby. I was impressed with how easily she talked with everyone as well as the number of people who knew her and seemed to admire her.

Eventually, we were called into the large room where the lecture would take place. The room was filled with row after row of non-cushioned folding chairs. I flashbacked to the time when I had sat in similar chairs at the John O'Donohue lecture and to how much my butt hurt by the end. *Oh well,* I thought, *I'm sure I'll be so intrigued with what she has to say that I won't even notice the chair.*

The chairperson of the festival came to the lectern to say a few words and to introduce the speaker. Annie Proulx approached the lectern at the center of the stage wearing a gray, nondescript pant suit and a slight smile. With her short stature, cropped gray hair, and thick black glasses, she could pass for anyone's grandmother. She greeted us in a soft-spoken voice, thanked the festival for having her, and briefly explained why she was visiting this remote area of Ireland.

"I'm fascinated with the emigration from this area to the even more harsh environment of Wyoming where the winters are brutal. I'm here to research these rugged, brave people and to understand how they came to travel from here to Wyoming."

She went on to describe her isolated life in Wyoming and how, due to her advancing age, the winters were getting to be too much for her. She mentioned the possibility of relocating to Florida. She didn't strike me as being the kind of person who would take to Florida. Clearly she was a loner and planting herself in such a populated area with its tourism, traffic, and shopping centers would come as quite a culture shock. I admired her individualistic spirit, but there was something distant about her. It was as if she would rather be back at her home in Wyoming.

"I've just finished a short story I've been working on for some time. I would like to take this opportunity to read it to you," she said, shuffling through a pile of papers on the lectern. She began to read. The story took place in Wyoming, as most of her stories do, and it involved some cowboys whose families were experiencing a streak of bad luck. Most of her stories contain those elements too. I wondered if she used the same plot or at least a variation of it in all of her stories and simply changed the characters' names. But who was I to judge such a prolific writer and National Book Award winner?

I sat in my hard chair as we listened to her read on and on—or at least we pretended to listen. I kept hoping for the story to end or to at least take on a more positive tone. But no, I reminded myself, Annie Proulx doesn't write hopeful stories. She writes stories where all of the characters meet a violent, tragic death in the end.

And sure enough, a good hour and a half later, she had successfully killed off all of her characters. She thanked us again with her little smile and stepped away from the lectern. The audience gave her a round of applause, but I couldn't tell if the applause was for her or for the fact that her gruesome story had finally come to an end.

"What the hell just happened?" I asked my group as I slowly pulled myself up out of my chair, sore butt and all. "She didn't give a lecture!" I stood and steadied myself. The others were doing the same. "She read aloud a very looooong short story that left us feeling depressed! She didn't even do a Q&A."

"Yeah, I know," said Wendy. "I'm really disappointed. It was advertised as a lecture, not a reading." Sue, Joanne, and I nodded in agreement.

"There's no excuse for that!" I said. "She showed a total lack of respect for her audience."

"That's right," said Sue. "Did she really think we wanted to sit on these hard chairs and listen to her drone on for so long? By the way," Sue whispered to me, "my butt's sore too."

"I don't think she cared," I said as we walked toward the exit. "She came across as self-centered and arrogant. I hate it when an author makes no attempt to engage with her audience. She took the easy way out by reading a story out loud that we could have read on our own instead of preparing a well-thought-out lecture. I know I sound harsh, but, geez, we paid good money to see her and where would she be without her readers anyway? All I can say is Annie Proulx, I don't like you."

We got into the car for the long ride back to Anam Cara. I wished that it were still daylight so that I could take in all of the spectacular scenery, but the night air was warm and comforting after spending so much time indoors. We settled in and Sue sighed. "Here we go."

It had been a long day for all of us, but especially for Sue. About halfway through the ride she announced, "Okay girls, you all need to do something to keep me awake. Sing, scream, anything."

We made a halfhearted effort to sing a Beatles song.

"No, that's not good enough," said Sue as she rounded another curve. "I'm not kidding, I'm going to nod off if you don't do something to keep me awake."

"Okay," said Joanne. "Let's start out with 'Old McDonald' and then sing every Beatles song we know."

So into the night we drove serenading Sue with several rounds of "Old McDonald." In spite of our exhaustion, we had fun making animal sounds. We made up animals as we went, and the sounds got more and more outrageous. We went on to sing every Beatles song we could think of. As we approached Eyeries, I closed out the sing-along with "It's been a hard day's night and we've been listening to Annie Proulx too long." Everyone laughed, and I thought to myself, *I'm finally with my people. Thank God, I'm finally with my people.*

I came to realize too that the negative episodes of self-discovery, such as loud cities, obnoxious construction workers, and, yes, even arrogant authors, are all encompassed with whatever is good in the prayer that . . .

And all shall be well, and all shall be well, and all manner of thing shall be well . . .

CHAPTER THIRTY-SIX

The Giant Eagle and the Goat Lady

THE AFTER-DINNER readings and critiques were intense but helpful. I knew that the only way I could become a better writer was to have other writers give me their honest opinion about what worked and what didn't work. During the course of my stay, I shared two essays—one about my experience at the B&B in Clifden and the other about my attempt to climb Croagh Patrick. Both were well received, but the other writers had a few problems with the Clifden essay. Some thought that I was stereotyping the Irish, which wasn't my intention, so we talked that out. I was obsessed with finding my own unique voice in my work. Joanne and Collette both told me that I already had my own voice, that I simply needed to replace a few clichés with my own words. "You tell a wonderful story, Diane," said Joanne. "Some writers are on one side of the fence trying to describe what's on the other side. You, girl, have already climbed over that fence." Having doubted myself and my ability as a writer for so long, her affirmation was like coming into a warm house on a cold day with a cup of hot cocoa waiting for me. I wrapped myself in the warmth of realizing that I had found what I had been looking for since my first trip to Ireland—a sense of community.

Sue had arranged for me to spend a day with a local photographer. He would take me on a tour of the Beara Peninsula and show me the best spots for taking photos. I hoped that he would be a better teacher than Sean had been, but if he wasn't, at least I would get a tour of the Beara out of it. We waited a few days for the rain to stop. He arrived the next morning for our tour. I'm sure my mouth must have dropped as he got out of his little blue car. He was a giant—big-boned and at least six feet seven inches tall. His dark, unruly hair resembled a dried mop, and his shorts and wellies made his legs appear longer than they already were. He covered a lot of ground with his long stride, so it didn't take him long to walk up to me. While he did, though, I whispered to Sue, "You didn't tell me he was a giant!" Sue laughed and whispered back, "Oh, just you wait. You're in for a real treat."

"Hi," he said, extending his huge hand for a gripping handshake. "I'm John. John Eagle. And what is your name again?"

"I'm Diane. Diane Hartman."

"Diane! Oh, that's right," he said, slapping his hand against his head. "Diane," he repeated. "I should have remembered that!"

"It's okay," I said, already wondering what I had gotten myself into. Was this photographer going to be as disappointing as Sean? *You're one odd bird, John Eagle,* I thought as we walked to his little car. I opened the passenger door and was immediately covered with dog kisses from an excited border collie.

"Oh, this is Susie," John said. "I hope you don't mind that I brought her along. You don't mind, do you?"

"No, I like dogs," I said as Susie put her front paws on my shoulders and tried to sit on my lap.

"Susie don't do that! Susie!" John yelled, but Susie had a mind of her own and kept at it until I gently pushed her into the back seat.

"She's still in her puppy stage," John said as if that explained everything. I tried not to stare as he folded himself up to fit into the driver's seat. First one leg in, then a bend at the waist, followed by the other leg, then a lunge for the steering wheel with both hands, and, finally, pulling his upper body in. It truly was a feat of acrobatic stealth. He started his little car, put the stick shift into gear, and we began our adventure while Susie rested her head on my shoulder and panted into my ear.

Our first stop was the Dereenataggart Stone Circle, a prehistoric site east of Eyeries. I was excited about the opportunity to photograph these huge standing stones. On our way up the hill, Susie decided to take her own route and sprinted off in the other direction.

"Susie!" John yelled. "Get back here!" Susie continued to sprint away. "Oh, Susie, please come back. Suusssie," he wailed.

"It's okay, John. She's bonded to you, so she'll come back . . . eventually," I added. "Besides, we're in the middle of nowhere. There aren't any busy roads out here. She's safe."

"How can you be so certain of that?"

"I've had dogs who have run off," I answered. "They usually run away from their owner and then circle back."

He seemed content with that answer, so we continued up the hill. I could see the massive stones in the distance. They looked like they had been planted into the ground by giants. One in particular, narrow with a rounded top, had to be at least eight feet high. Just like the beehive huts in the Dingle Peninsula, I wondered who had put these here. And why? I pulled out my camera and began to take some shots.

"What is your ISO set at?" John asked.

"One hundred, I think."

"You think? You mean you don't know?" John saw the surprised look on my face and quickly backtracked. "Oh, I did it again. I shouldn't have said that!" Once again he smacked his hand against his head. I was surprised he didn't have a permanent palm mark on his face.

"It's okay," I said. "Let me check my settings. Yeah, it's at one hundred."

"Ye will want to set it at two hundred here so the stones won't look too dark."

By now I had figured out that John probably scored fairly high on the Asperger's scale. Either that or he was just plain eccentric, but I suspected the former. Knowing from my teacher training that people with Asperger's have few social filters and, in general, process information differently, I didn't take anything he blurted out personally and treated him gently, but firmly. Therefore, when he started obsessing about a pan he had left on the stove too long, how the food had burned and smelled up the whole house, and how stupid he was for forgetting that he had put the pan on the stove, I gently, but firmly, reminded him that he had repeated that three times now, that everything was okay, and that the smell would go away.

We spent the rest of the day circling the peninsula, stopping at Healy Pass, the Hag of Beara rock north of Eyeries, an old church cemetery, and a fairy forest. The rock is named for the mythic Irish goddess. Similar to the Cailleach in Sligo, or Hag's Head at the Cliffs of Moher, the rock represents the fossilized face of the hag staring out at the ocean waiting for her husband, Manannan, god of the sea, to return. Visitors leave trinkets as offerings to placate the hag and stay on her good side. I left a pebble I had picked up from the creek at Anam Cara. I was intrigued with the carvings on the tombstones in the cemetery. There were cats and gargoyles along with angels. The place had an ancient feel to it despite having many recent burials. John took me to his mother's grave.

"There she is, me mam." John lowered his head for a moment, then bent down to wipe the tombstone clean with his hand. I watched as his large fingers gently touched her name carved into the stone. "Holy Jesus, I miss her."

"I'm sorry, John," I said. "Losing a parent leaves a hole in your heart, doesn't it?" I bent down next to him. "I lost my dad a long time ago when I was a child, but it still hurts."

"What about yer mam?" he asked as we stood up. I felt the wind picking up and saw rain clouds in the distance across the bright-green hills.

"My mom has non-Hodgkin's lymphoma and other health issues. We don't expect her to live much longer."

Susie came bounding down the hill to join us. She stood on her hind legs, resting her front paws on my stomach, and jumped so that she could plant a wet lick across my face.

"Susie, no! Don't do that, Susie!" John yelled. As always, Susie ignored him. I backed up a few steps and laughed, wishing I had the same energy and sheer exuberance as Susie.

I had no idea where we were when John pulled the car onto a dirt drive alongside the fairy forest. There wasn't a house or car in sight. The forest of pine, oak, ash, hazel, and birch was dark, with shafts of sunlight filtering through to the forest floor of moss, fern, and wildflowers. Straight ahead was a path of sorts covered with pine needles beckoning us in.

"Watch out for the fairies," said John, calling from several steps ahead of me.

"Fairies? Do you really believe in fairies, John?"

John stopped and turned to face me. "You think I'm joking, don't ye?" Before I could answer he continued, "Everyone in the Beara agrees that fairies live here. There are many stories about folks hearing strange voices that lure them off the path. Many have gotten lost in here."

"Well, it sure looks like a fairy forest," I said, trying to keep pace with him. "An enchanted fairy forest."

"Right so," John said. "Just stay on the path and don't do anything to piss them off."

The forest did feel enchanted. It was far more beautiful than the fairy forest in Clonbur. The smell of the damp dirt mixed with pine needles gave off an earthy, comforting aroma. The only sounds were the wind rustling the leaves and songbirds flitting from tree to tree. I followed John's instructions to stay on the path. Both of us were busy with our cameras, but, unlike Sean, John took his time with me and turned out to be a much better teacher than Sean. *I'm learning more from him in a few hours,* I told myself, *than I learned in three days with the award-winning photographer.*

We had been walking for several more minutes when I began to hear the faint sound of rushing water. John motioned for me to follow him toward the sound. The water became louder and louder as we approached a small clearing bordered by a rickety old wire fence. *Maybe a property line marker?* Just beyond the fence was a small, but forceful, waterfall.

"Oh, damn!" I said as I approached the fence. "I want to get a close-up of that without all the other stuff in the way."

"If ye want to do that, ye'll either have to stand on the fence or climb over it," he said. He gave the fence a little shake. "Ye can't climb over this, it's not sturdy enough."

"What if I climbed halfway and balanced myself?"

"How are ye going to get a good shot using a fast shutter speed when ye won't be able to stand still?"

"Good question," I said. "Let me give it a try though. I'll brace myself against the fence and you push against my back so I don't fall backward."

"Okay," he said with a sigh. "Let's give it a go."

His hand on my back did the trick until I wobbled too much and had to jump down. "I think I got it though," I said. John shrugged his shoulders. "With a little fairy luck, maybe," he said dryly.

Susie was having a great time running and barking through the forest, causing havoc with the birds and whatever else she came across.

"I'll bet she's pissing off the fairies," I said.

"Right so. We'd best get going. It's getting late besides," he said.

I gazed out my window at the lovely scenery on the ride back to Anam Cara. Susie had worn herself out and was spread out in the back seat snoring away. I was worn out too. For an introvert such as myself, socializing takes a lot of energy—and that's under normal circumstances. Socializing with someone most likely on the Asperger's scale with a spirited pooch was just plain exhausting. Exhausting, but so much fun. Having a person who had lived in the Beara all his life show me the hidden, special places of this gorgeous peninsula was more than I could have hoped for. And learning some new photography skills as well really lit the candles on the cake for me. I wouldn't have had this experience if it hadn't been for Sue arranging it. I had her to thank for so many things. Synchronicity came through again.

I took a leisurely walk into Eyeries the next afternoon. I arrived at a field outside the village just in time to see a chestnut mare urging her newborn foal to his feet. Fortunately, I had my camera with me. I took several shots of this unexpected, tender scene. (I had seen the mare several times but didn't realize she was pregnant. Such was my knowledge of horses.) It didn't take long for the foal to stand on its own and trot alongside his mother. She came to a stop and he nuzzled against her in what resembled a cheek-to-cheek hug. I stood watching them in awe, praying that my photos would do justice to this sacred moment, and marveling at the synchronicity that had brought me here at this exact time.

I took a different route on my way back to Anam Cara—a back road that ran parallel to the main road. I saw a small field up ahead with two Toggenburg goats. I knew their breed because I used to dream of having a dairy goat farm, and Toggenburgs are one of the best dairy breeds. I approached the field and the goats walked to the fence to greet me. I was engrossed in taking pictures when a thin, naturally pretty woman approached me from the house across the road.

"Do you fancy goats?" she asked. She had a sweet smile and high cheekbones. Her ash-blond hair was pulled back with a hair clip, her dress a well-worn blue gingham shift.

"Yes, I love goats," I answered. "Are these yours?"

"Yes, this is Evie," she said, pointing to the darker brown of the two. "And this is Bramblennie." Both of the goats seemed to recognize their names and nuzzled closer to the woman. "See, she is a bit shorter and has a longer white line down her face."

"Yes, I see. How long have you had them?"

"I got them both four years ago. So tiny, they were. They're my babies."

"They're darling," I said, petting Evie behind her ears.

"So who are you?" the woman asked. She came closer, almost in my face. I was caught off guard for a moment by her directness. Had I encountered another eccentric Irish person?

"I'm Diane. I'm staying at Anam Cara."

"I'm Harmony. It's lovely to meet you, Diane. Then you know Sue. Isn't she lovely?" She talked very fast, nervously, and before I could answer she said, "Then you're a writer! Brilliant! Oh, we do love having you writers here. So how long are you staying?"

"Just a few more days," I said quickly, hoping to get a word in. "I've been here for almost two weeks."

"And you do love it here, don't you?"

"Yes, I do," I said. "And I love that I saw your goats and got to meet you."

"Oh, how sweet." Harmony rushed on. "I don't have any children, ye know, so Evie and Bramblennie are my babies. Aren't ye girls?" Brambleenie rested her head against Harmony, but Evie was more standoffish and moved away. "Evie don't do that. Come back darling." Evie slowly walked back to Harmony. "That's me girl."

"Your goats are very lucky to have you," I said, moving over to pet Brambleenie.

"Oh, thank ye. They are such a joy to me." She leaned even closer to me and said in a low voice, "My husband doesn't like the goats. If he ever gets rid of them, I'm coming back to haunt him."

"Oh," I said, taken aback at such a strange, direct comment. "Well, I hope you won't have to do that." I smiled nervously and moved a few steps away. "I guess I'd better get back to Anam Cara. I have some writing to do before dinner."

"Enjoy your last days here, and have a safe trip home," said Harmony. "When will you be coming back?"

"I don't know," I answered. "I'm not sure if or when I'll be back." I didn't want to go into detail about my lack of travel funds and how I loved Ireland but, after four trips, I was tired of traveling alone.

"Oh, ye will come back. I'm certain of it."

"Well, maybe you're right. It's been great talking to you, Harmony. Bye now," I said, giving Evie and Brambleenie one last pat. "And best wishes to you and your goats." *I hope your husband doesn't get rid of your goats,* I thought. *I don't doubt that you would haunt him.*

I told Sue about my encounter with the goat lady.

"She showed up at my door one day with a dead bird in a casket she'd made for it and asked if I would take a picture," said Sue.

"What?" I laughed. "And did you?" I asked.

"Yes, and she was so grateful." Sue smiled. "I have to admit that her visit threw me off guard, but I pretended that her request was perfectly normal. I've learned that part of living here is to accept everyone, even the more eccentric ones, just as they are."

I sat in the swing outside that night after putting the ducks back in the enclosure and thought about what Sue had said about accepting everyone just as they are. I knew I was getting better at this and that by doing so I was learning to accept myself just as I am. Learning, but still so much growing to do.

Tomorrow I would be going to Dzogchen Beara to meditate and to see Luka perform. I knew it would be a day of reckoning for me. Part of the Buddhist teaching of mindfulness means to accept oneself in the moment, right here, right now. I hoped that spending the day at a Tibetan Buddhist retreat center would help me learn to do just that.

CHAPTER THIRTY-SEVEN

Letting Go

"I'VE NEVER seen anything like this," I said to Joanne as our cab headed up the narrow drive leading to Dzogchen Beara. The modern, white building had several tall, peaked roofs and rounded corners. Built on a hilltop overlooking the Atlantic, its numerous large windows were trimmed in red, and strings of prayer flags cascaded from the rooftops.

"It sure is an interesting building," said Joanne. "Beautiful. You can tell a lot of work went into building it. Wow! Look at that view."

By now the cab had pulled up alongside the building. We said goodbye to our cabdriver and walked to the end of the building for a better view. The sun peeked out from behind the clouds, casting light on the waves crashing onto the rocks far below. Only nature could reveal such beauty. Joanne and I stood in awe taking it all in.

"I can't believe this," I said, tears filling my eyes. "I wasn't expecting it to be so beautiful."

"Neither was I," said Joanne. "It's breathtaking."

"I'm gobsmacked," I said.

"Yeah."

We pulled ourselves away and walked into the building. Its thick walls sported the same colors and was as modern as the outside. We had arrived several hours early so that we could attend a poetry reading and still have time to sit in the meditation room before the concert. I was happy to have Joanne's company even though she wasn't familiar with Luka's music. ("Is he a local singer?" Joanne had asked. "No," I replied. "He's known internationally, and he has several albums on the Warner Brothers label.") Sue was a fan and would have come with us, but she had some business to take care of in Kinsale. Having another fan with me who understood my excitement and my anticipation would have made the night even better.

I was excited about the poetry reading. Three poets published by Salmon would be reading from their works—Paula Meehan, Theo Dorgan, and Tony Curtis. A guide took us to a large room with a window overlooking the Atlantic. We settled into our seats and the poets entertained us for the next hour and a half by reading some of the best poetry I had heard in a long time. My favorite was Tony Curtis, whose curly dark hair resembled the actor of the same name. Dressed in a white button-down shirt with a black vest and pants, he recited his poetry as opposed to just reading it. He was funny and charming, and his poetry, with lines about ponies smelling like fairy dust, old churches, old books, and riverbanks, resonated with greatness.

"We still have a few hours before the concert," I said, looking at my watch. "What do you want to do?"

"Why don't we go for a walk? The weather has cleared, and I need to stretch my back."

"Good idea," I said, rummaging in my bag for a guide to the trails I'd found earlier in the lobby. "Look, this trail would take us closer to the ocean, and there's no climbing involved."

"Let's do it," said Joanne.

I read aloud from the guide as we set out. "Listen to this," I said. "At the point just east of the building is a spot where it's traditional to think about what you would like to let go of in your life and, if feeling moved to do so, throw one of the stones in the rock pile down the hill and out to sea, thus symbolizing ridding your life from that which is holding you back."

"What a great idea," said Joanne as we approached the rock pile.

"Yeah," I said, "but I think it would take more than throwing a stone to rid myself of what is holding me back."

"I know," Joanne said. "I feel the same way, but it won't hurt to try, right?"

"That's right, we've got nothing to lose. You go first."

"Okay," she said. "Hold on. I have to think this through for a minute." She stood still with her eyes closed before saying, "I'm thinking about my mother and all the anger I still feel toward her for constantly belittling me. From the time I was a child up until the time she died three years ago, nothing I did was good enough for her. God knows, I tried to please her, but that was impossible. She did everything she could to make my life miserable. I loved her and hated her at the same time." By now she was sobbing. "So I'm throwing this rock and letting go of all of the hate and anger." She picked up a large rock, pulled her arm way back and, with a shriek that could have woken the banshees, hurled it out to sea.

"Well done!" I said as I walked over to hug her. "Do you feel better now?"

"Yes, I feel relieved," she said, rubbing her arm. "Now, it's your turn."

I stood with my eyes closed too. "I came over here to find my life, a life of my own. A life where I feel confident, valued, and encouraged to do what I want to do, not what everyone else expects of me. I feel so much anger about things that have happened in my past. Things I had nothing to do with—my dad's suicide, all of the teasing that happened during my childhood, and the emotional abuse from my ex. All of this anger is doing nothing but holding me back from being the person I was meant to be. I need to let it go!" I picked up the largest stone I could find. It was dark gray, almost black. It was heavy, but holding it felt right. I bent down, holding it between my knees, and with a loud grunt, heaved it out to sea. I instantly felt that a weight had been lifted. I hoped it would stay that way, but I knew from my experience at the Cliffs of Moher that purging myself of the anger that had fermented inside me for so long would be an ongoing process.

We had a few hours before the concert. After taking a tea break, we entered the circular meditation room. Red cushions were sprinkled throughout on the matching carpet. A red-and-gold Tibetan Buddhist altar was in the back, but it was the front of the room that took my breath away. Floor-to-ceiling windows covered the front half of the room overlooking the water. The view was magical. It was as if the room extended out over the ocean. All I could see was sky and water. Joanne and I looked at one another as if to say "Can you believe this?" before finding our own cushions and sitting in silence.

I knew from reading books about meditation that most of it is about the breath. The ability to concentrate on one's breathing keeps the "monkey mind," or chatter, at bay. The goal is to clear one's mind, and I failed miserably. I could concentrate on my breath for short intervals, but then I would open my eyes and watch the mist ebb and flow on the water. Finally, I gave up the breath thing and fell into a trance-like state by watching the water. My monkey mind was still there with reminders of how nervous I was about the evening's concert, whether I would be able to talk with Luka after the show, and what this whole Luka synchronicity thing was about. I didn't believe for a minute that Luka's presence in this remote part of Ireland at the same time I was here was a coincidence. What did it mean or did it mean anything at all? I didn't know. "Just let go and accept it as it is," said a calm voice inside my head. After that, it felt as if the mist outside had come inside, enveloping me in a blanket of peace.

An hour had passed by the time Joanne and I quietly exited the room. She shared a poem she had written while sitting. I told her about feeling as if I had been blanketed in the mist.

"I'm glad we did this," said Joanne, brushing back her short brown hair with her fingers and rearranging her shoulder bag, "especially after throwing that rock."

"Yes," I said. "It felt right to be meditating after lightening our load."

"Right," said Joanne, stopping to look around. "Which way is the tent?"

"I think we have to go outside and walk around toward the back."

"Are you excited?" Joanne asked as we approached the large white concert tent.

"Oh my God, yes," I said. "I'm always excited to see him but seeing him perform in a place like this is so surreal. I wasn't expecting this at all."

We entered the tent early so we could find the best seats. A lone microphone and acoustic guitar took center stage, while colorful Tibetan banners adorned the wall behind the stage. I walked toward the front a little faster and managed to snag two seats in the front row. I hadn't been questioned about my camera, so I took it out of the case and clipped the strap around my neck. Joanne and I gabbed away, and I glanced at my watch about a hundred times. The tent was completely full. Finally, without any fanfare, Luka walked onto the stage, took his guitar from the stand, waved to the audience, and began to play and sing.

> "I go down into the water, and dive as deep as a man can go
> Into those dark places, watch the underwater flow."

By the third song I had come out of my Luka-induced trance and began snapping some pictures. I was looking at him through the lens, trying to get the best shot, when all of a sudden he paused. I clicked the shutter and lowered my camera. He was looking straight at me with a small, bemused smile.

Oh my God, he's thinking that I followed him all the way over here from Chicago! Or maybe Anne told him that I was staying here. I don't know. But I can't believe he stopped the song and is staring at me.

And then I did something really stupid: I winked at him. I winked on impulse without even thinking about it. And the moment I did it, I regretted it. He looked out over the audience again and picked up where he had left off. Joanne grabbed my hand and whispered in my ear, "Diane, he was looking at you!"

"Yeah, I know," I whispered back.

Damn and Jesus H. Christ! I know I was just acknowledging his attention, but why did I have to wink at him? Why couldn't I just have given him a little wave as if to say "Hi, Luka. Yes, you're friend Diane is here. How ya doin?" Crap, he's probably thinking that I was flirting with him, like so many other women do. Way to go, Diane. Bet you'll be hurling that *stone into the water too.*

What was done was done. I willed myself to keep my camera down and enjoy the rest of the concert.

Joanne leaned over occasionally to say, "He's really good!" as if that were a surprise. I nodded and immersed myself into my Luka world of song, trying to forget the embarrassing wink. Ironically, as if to answer my thoughts, Luka broke into his song "Don't Be So Hard on Yourself" and I smiled at the synchronicity.

"What time is it?" asked Joanne as we left the tent.

"Ten thirty."

"Ten thirty!" Joanne practically screamed. "We have to walk down the hill to catch our cab. He's been waiting since ten fifteen!"

My heart dropped with a thud.

"Well, I was planning on talking to Luka for a while after the show," I said.

"We can't keep our cabdriver waiting," she countered.

"Well, can't you call him and ask him to wait a little longer? I'll pay the difference."

"I don't know his number. Sue made the reservation."

"All right," I said, and we walked toward the hill. Feeling frustrated and dejected, I wished that I had thought to tell Joanne to go ahead and ask the cabdriver to come back and get me later. But I didn't. Instead I let someone else tell me what to do instead of listening to my inner voice. The voice that was telling me that if I talked to him our friendship would deepen. The voice that was telling me that I should take this risk.

On the way I saw Luka standing several feet away posing for pictures with a group of admirers. He saw me and smiled and waved as if he was expecting me to come join him. I smiled, waved back, and reluctantly continued down the hill, my heart heavy with regret.

CHAPTER THIRTY-EIGHT

Homeward Bound

"I'M GOING to have a hard time of it when I get home," I said to Sue. We were drinking tea at the kitchen table waiting for the driver to pick me up.

"How so?" asked Sue.

"I've been preparing and building up for this trip for so long that I'm bound to feel depressed now that it's over."

"It's normal to feel let down after such a long journey," said Sue, before taking a sip from her bright-orange mug. "Just rest for a while. Let the trip sink in. You have a lot to process. Then write in your journal and keep as busy as you can. In time you'll settle into your old routine."

"Keeping busy won't be hard," I laughed. "I start another school year in about four weeks. In the meantime, I need to reconnect with friends and family, edit my photos, and email them to you and a bunch of others, plus prepare a slide presentation for the Teacher Creativity Fellowship dinner in September."

"And don't forget to keep writing, Diane. You have a very strong voice and a natural way of telling a story. I'm looking forward to reading your essays."

"Thanks, Sue. You've been wonderful, and I am so grateful." I reached across the table to take her hand. "I never dreamed that I would meet someone like you. I never dreamed that I would be staying in a place so much like paradise. I'm really going to miss you."

"I'm going to miss you too," Sue said, squeezing my hand. "You should plan to come back next summer. Remember, return guests have a ten percent discount." She smiled.

"I'd love to do that, but with my mom's poor health, I can't make any promises right now."

"I understand but try if you can."

Just then we heard the van pulling into the drive. Sue helped me carry out my luggage, and we stood in the driveway hugging each other as the driver loaded my bags.

"Goodbye, my friend," said Sue, wiping away her tears. "Email me when you get home. Promise?"

"Promise," I said, giving her a long, loving gaze through my tears before climbing into the van. I didn't look back as the van pulled away. I knew that if I had I would have been a weeping, inconsolable mess.

I spent the night in a comfortable hotel recommended by Sue close to the airport. My flight home would be later the next morning. I stayed up late writing in my journal in an attempt to process all that had happened on this trip. But I had experienced so much kindness, love, friendship, synchronicity, and adventure that I knew it would take a long time for me to understand the full impact of this journey and how it would affect my soul and my future.

In fact, it would take years to process all of it. Years of living my life as I had before but with a deeper sense of appreciation, gratitude, and acceptance. Years of grappling with the Black Dog of depression but finally accepting it and understanding that without it, I wouldn't be the resilient person I am today. Zero possibilities for romance, but as my mother always said, "Never say never." Five years of struggling in my career with ageism and unfairness, but mostly taking the high road, knowing that this too shall pass and that retirement would offer new possibilities I never dreamed of. Years of deepening friendships, forging new ones, and letting go of those that no longer served me. Grieving those whom I lost—my mother, my youngest brother, best friends, and even dear John Eagle and Patricia Monaghan—but knowing in my heart, amid the wrenching grief, that time is an illusion, that they are with me in spirit, and that we will be together again. And watching, as any parent will understand, with love, fear, joy, trepidation, and pride as my daughters blossomed into women with children of their own, thus allowing me to experience the greatest gift of being a grandmother of five. And, of course, years of writing and loads of gratitude for being led to my writing community in Montana, a community of diverse souls who continue to support and champion my writing.

And Ireland? Though I haven't returned in over ten years, Ireland will always remain in my soul. My journeys throughout that beautiful country gave me the self-confidence I desperately needed to move forward. The friends I made there are still my friends, and I'm thankful for every one of them. They're always asking me when I'm coming back. "Someday . . . hopefully soon," I reply. And I do want to return. I miss my friends and the Irish countryside. I can picture myself doing a book signing in Jessie's new bookstore in Ennistymon, walking the beach with Anne and Luka, adding my book to Sue's library at Anam Cara, and visiting my beloved Burren and Beara once more. But whether or not I ever return one thing is certain:

And all shall be well, and all shall be well, and all manner of thing shall be well . . .

Acknowledgments

THIS BOOK has been a work in progress for many years. I was fortunate to have many people help me to bring this story to life.

First and foremost, I would like to thank my mentor, editor, and friend, Laura Munson, for her continuous support and for helping me to bring this book to its final form. She was the first to recognize that my story was a memoir, not a collection of essays about my travel experiences. Her admonition to "go deeper" finally paid off. Without her and the support of my Haven Writing Retreat friends, this book would not exist. I'm particularly indebted to my Haven monthly writing group members, Helane Davis, Erika Putnam, and Josefina Barbero, for being my constructive critics and cheerleaders. You've all made me a better writer.

To She Writes Press and its extraordinary staff, especially Brooke Warner, Lauren Wise, and Shannon Green. Thank you for bringing my story to the world.

The journals I kept during my travels in Ireland were instrumental in providing details I would have otherwise forgotten, but I am also greatly indebted to my friends in Ireland for their willingness to jog their memories and provide more details: Sue Booth-Forbes at Anam Cara Writer and Artist Retreat, Jessie Lendennie at Salmon Poetry, and musicians

Anne Rynne and Luka Bloom. Synchronicity brought you into my life, and I'm forever grateful for your kindness and support. I hope to wander the back roads of Ireland with you again soon.

A special thank-you to my friend since junior high school, Lynn Schilling, for reading parts of the manuscript and offering a male point of view.

To the many mentors in my life over the years who believed in my writing, some of whom are no longer here but will remain forever in my heart: Earl Conn, Patricia Monaghan, John Eagle, Dan Wakefield, Charlene Ann Baumbich (love you Cuz), Vicky Phillips (a.k.a. Daisy Pettles), Tracy Line, and Shari Wagner.

The Indiana Writers Center and the Midwest Writers Workshop presented an opportunity for me to hone the craft of writing and to become involved in their writing communities through their classes and conferences. I am also indebted to Lilly Endowment for granting me its 2009 Teacher Creativity Fellowship, which allowed me to explore Ireland without having to worry about my bank account.

Finally, to my daughters and the rest of my family for your love and support. *Tá grá agam duit.*

Citations/Permissions

Yeats, W. B. "Into the Twilight" 1913. https://www.poetryverse.com/william-butler-yeats-poems/into-the-twilight, accessed October 21, 2024. (Public Domain)

"I'll Tell Me Ma" (Traditional Folk Song), https://archives.vwml.org/record/RoudFS/S239172, accessed October 21, 2024. (Public Domain)

Carl Jung Quotes. BrainyQuote.com, BrainyMedia Inc, 2024. https://www.brainyquote.com/quotes/carl_jung_114806, accessed October 21, 2024.

"I'm a Bogman." Luka Bloom Between the Mountain and the Moon ℗ 2007 Big Sky Records ℗ Skip Records Released on: 2001-02-03 Reprinted with kind permission of Luka Bloom.

"Blackberry Time." Luka Bloom Salty Heaven ℗ 1998 Sony Music Entertainment (UK) Ltd. Released on: 1998-05-11 Reprinted with kind permission of Luka Bloom.

"Exploring the Blue." Luka Bloom Acoustic Motorbike ℗ 1992 Reprise Records Released on: 1992-20-01. Reprinted with kind permission of Luka Bloom.

About the Author

photo credit: Lynne Medsker

DIANE HARTMAN is a retired school library media specialist, photographer, dog rescuer, bird watcher, and lover of Ireland. She has received honors for her writing from Midwest Writers Workshop, Daisy Pettles Women's Writing Award, and the Griffith Writing Fellowship at the Mary Anderson Center. Her photography has garnered several awards, including the Indiana Governor's Award. Diane is an alumnus of Laura Munson's Haven Writing Workshops and Retreats. She lives in the Indianapolis area with her rescued corgi, Winston. This is her first book.

www.dianehartmanauthor.com
Instagram.com/dianehartmanauthor
Facebook.com/dianehartmanauthor